SIBLINGS
Our First Macrocosm

WISING UP ANTHOLOGIES

ILLNESS & GRACE, TERROR & TRANSFORMATION
2007

FAMILIES: THE FRONTLINE OF PLURALISM
2008

LOVE AFTER 70
2008

DOUBLE LIVES, REINVENTION & THOSE WE LEAVE BEHIND
2009

VIEW FROM THE BED: VIEW FROM THE BEDSIDE
2010

SHIFTING BALANCE SHEETS:
Women's Stories Of Naturalized Citizenship & Cultural Attachment
2011

COMPLEX ALLEGIANCES:
Constellations of Immigration, Citizenship, & Belonging
2012

DARING TO REPAIR:
What Is It, Who Does It & Why?
2012

CONNECTED:
What Remains As We All Change
2013

CREATIVITY & CONSTRAINT
2014

SIBLINGS
OUR FIRST MACROCOSM

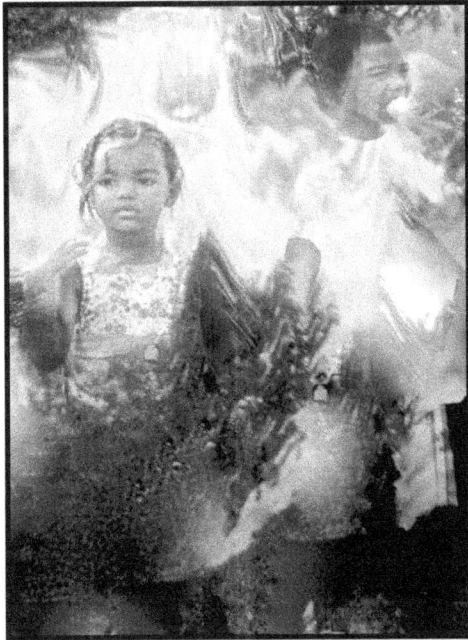

Heather Tosteson, Charles D. Brockett
Kathleen L. Housley, Kerry Langan, Michele Markarian
EDITORS

Wising Up Press

Wising Up Press
P.O. Box 2122
Decatur, GA 30031-2122
www.universaltable.org

Catalogue-in-Publication data is on file with the Library of Congress.
LCCN: 2015945302

Wising Up ISBN-13: 978-0-9826933-5-3

DEDICATION

To all our siblings

Becky, Beth, Carrie, Catherine, Ingrid, Jim, John, Joshua,
Lainie, Larry, Liz, Lucille, Mel, Shannon, Steve, Stu, Sue, Tor, Zoë

TABLE OF CONTENTS

II. BONDS *&* BOUNDS

III. BROTHERS, SISTERS, KEEPERS

HEATHER TOSTESON

SIBLINGS: Macrocosms and Pluriverse

Macrocosm: The whole of a complex structure, especially the world or universe, contrasted with a small or representative part of it.

I

All our anthologies are both highly personal and composed almost entirely of the voices of strangers. I'm not sure what triggered the idea for this anthology, but I knew immediately that many people would find it as evocative as I did. It was only later that I realized that in all my own writing, I have never actually written about relationships between siblings, which is a little surprising since I have many and my relationships with the three I grew up with are complex. I use birth order often to understand how people function in the world and listen with interest as my friends and spouse and strangers on airplanes tell me about their own sibling bonds and schisms, and I share my own experiences, at length, as well. But the idea of this anthology wherever it came from, just the sensory intuitive *feel* of a macrocosm, not a story, not a relationship, a *macrocosm*, was liberating to me—as was the idea of exploring this experience openly with total strangers.

Another unanticipated result was that I suddenly felt truly free, after a hiatus of many years, to encounter again as a group all three siblings with whom I was raised. This was a spontaneous, not a deeply considered decision. Suddenly, one day it just wasn't a question or an intention. It was just flow. I knew I had a container for whatever responses I might have, which meant I had no need to reconcile my responses with theirs. My container was the call for the anthology itself and its audience—the world at large, or more exactly, the world of those who resonated with these questions, which didn't necessarily include, this probably goes without saying, my siblings themselves.

❖ *How much of the experience of our first macrocosm do we carry out into the world as part of our deepest, inchoate expectations of the world or of ourselves?*

❖ *Is birth order destiny?*

❖ *How are we shaped by the constellation we're born into, whether dyad or nebula?*

❖ *What is the appropriate sentiment to have towards those with whom we may share only genes and environment? Towards those who knew us before we had a sense of self?*

❖ *What does choice have to do with sibling relationships?*

❖   ❖   ❖

The most evocative image I have of that unplanned reunion involves only me, swimming alone early one morning in the empty pool at our modest hotel, turning over on my back and staring up at the clear, cloudless Florida sky, feeling an openness, an embrace, a lift that I had never experienced before as I thought about my siblings, now all over or approaching sixty. Oh, I can still feel what it felt like cradled in that clean still water, breathing deeply, the wide sky arching above me. *My* macrocosm. It had room, once again, for the inchoate mystery of each of us.

This spaciousness existed, I realized, because our parents were at last good and truly dead. We had never met, the four of us, out from under their shadow. I loved it. As I age, I feel deeper and deeper sympathy for my parents, for the circumstances and the choices that made them who they were. But I hated and still hate the structures they created, my mother's distorted by her addictions and depression, my father's by his narcissism, hypocrisy, and need for control. I left home at sixteen during the year of my parents' acrimonious divorce to evade both my father's request that I "take care of the children" and my mother's nightly alcoholic tirades. When I chose, at eighteen, to marry, it was not only to make a safe home for myself but also to be able to provide one for my younger siblings if they needed it.

I wanted to create a new world, *my* macrocosm. That was *my* need. It wasn't necessarily my siblings'. My older half-sister, sent off abruptly to Switzerland at fourteen to live with a father she didn't know and his fifth wife and her children, developed a deep distaste for conventional families and bonds and has made her home as an international civil servant in France and Africa. For me, the role of single mother best transformed the black sheep and little mother roles of my childhood. My brother, late in life, married and has led the life he wished his much admired father had—scientist, devoted husband, attentive father willing to live through his children. My younger sister left the U.S. at nineteen to create a warm extended family for herself among her husband's five parentless siblings in Caracas, Venezuela.

But for both my brother and younger sister, the idea of "our" family, "the" family, however deconstructed/reconstructed, centered around my father and held high numinosity for them. *Their* first macrocosms had been shattered at eleven and thirteen by my parents' divorce in a way my older sister's and mine had not. But now, my parents dead, the conflicts we had had in the past, which turned around our parents and, more importantly, the *structures* they created, were irrelevant. Now there were only *our* macrocosms, each perfect and perfectly irreconcilable, turning in a big, beautiful, Jamesian pluriverse.

I thought of each of them, my older sister here from her home in Dakar, Senegal; my younger brother down from Hanover with his wife and son and daughter; my younger sister in from Venezuela with her husband and son, summering in her Florida condo and acting as casual host. What filled me with peace was being able to feel the lives they had created for themselves in their long, active adulthoods, how richly organized they were around what was most true and good and faithful in each of them—just as mine now was, that each of us had created from the various influences of our difficult childhoods a new, more promising macrocosm that fit us like a glove. One that allowed the best in us and those around us to thrive. I liked the coherence of each of these worlds of meaning, like large iridescent soap bubbles rising leisurely on a summer day, reflecting the world around them on their surface. And, truth be told, what I especially liked was having no essential part *within* any of them. This also felt accurate to my experience of the world with and through my siblings, that private world that existed to some extent independently of our parents as we were growing up.

Earlier, when my younger sister and I were considering getting together with my older sister and brother, whom I see rarely, I said, "I'm not considering hosting anything until they ask me a personal question."

"That will never happen," she said simply. I knew she was right. They still hadn't. Wouldn't. It wasn't personal, it just wasn't in their make-up. But staring up at that perfect sky that June morning in Florida, that was perfectly fine with me. I was, miraculously it felt, freed of the need to share or reconcile our worlds—and thus free to savor the contours of them all, including my own, to loose it, too, to the whims of the wind.

❧ ❧ ❧

As I started to write this introduction, a year after my release into the sublimity of the pluriverse, and after the reading of hundreds of submissions and a number of interesting books on sibling research from sociological, psychological, and intimate perspectives (including Dalton Conley's *The Pecking Order*, Jeffrey Kluger's *The Sibling Effect*, Clea Simon's *Mad House*, Andrew Blauner's anthology *Brothers: 26 Stories of Love and Rivalry*, and Anna Quindlen and Nick Kelsh's photo essay *Siblings*), I returned to thinking about this intriguing quality among my own siblings, their lack of interest in what went on inside each other's heads. This was true among my husband's siblings, whose relationships tend to be more benign, and as I made an informal survey of friends, I found true of their own experiences of their siblings, especially as children but extending into adulthood as well: they were all profoundly *in*curious about each other. Incurious, I mean, about motives, beliefs, otherness and macrocosms. Even if they would naturally discuss motive and intention when discussing the actions of friends, spouses, or parents, they didn't do so about the actions of their siblings. Do siblings actually have intersubjectivity, a theory of mind, a sense of the Other about each other? I began to wonder. Did this lack of interest have to do with knowing them, or being known by them, before we *had* a self?

I wouldn't presume to speak for my siblings about their interior worlds. I know they can't speak for me. There are so many ways our experiences and our understandings of our childhoods, our abilities, our callings and the meaning structures of our lives are inconceivable to each other. I know the forces that shaped me most profoundly as a child and shaped my own understanding of the world and my place in it, the possibilities I felt it held out for me: my birth order as the first of my father's children, second of my mother's; being both a target and a favored child; losing my primary caretaker before the age of two; constant moves inside and outside the U.S.; my age at the dissolution of my family; being asked to be a secondary parent; family secrets; parental infidelity; early physical and sexual trauma; the kindness of strangers; academic success; social acceptance; social exclusion; my gender; my class; learning to read; learning to write; finding my creative voice. I know all these forces and more, including life-threatening childhood illness, other fathers, stepfathers, stepmothers, other divorces, and changing economic conditions, shaped the lives of my siblings and created very different worlds of meaning for them.

That doesn't negate the truth or value or reality of any of our early macrocosms. It does put into high relief the mystery that the very same events, and same stream of events, places, people can create innumerable stories and belief systems—that the same words, the same act can not only be seen but *be*, simultaneously, unambiguously salvific and desolating. No wonder then that silence, *in*curiosity, is perhaps wisest. No wonder, then, that with events so formative and core, so necessary for us to faithfully absorb, to test, to turn over and over, we keep forgetting that and as adults keep coming back, trying to match, to meld, forgetting repeatedly that there are as many families in a family as there are individuals within them.

We return because there is another experience at work here. One that is non-verbal, although conceptual, accessed in and through image and sense impression, that was created by the far from simple experience of *being* together. What *were* we really like as children? I ask myself as I look at early photographs. I think we lived fully in our own tumbling streams of consciousness—rather like the heterogeneous ideas of a metaphysical poem without a poet to yoke them. I don't remember having direct conversations with my siblings, certainly not about states of mind. I don't remember asking myself why they did what they did.

I don't remember being alone with any of them for any length of time except my older sister. Between the two of us in my preschool years, there was a secret world invisible to our parents, one that was not necessarily safe or comfortable. She would use me as her doll, cut off my curls, force me to cover my head with my beloved red flannel blanket each night and descend the stairs and interrupt my parents' late candlelit dinners saying, "I am a ghost, give me a piece of bread." Sometimes my parents would laugh and give me the bread, promptly appropriated by my sister waiting out of view at the top of stairs. Sometimes, exasperated, they would send me back, embarrassed and empty-handed, to face her wrath. I'm so sure she remembers none of this, I have never bothered to ask.

From school age on, when I do think of the four of us together, it is usually being corralled by my father to play a game, go sailing, take a hike, do chores. If left to our own devices, it is more likely that each of us was absorbed in our own book, or talking a mile a minute over each other at the dinner table, going off with our own friends, or gathering into large tribes of children from the neighborhood to play games, climb trees. We didn't interact. We just *were* to each other.

I believe this is very true for many siblings. What they share, what *we* shared, is the reality of having been in the same place and time. This is a profound bond. One woman I interviewed for another book described her relationship with her siblings as like all being present at the scene of the same car wreck, but seeing it from a different corner. But they shared the same air, the same shock waves, the same rises and falls of energy, the same real mangle of metal.

The other image I have of that meeting with my siblings last summer was the four of us sitting around my younger sister's dining room table with my brother's son and daughter. They are beautiful young people. They resemble each other but my nephew also looks startlingly like my brother as a young man, and my brother, in his early sixties, now looks startlingly like our father. There is obviously a strong, bemused, and comfortable relationship between the two siblings and between them and their parents. I have seen the children perhaps four times in twenty years at larger gatherings. That evening may have been the first time they ever experienced this particular constellation, what we have started to call "the first four," alone together and they were intrigued. My siblings and I fell into a conversation about our childhood, a natural casual one. I think it started with someone checking a random detail about a house we lived in, maybe in St. Louis, or perhaps Denmark or England. My brother suddenly asked my older sister, "By the way, can you remember ever holding me up over the rail of that ocean liner and asking me if I was afraid of falling?"

"I would never do that," my older sister protested.

"Of course you—" I started, touching the scar on my eyebrow where she hit me with a swing, the hair from which I still cut all the curls. But the look on her face was shocked, bewildered. She was hurt by the very idea. I thought of her telling me earlier that afternoon about how she liked Senegal, felt truly at home there, that the tribal chief in her village called her his daughter, what that meant to her. I thought about this whole precious world of hers whose taste and smell I can't begin to imagine, about how obviously this sense my brother and I had of her as a child, however validly based it might be on our experience, had no place in her here and now. Or in ours either.

My brother shrugged. "I don't know why that image came to me. I just thought I'd check." He went into the kitchen to wash the dishes. His son and daughter stayed at the table, listening intently as my sisters and I exchanged more stories, wilder ones. Our mother's drinking. Our father's misalliances.

They exchanged glances. It was all new to them. I was aware my brother did not try to deflect the conversation. There were no reputations he had to protect, no illusions to preserve. *We were good and truly out from under their shadows.* But I was uncomfortable. I wasn't sure what I wanted this niece and nephew I hardly knew to hear.

I suddenly recalled how two years before at the same table, with women friends, I'd gone on a free association binge about my family, all the splinters that were left, words I couldn't forget, acts I wouldn't forgive, and afterwards I thought, *never again.* I'd made a list of all the unforgiveable events, unretractable words and thought: I need to make a *good* story that can hold them. But that evening, watching my niece and nephew exchange glances, I thought, what matters here is *only* the laughter. It wasn't covering anything. It was its own reality. What story could capture that?

The psychologist Daniel Stern, in his book *The Present Moment in Psychotherapy and Everyday Life*, talks about the present moment as being a non-verbal experience, the raw material for verbal and narrative recounting. He talks about the role these small shared present moments have in creating a sense of intersubjectivity, that profound sense that we are of the same stuff as others. Small children have no theory of mind, but they do have direct experience of each other's energy states, they are hard-wired to perceive intention (if not motives) in actions, they know what it feels like to share focus. This non-verbal world they experience in and with each other is to some extent invisible, and inexpressible, to adults.

For all but the first born child, this nonverbal macrocosm precedes labels like family, brother, sister. The meaning of those concepts is intrinsically different if they begin in a sensory way, what Jerome Kagan in *Surprise, Uncertainty and Mental Structures* calls schematic thought, generalizations made directly from sense impressions as symbolic images or stories, than if they begin as syntactical thought, grown-up words and logical constructs. For example, what "sister" means to our two-year-old granddaughter, Nora, who was introduced to her new role and what it required through the word "sister" and *then* through the sensory reality of a tiny, brown-haired, nipple-grabbing, snuffling being named Ellis is quite different from what "sister" will mean to Ellis when, after having experienced a year of pokes and strokes by blonde, blue-eyed, ambivalent Nora, she is invited, perhaps by Nora herself, to match a sound with such a richly nuanced, sensorially dense, and ambiguous experience. For Ellis, like most of us born second or tenth, all words related to siblings will have these two senses, what the world tells us and what we know for ourselves before we're told, with the experiential dimension dominant.

The point I want to make here is that these two ways of knowing require different things of us and also provoke different responses. In schematic thought, concepts born of experience can fuse, transform like images in a dream, like our real life flow of impressions. The unexpected is greeted with surprise, but remains part of the sensory continuum. When we're working with verbal concepts, by definition they can't become their opposite. The unexpected makes us uncertain, dogmatic. When we are working with verbal concepts we fight to delineate, to make uniform. We can shift between these worlds by just using a proper or a common noun. What I say, think, feel, when I talk about my sister using her name, Zoë, is qualitatively different from those same things said about "my sister" or "my younger sister." What is *possible* between us changes. We naturally grant a much wider range of potential action to the unique individual than to the role. We need one system to know what is expected of us and what we might expect in the world at large; we need the other to know what to expect up close. We *are* both.

To blithely say that we are all part of a prolific pluriverse is not sufficient, for we all need to feel that we are also part of a coherent, unbroken continuum of meaning as well. A good friend who I once bribed to go with me as an emotional bodyguard to some family function had a marvelous time and said to me afterwards with a little shrug, "Whatever you want to say about them as a family, they are all very bright and interesting people." I looked at him bleakly then, but I have to smile now because of course he is right. Each of my siblings, if you listen to his or her rapid, varied, incessant stream of consciousness, is fascinating. It's just when you try to listen to them all talking at once, which is still usually the case, *and* try to listen to yourself as well to hear what, if anything, this has to do with you, you quickly get a migraine—or turn to art.

I realize that much of my artistic drive comes from taking different streams of consciousness and folding them into a coherent whole, one that, for a single, perilous, fleeting moment promises to hold all, *all*—whether I'm using collage, complex overlaid photographic images, stories with many points of view . . . or anthologies. For that is also what I received from my siblings, a deep internal need to understand those different temperaments and energies within a new, personally meaningful constellation, without distorting their original momentums and unique trajectories. Which brings me to this latest Wising Up anthology.

II

All our anthologies are both highly personal and composed almost entire of the *kindred* voices of strangers. We select a broad range of stories, poems and memoirs from many different individuals with different experiences, voices and sensibilities—but ones who share two things with us: an interest in the theme and the need to explore it by making a personally coherent narrative. Our contributors don't write works specifically for our anthologies, rather they write out of a sense of inner necessity and then discover a kindred sensibility in our theme. The fact that we received so many submissions for this anthology tells me that there is a strong need at almost every stage in life to explore the mystery of our sibling relationships and how they have shaped our experience of the larger world. The need to explore this subject is often felt by those who had less power to define their own experience within their family unit, or those whose experience is farther from the social norm.

We never imagined there were so many twins who need to give voice to their individual experience—or that birth order had such salience for them. At least twice as many middle or younger children as oldest ones felt a need to write. Two-child families provided such a quantity of passionate, often invidious, compare and contrast that we began to consider having a free standing volume called *Incessant Comparison*. Again, our writers range broadly in age, from barely twenty to over eighty. I do invite you to listen to how much or how little the narrators are aware of the interior life of their siblings, also to how shifts between experientially-based expectations of siblings as individuals and normative expectations based on roles ease or intensify conflicts.

The works we selected fell into several broad themes. In each of them, we include stories from across the developmental spectrum. The historical reach, given the age range of our contributors, is also broad. From a young gay millennial, high on various forms of ecstasy, dancing in an Atlantic City nightclub with his stepsisters, to a single-parented black family making their way resiliently through the race changes of the last half century, to Canadian women now reestablishing relationships with a sister given up for adoption during World War II, we can feel how differences in broad social conditions shape the inner climates of families.

I. World

Our first section deals most directly with the feel of our early macrocosms, its totality. All the selections here evoke the sense of an intact world, one that often gleams with the polish of time, the poignant pull of belated understanding. The emphasis is on description, capturing an atmosphere, the sensibility and level of understanding present at that time.

"I did not wonder then," Gary Young writes about being asked to rescue his sister in a fire. "It was my house; I knew where I was. I could find my way even in the dark."

"I have no memory before her," Sharon Munson writes of seeing her little sister in her playpen. Her self begins here with this private game of give and take. "Your hands were the first to find me," Lori DeSanti writes of her twin in the womb.

In Steve Koppman's "Morning Again," a young boy haunted by angry, obsessive thoughts struggles to understand the changes in his family and himself with the arrival of his sister: "Ever since Mom was sick when Ruthie was born, it was disaster after disaster." Beth McKim, on the other hand, relishes remembering the imaginative retaliations she exacted on her younger sister when she tired of the exasperating role of the good big sister. Katie Bush, in "Queen of the May," describes the imaginative kindness of her older sister, who helps heal the slights she had experienced at school through their private ceremony.

Rose Hamilton-Gottlieb's story "Favorite Son" describes the growing awareness of an eleven-year-old farm boy. The story beautifully captures the painful equipoise in the family, the safety Willie feels knowing "his father was downstairs standing between him and the world outside the farm" and his realization that he must protect his sickly younger brother from his father's wrath: "It was up to him to keep Stefan safe, to stand between his brother and the world." The world that was their father.

Brian Burns's story is an exuberant celebration of the acceptance he receives from his older stepsisters: "I saw all the work it took to be a girl. I worshipped them, knowing them as my sisters but understanding them as women." In her poem "Candidate for Statistics" Loretta Walker similarly praises her brother and the world he invites her into: "He can balance a world/of white and black,/peel disappointment/from skinned knees,/pray when others curse/his choices."

Patti See in "Like Me Best" describes the strength of her family, the cohesiveness of the eight children, in the face of their mother's imminent death by Alzheimer's: "'This is how I hope she dies,' I say to my brother, 'with lots of us sitting around telling stories and Mom in the middle.'"

II. Bonds & Bounds

This is the longest section of the anthology and explores one of the most important dynamics between siblings: identification, de-identification, and limit setting—and how self-understanding, the coherence of an individual macrocosm, develops through these dynamics.

In Jill Smith's "Play, Playing, Played," we see the power an older brother's innocent teasing has to define the world for his trusting little sister: "The innocence of a child's game has turned an idyllic world into something less than perfect. I have tasted fear, felt the sucker punch of recognition that someone is other than he seems."

Christa Champion's "The Sun is the Center of the Universe," traces the healthy development of a younger sister who idealizes her older sister but learns to establish her own complementary identity, from which she gathers a new sense of her older sister: "How she viewed me at the time, I have no idea. It never occurred to me to think about it from her perspective. When the sun shines on us, do we think about how the sun feels?"

Grey Held's poems vividly convey the intractable energy of sibling rivalry—both between him and his older brother and also between his own sons. He asks, "And even if I could/love them equally,/all the time, would they/ever see it that way?"

In Diane Gillette's "Balloons Adrift," a younger sister remains loyal to her older brother—and her own definition of family—even when her father sends him away. The story shows the shifts in understanding needed for all of them to absorb a new, more tenacious and ambivalent understanding of family.

In Katharyn Machan's poems and Tania Moore's story, the limit setting is more ambiguous and more necessary. Machan writes of the lasting legacy of ambivalence and pain from sibling incest. The narrator in Moore's "The Messenger" ponders the impact of her troubled sister's accusation of sexual abuse on her relationship with both her sister and her father:

> I might put my head in my hands and cry. Other times I ask for forgiveness, even if I'm not quite sure why. Perhaps for not knowing who to believe, or for the acceptance that I never will. Often I raise my arms and offer my father and my sister to the light filtering down from above. I turn them over again and again, and sometimes they are lifted.

Sarla Nichols, in her memoir "Mother, Sister, Friend," struggles with her feelings of guilt at not meeting her younger half-sister's expectation that she serve as a surrogate mother. Here we see how external conditions, poverty and addiction, can shape relations within a family—and how different interpretations of the same events create deep rifts. The older sister, who chose to leave the family circle to advance, insists on the power of the individual to define her circumstances. The younger sister, who remains attached to their family of origin, emphasizes the shaping role of larger social forces in the circumstances of her brothers, but holds her older sister individually responsible for what she experienced as abandonment. Both voices ring painfully true.

Older brothers set limits in both J.S. Kierland's "A Quick Kill" and Donald Vogel's "Esau and the Laodicean." In Kierland's story, the older brother refuses to sugar coat the impact of their father's behaviors, which he feels his brother is repeating with his own children. What is fascinating here is the response of the narrator when his brother does respond to him as if he may have had a different experience:

> Then he did something he'd never done before. He looked straight
> at me, waiting for an answer to his question. It was absolutely terrifying.
> "No," I said. "I don't think we ever did get through those years in
> the Bronx. We only thought we did, but never quite made it."

Vogel's narrator questions the whole structure of his poorly blended family, where his drunk younger brother is viewed more favorably than his loyal, well-behaved stepbrother—and, most importantly, questions his own role in sustaining the system.

Ruth Latta in her gentle story "The Family Together" shows both the resiliency of sibling bonds and the innovative ways people move beyond the negative labels of their immediate family, creating healthier new worlds of meaning.

III. Brothers, Sisters, Keepers

This section includes some of the strongest and most moving work in the anthology. Almost all the pieces are told from the point of view of a healthy sibling and describe the impact a mentally ill sibling has had on her own understanding of the world. In many of the selections, narrators have a meticulous exactness in their observations of their own responses—one that moves us to a world without labels perhaps unique to siblings.

Susan Mahan says of her older sister, permanently hospitalized for mental illness when she was sixteen, "We were close in age, and Cynthia was often the bane of my existence, but untouched as she was by the ordinary constraints of life, she sometimes served as my window on the world of possibilities."

"Childhood tasted like my brother's rage," Alison Stone writes bluntly in her poem "Asperger's." In Emily Rubin's story "Crazy" a younger sister describes what it is like to no longer be allowed to live in the same house with a brother whom she loves, is terrified by, and feels responsible for, but is unable to protect when "his brain gets taken over." In this story, the siblings do try to share mental states. The sister hopefully tells her parents, "If Nelson was truly crazy, I don't think he'd care about how I felt."

In Jane St. Clair's funny and deft story "Talking Berkeley Down," a sane brother has become adept at responding to his brother's suicidal depressions with humor and rapid attunement. "I wish you could see things the way I do," his suicidal brother tells him. But the exhausted brother observes, "I'd need a Seeing Eye dog in his world. In his world, I'd just be the blind person with a Seeing Eye dog."

Andrea Rosenhaft shares an unusually aware and appreciative account of how her brother has supported her throughout her years of serious mental illness in her essay, "I Love That You're My Brother."

IV. Discovery

The works in this section turn on unexpected reversals of meaning that reshape the narrators' macrocosms. In Sharon Leder's amusing "In Sisterhood," two sisters who have developed in reaction to one another, the older a young graduate student living in a feminist commune and the younger leaving a Christian cult to work in a deli, begin to discover their complementarity.

Elaine Morgan describes how, at fifty-five, she assumed care of her mentally disabled younger sister and managed to greatly expand her sister's range of competencies: "I also imparted my philosophy for living to her, 'If you can't do something one way, there's always another way which will work for you. Let's see if Mom was wrong. Okay?'"

In "Am I My Sister's Daughter?" Deborah Burch-Lavis explores a question posed to her after her sister's death by the women she has been raised to believe are her nieces. Her answer finally rests on her direct experience of her sister *as* a sister, which was decidedly non-maternal, and concludes, "The truth we lived was the truth they created and the only reality I know."

Both Loretta Walker and Maureen Flannery explore what it meant to them to discover an unexpected sibling after the deaths of their fathers. Flannery decides, "Invite them all to the table/the altar where we're all related." She accepts the "0% probability that my childhood can actually have been/ what I believe it to be."

In "The Sister Who Wasn't There," Heather Storey describes meeting the sister her mother put up for adoption during World War II and her decision (unlike the sisters she grew up with) to create a present-time relationship with her: "My fantasy that Jacqueline, the sister who wasn't there, would one day find me has given way to a deeper and richer reality. Her name is Sandy and we have found each other."

Charlotte Jones in "When Things Come to Light" describes how, when her beloved older sister dies, she discovers her sister may not be the person she thought her to be. Her sister's many many lies make Jones wonder if she ever really knew her. She finds some kind of resolution in the vivid childhood memories she has of her sister, how they "plotted our rendition of *Chopsticks* specifically designed to drive our folks crazy."

Paula MacKay's elegantly poised and thoughtful memoir "My Sister's Shoes" describes her relationship with her fraternal twin over fifty years and how their relationship as twins, which had so completely shaped her own understanding of both of them and their place in their family and in the world, shifted: "Most of all—and this had taken me a half a century to understand—I didn't know what it was like to be Pam."

V. Loss

In some of the stories in the first section, we feel the polish of time, a cherishing of ways of being and feeling soon to be lost. In this final section, writers grapple with the actual loss of siblings at different ages. "And yet, and yet, as Issa says/and yet we sensed some new thing there/not there before, an unseen path," Tim Myers writes in his poem "The Night We Talked," which explores the explosions of grief and revisions to the family's macrocosm that follow the death of his sister.

Greggory Moore's "How They Say It" evokes the unresolved grief the narrator still feels years after the death of a beloved seven-year-old sister who died the semester he studied abroad, a macrocosm shaped equally by love and guilt.

Roseann Lloyd and Christine Sikorski grapple with the death of brothers.

Sikorski enlarges the experience as a way of containing it in "For the Brothers":

> *For Cindy's, struck by lightning*
> *For Janet's, leapt from a bridge*
> *For mine, hit by a car*
> *For my mother's, blown up in the war*
>
> *For yours, if he's already gone*
> *I have made a little song . . .*

In "Finding a Sister" Elizabeth Farrell claims the beloved sister whose death by suicide she was never allowed to mourn as a child, recognizing how she has, through all these years, kept the positive legacy of her sister alive through her women friends. In "Sing" Kavanaugh celebrates the sister who protected her during her childhood. "I loved her in a way that can only be described as primal," she says. Her sister was her lifeline but also something more: "Jean hoped to see a flower bloom—she would wrench my dreams out of me and then she'd champion every one of them."

Alexandrina Sergio in "I Tell Her" keeps her relationship with her sister alive by sharing her own vivid memories of experiences they have shared: "I scramble to gather up the pieces she's dropped,/give them back to her,/but when she turns/she takes only stories." The sensory world made whole again, complete in itself, as it was at the beginning.

What we hope you take with you from this collection is a sense of it as a whole, a macrocosm, and also the power of each of these stories to evoke the completeness of our present moments, to invite us all into the recurring mystery of the question which began our call: How much do we carry the felt experience of our first social macrocosm into the world as part of our deepest, inchoate and *graced* expectations of the world and of ourselves?

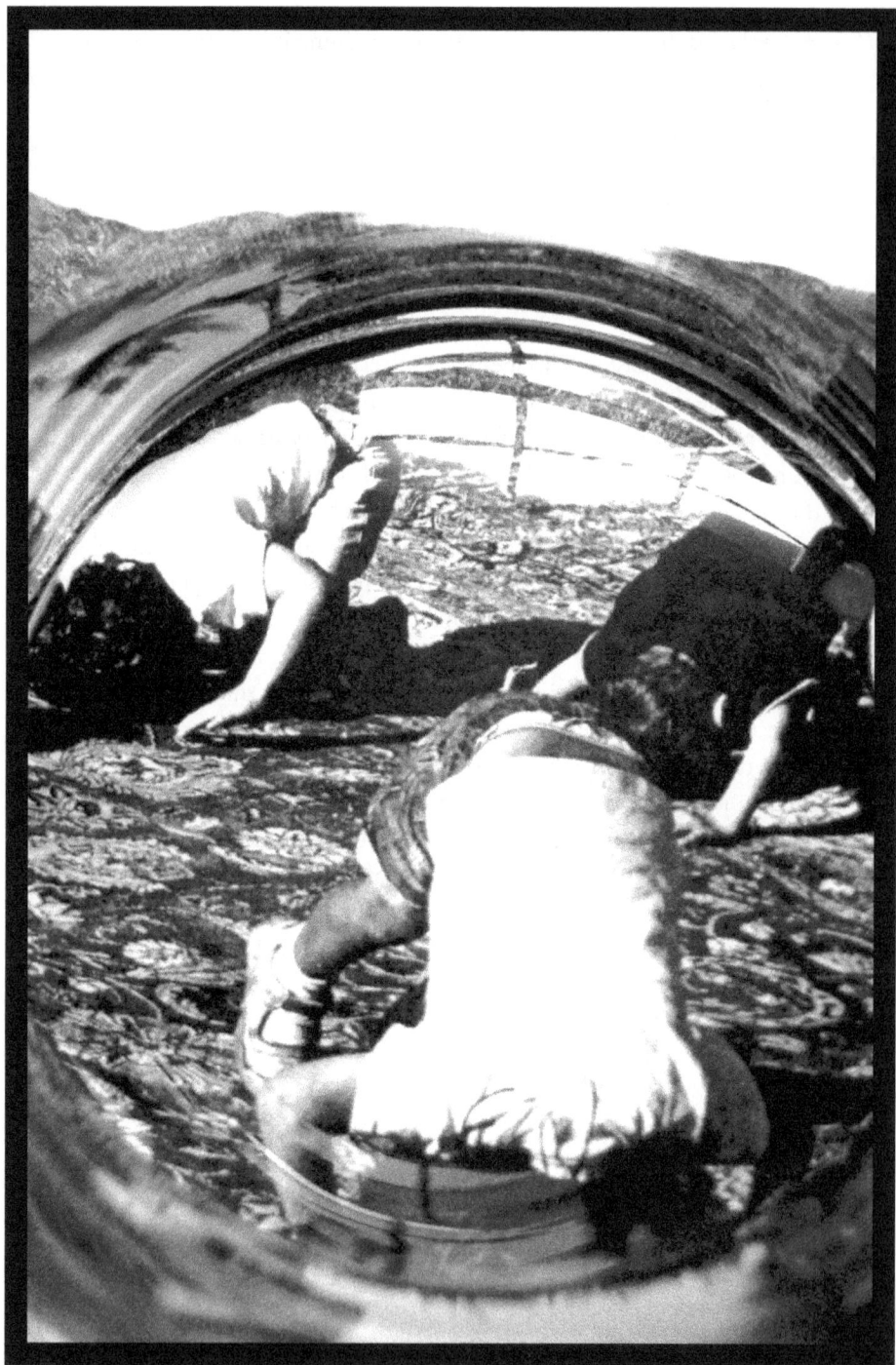

I
WORLD

GARY YOUNG

FAMILY MATTERS

My brother's in Wyoming, and I've had that dream again. We're fishing. The trout rise, take our bait, and keep rising. In love once with a woman, and with my own capacity for pain, I fell in with some cowboys, and broke my neck riding bulls in a little rodeo. That night, drunk in the bunkhouse, not knowing how badly I'd been hurt, I thought it can't get worse than this, but I was wrong. That was twenty years ago. Thunder rolls down South Fork Canyon. The Milky Way is a great river overhead. My brother is in Wyoming. I miss him more than ever when he's there.

✤

The burning house turned our nightclothes yellow. Standing at the curb, my brother batted ashes with his hand. We had a puppy, and my mother shouted, where's the dog, and then, my God, where's Cathy? I remember the sound of breaking glass, and walls too hot to touch. I remember pulling my sister from her bed, and leading her out into the world again. I did not wonder, then, how I'd found her, or how my mother could have turned so easily to send me back into the smoke and flames. It was my house; I knew where I was. I could find my way even in the dark.

My father would say, you need a memory lesson, and he'd beat us, first me, then my brother. And I do remember, the little scratches on the banister in the upstairs room, the copper lamps and the flame-shaped bulbs, dark knots on the varnished wall; bamboo curtains creaking as the wind pushed through, the taste of salt, and my brother, shaking as he waited his turn. I took my comfort there; I knew where I was, and what was coming. My father once broke his belt against the back of my legs, and when he saw the welts and the drizzle of blood, he began to cry. I was so frightened to see him change like that, not shouting anymore, but on his knees, sobbing.

✤

My brother was playing in the car when he slipped, pulled the handle, and cut his thumb off in the door. My father heard the scream, and ran naked from the house. My bike was on the porch, and without breaking stride my father picked it up and tossed it aside. I remember it hovered in the air. I remember my father flying, too. He took off from the porch and sailed above the shrubs, the grass, the newly staked trees, and at last came to rest by the car, where he knelt, and pressed my brother's bloody hand into his chest.

❧

I waited for my mother in the greenhouse. It was warm, and I could feel the presence of the air. I practiced words in my breath on the windows. I thought I was alone, but an older boy in the corner called my name. I asked, how do you know me? And he said, I'm your brother. He said our parents had sent him away, but he knew me, and watched me every day. That night my mother said, someone is playing a joke on you, but I knew she was lying. I believed him, I still believe him, an orphan, a boy I could never be.

CAROL BARRETT

IF I WERE ADOPTED

It would explain all this: how my sister Kathy who loves roses and can diagnosis a stem fungus yards away, cleans her linen closet every few months, not just with bleach after the pressed guest towels have been stacked in the kitchen by the phone she disinfects daily. She *repaints* the interior, some color coordinate of whatever daisies or asters are fresh and sparkling in her garden just then, whereas I let the tumble of sheets and unmatched pillow cases accumulate until I move to a new place several states away, Idaho or New Mexico, the foothills of Colorado or the San Diego zoo, and begin again.

It would explain how my sister Patty grows lemons the size of toddler footballs, Crayola yellow, no added dye, ships them to all of us for tea and fishcakes, whereas I cannot remember to water the prickly cacti that require only an occasional drizzle, their sad torsos stiff and browning on the arid windowsill. She tells me it's easy, the sun a natural ally, you just need to take notice once in a while then enjoy the harvest. Apparently I keep noticing something else, the mold in the shower, how I forgot the mail again, or whether my nails are too long to type, requiring clippered action. I cannot fathom *watering can*, even when I buy a little mini to sit right beside the furry stems.

It would explain how my sister Susy is a VP at Bank of America, keeps getting promoted when those around her are laid off, or given a choice of Longview, Texas, whereas I hate dealing with dollar signs so much I take my end-of-year pay statement to an accountant on the last available appointment before April 15th, and he slices it open like a tomato, and I wince at the juice. It would explain how she just happened to buy an old mansion in New York and down in the basement found a grenade from World War I that was ready to go off, and the police came and carted it away in a bed of cotton, blew it up after photographs on a landfill the other side of town, and it was in all the papers. She was famous overnight, her blond coif and shy smile right beside that dark mystery, which pairing inspired a host of callers and suitors, whereas I can't get the library in my hometown to sponsor a reading, let alone interview me about what's in my basement.

It would explain why I love my brother Bill as if we are not related, no matter he is twelve years my junior. I still lament the day my father took him to a barber, unbeknownst to any of the women in the family, which is all the rest of us, who snipped off the long red curls dangling from his darling face. It explains why he can fix anything, my toaster, or blender, or garage door opener, when I have one, or my car, like when it was making a sudden scraping noise that was kind of a rattle, more of an uneven snare drum but without resonance, and he came to work his magic and found I had picked up a limb from a vine maple in its underbelly and everything was OK, but I never thought to look down there.

It would explain why my sister Nancy is passionate about tracing ancestors and forebearers, their cousins' cousins, can tell you exactly how we ended up related to both Lewis and Clark, though one of them never married, and precisely how many retarded or illegitimate children swung from the family tree, how many women died in childbirth, or shortly after, who was a criminal and who kept their nose clean as a bobby's uniform in Swindon, England. She spends vacations ferreting out electronic newspaper clippings to add to her arsenal of strategic information, whereas I can't be bothered with all the roots and branches and little leaves of adultery and legally sanctioned couplings in corn rows or hay barns or stone rooms in a damp castle in France.

Maybe I am afraid to find something out. Maybe I know deep down no research can trace what I am really made of; there is simply no way to tell who I am or may become. Then again, maybe all my siblings were adopted and I am the one true genius, descendant of Lewis and Clark, destined to explore the inner cavities of personal landscapes, now and forever.

LORI DESANTI

JUMELLE
For Lisa

You are an element of me—
you were born fire, and I
was born sky and in the womb

your hands were the first to find me.
We learned how to breathe water

and I knew the safety of your palms
before our eyes ever opened.
You mastered the art of sleep

and I held you at all hours of the night,
us curled into each other like Koi fish.
Water still brings you peace, and I hear

you hum water songs in the dark. Our
mother tells us you always blew bubbles
against your side of her ribcage;

and I still find comfort in the sounds
you make when you sleep.
The sound of fire you breathe
in your dreams and this,
this is home.

LAURA APOL

TWIN SISTER, STILLBORN

> *liana—(Fr. to bind): Any luxuriantly growing vine that*
> *roots in the ground and climbs, as around a tree trunk.*

I am the one who knew you,
the only one who will ever know.

I felt the push of your new heart,
the swim of your limbs, the turn of your self
as you turned toward me. We were wild fish,
smooth wet dancers side by side,
entwined. Our cells divided

then our selves divided and
in a liquid mirror we were a double face
with identical sightless eyes,
same nubby fingers, same zippered spines.

If they had known we were us,
had seen through the stretched wall into
the cave of our shared life,

they would have seen two shadows
bobbing and would have sung lullabies
twice. They would have found
a name that could divide

not into half, but evenly into itself.

And then they would have seen
one shadow quiet,
one wild fish fail, forever imprinting loss
in the growing bones of the other.
By the time I rushed us into the world,
one name was all we needed—
a name for me.

Forty years later,
I choose our birth—death—day
to name you now.

Lianna, tenacious vine holding me,

I have called your unnamed name
across the years, never knowing you
were the absence I was trying to fill, the end
of a sentence I didn't know how to begin.

I am echo to your silence;

you are the loss I took all these years
to find.

SHARON LASK MUNSON

LITTLE SISTER

It's my baby sister behind bars,
locked in for safety
or convenience.

Probably both.

I'm three, standing outside the wooden playpen,
too old to be trapped
by the jail set up in the living room.

Through wooden spokes I slip in
my red rubber ball, a cloth alphabet book,
her favorite Raff the Giraffe rattle.

She inspects the offerings carefully
before passing them back,
thinks it's a game.

She holds the doll over her head and laughs.
A sultry summer wind
wafts in through open windows.

White eyelet curtains flutter.

Late afternoon sun filters through
creating shadows.
The grandfather clock chimes four.

Dust motes hang in the catch of light.

My baby sister grips the bars
and tries to stand.
Letting go she laughs again.

I have no memory before her.

JULIE PREIS

CENTER OF ATTENTION

At first it is enough simply to be
a squirming bundle in the crib, to feel
the out-of-focus world assume the shape
of comfort in the daily lifting up
and laying down, the warm surprise of breath
upon my belly, the enticing wreath
of light around the faces leaning close
to mine. Sweet baby, little one, papoose,
I gum a smile as all eyes turn toward
me. So far, newness is its own reward.
And every day my sister, brother, four
and three, push their small noses through the bars
to sniff me out, to see how well I learn
about belonging, order, taking turns.

BEST BEHAVIOR

The order of belonging: took my turn,
distinguishing myself by being born
after the one time she miscarried, so
began successful. Slid right out, although
I weighed nine pounds, eleven ounces; won
advantage points for that good deed alone.
Cooperated, raised no ruckus, gave
no lip, never provoking push to shove.
Named for a saint who founded convents, I
gained favor early in the arms and eyes
of nuns, my mother's friends. One photograph
shows Sister Michael cradling me; the stiff
wings of her veil surround me like a tent.
I sleep, already vowed, obedient.

TOGETHERNESS

The edges beckon, but perimeters
of family contain us. Birth order,
name, age—these fundamental facts are how
we answer when we're asked, *Which Preis are you?*
(Age twelve, third oldest.) *You all look alike,*
as if we shouldn't. Each Sunday we pack
the front pew. Ladies smile approvingly
—*such good kids!*—at our pious group display.
At home we do our chores (assigned by size)
and make up secret words known just to us.
We chant our names backwards: *Gem, Kram, Eiluj.*
Eiluj, girl troll, hides underneath the bridge
and spies upon us as if she, and she
alone, has powers to escape the *We.*

THIRD AND ELEVENTH

Settling her body into mine, the last
of many siblings finds repose against
my chest. I lightly stroke the fontanel,
nuzzle her scalp as I have done with all
of them. I've oiled their bottoms, trimmed the soft
translucent nails, cradled the tender heft
of their heads in my palm. The songs I sing
to this one, written in our mother tongue
and minor key, draw lyrics from the same
shared well. Sibling: unwritten synonym
for unsought love. I cannot help but praise
her body and my own. My wish for us:
that each one carry with her future self
the simple knowledge that she is enough.

STEVE KOPPMAN

MORNING AGAIN

Dad slammed the door, and the boy felt the apartment shake. He had lost. Sitting there on the bed, the fresh little boy had lost again. Started a whole horrible ruckus. Out of what? Out of nothing. He didn't want to wear a sweater, he knew how he felt, he didn't need anybody to tell him. I just wish you'd put it on—The chill goes right through me—Such a nice sweater—Won't you just do that little thing to make me happy?—Such a little thing. But it went beyond that in seconds. Listen to your mother—You think you're so smart—Little ingrate—After what we've been through here the last few weeks—Can't you just let things be—You just have to do it—Shirley, he just has to do it—He has to be this way—He just has no appreciation. Dad screaming about him to Mom, shaking the house with the violence of it—doors slammed and cups crashing and coffee spilled all over Dad's new suit—with the sounds of the Kaddish in the synagogue still soft sad golden in his ears. He loved that melody, those perfect Hebrew sounds, mysterious but familiar as his heart, that meant peace with the other world, peace with Grandpa and everyone who had died. And now this—it always had to follow—there was no getting around the fights. Ever since Mom got sick, it was Get Tough on Bobby. And the Kaddish kept coming to him, and the words flowing uncontrollably through his mind— "Ruthie is a fat rat"—"Ruthie is a fat rat"—and he kept adding "NOT" at the end each time but that didn't stop them. Then he'd say it deliberately to himself as many times as he could, "Ruthie is a fat rat. Ruthie is a fat rat. Ruthie is a fat rat." If he could say it himself, over and over and over again, it wouldn't bother him so much, and God knew he didn't mean it. He talked to God inside his head, and God understood, God knew it was all right, that he didn't mean it, couldn't help it.

Ever since Mom was sick when Ruthie was born, it was disaster after disaster. Nobody knew when she'd be back, and the hospital wouldn't even let him visit. He'd wanted a little sister, but things hadn't worked out the way they said. And even when Mom finally came home, she had to keep going back, with Mrs. Clark and Mrs. Steiner coming to take care of him and Ruthie. He hated them. He only wanted Mom back, for good.

All kinds of strange things happened with Mom away. The bed shook in the middle of the night and he didn't know what it was and he was scared to look under and there was nobody to tell. Dad was always angry, yelling at him about talking back and getting to bed late and stop teasing your sister, you're older you should know better. And then Mom coming back, weak and tired and sleeping all the time, and then back to the hospital again and again.

Then Grandpa got really sick too. Mom told him it was some sort of "malignancy," which sounded really bad, especially since they only let him see Grandpa once the whole year and he looked like a shriveled-up ghost in his dark airless room, always sleeping, wrapped in sheets, watched all the time by nurses dressed in green instead of white. He couldn't even see Grandpa's face any more. When would things go back, the way they'd always been before, when everyone was all right?

It was summer so they sent him to day camp. He waited in front of the building every morning for the bus to come take him away for a day of fun with nice children he hated. Lining up in order at the start of the day, eating peanut butter and jelly sandwiches on benches in the woods. Boys who were bigger and stronger and knew what they were doing., who could swim, while he felt sick at the sight of the pool. He missed home all day and couldn't play ball any good and they'd even laugh at him when he'd talk cause he'd stammer and it was day-to-day torture. He just wanted to be home, reading, or something safe. One night he sat in the middle of the hallway next to the kitchen and screamed and cried as hard as he could, and Dad wasn't home, and Mom was weak now, she couldn't fight with him long, so really, If you hate it so much what's the point? So then he'd go sometimes and feel better cause if it was too bad maybe he wouldn't go the next day, and sometimes it would be good anyway cause he'd come home so tired he'd just fall asleep as soon as he got in. Nothing could really be good at home since things changed. Ruthie would cry all the time, and always had to be taken care of, and when he'd look at her—"Ruthie is a fat rat"—"NOT!"—"Ruthie is a fat rat"—"NOT!"—so usually he'd turn away and leave her alone. She'd started walking a few months before, she toddled back and forth through the apartment all the time now, chattering, tiny feet bouncing across the green carpet, and usually he felt he loved her, but she'd cry so much when he was around and then he'd hit her sometimes cause she'd cry and then she cried more and he didn't know what to do. Mom promised before Ruthie was born they'd never yell at him in front of the baby, but no sooner was she there alive in front of them than all that was forgotten. They never broke promises before. That old world was like some good dream from long ago now.

Finally Grandpa died, and it was strange, he didn't feel that much. It had taken Grandpa a year and a half to go through the whole thing and everyone said how strong he was and told Grandma what a great will to live he had to keep on so long, but he died anyway. There didn't seem so much to feel cause Grandpa had seemed gone a long time already as far as he could tell. Disease and death were everywhere now, and you didn't have to be old to die. Rudy from upstairs got hit in the head running between two cars just the other day, and could've easily been killed, his fat Italian mother screamed, but for the slow speed and caution of the driver. There were the Russians, with the A-bomb and the H-bomb, and leukemia, and cancer, polio and fires, red-faced bleeding men in the park across the street shouting wildly before they were carried away.

But none of that mattered when something sudden happened in the house. That was one good thing about the screaming, it took his mind off his chances of dying tomorrow or Mom's dying or God punishing him or "Ruthie is a fat rat." When Mom told him to put on the sweater it was chilly and he didn't want to and then Dad got in the act—he always had to—and Grandpa had just died—the week of mourning just over—Couldn't he understand?—Didn't he love them?—Why wouldn't he just listen? He has to be this way, Dad yelled, he just won't listen. And the door slammed and Dad would keep screaming behind it, first at Mom about him and at Mom for spoiling him and on and on and he couldn't stand it. He started singing the Kaddish, very quietly at first. *Yisgadal v,yiskadash sh'may rabah.* Mom said, While you're living, pray for the living, but she didn't understand what the Kaddish meant to him and now Grandpa was dead anyway, so it must be OK to sing it over and over. He lay back on his bed. He felt sick in his stomach and head and all over. He was really looking forward to school starting; it had to be better than this. When would things get right again? Could it really go on like this forever?

Discordant notes sounded from the piano in the living room. Then little steps. He looked up and she was slowly pushing open his door, hesitantly at first, as if hiding behind it, then toddling cautiously in. Her big blue eyes were circled with red from crying like she always did when Dad screamed. Her hair was parted in the middle, flowing over her ears. She stepped to his bed, standing next to him, and stared into his eyes, first with a sad, serious expression, then after a few seconds breaking with him into a little smile, then an uncontrollable giggle. She laughed and laughed and he even started giggling a little, he didn't know why, he couldn't help it, as she ran excitedly around the room, then jumped over and over against his bed.

"Hi," she said, straightening up for a second, then giggling again.

"Ruthie," he said.

"Love you," she said with a lilt, still giggling.

He put his hand around the back of her neck. "I . . . love you . . . too, Ruthie."

"Ruthie is a fat—" started through his mind.

"Love you, Bob-ert," she said, patting the top of his head. "Much much."

BETH McKIM

A TALE OF TWO SIBLINGS

Sibling rivalry was not allowed in our family. We were expected to *act nice*, *be sweet*, and *never argue with each other*. As the older sister to Meg, I had the special responsibilities of being a good role model, entertaining my sister, sharing my things with her and teaching her how to be a *good girl*, like I was. The story was always told that I was a mature and generous older child but I had my own methods of exacting revenge for having to sacrifice so much of what was mine.

You see, I became a storyteller. One of the earlier stories, when she was about five, was about how she had come to live with us. This one, although not entirely original, seemed to be effective for the purpose I had in mind. I told her we found her in a basket on our front doorstep with a note attached saying, *Please keep this baby for us until we come back to get her someday. You can name her whatever you would like for now.* Since my name was Beth, we decided to call her Meg since it *sort of* rhymed with Beth. Meg cried each time I recited this and told our parents, who assured her it was not true. When questioned, I promptly denied having told her that and suggested maybe she had dreamed it.

Another story I enjoyed telling was that Mom and Dad had borrowed us from an acting school and we were actually auditioning to be in the family. If we did not act right or play our parts well, they would be turning us back into the school for better kids. This one seemed to work fairly well because she was too afraid to even ask the adults if this one were true because of her fear of flunking the tryout.

I figured out there was no Easter Bunny when I was about seven and Meg was almost five. I went to her and asked her why she believed one little rabbit could hop all over the world delivering candy. She said she did believe it and I shook my head in arrogant disbelief that she could be so silly even though I had believed it just one year earlier.

About a year later, after learning the *truth* about Santa Claus, it took me two years to convince Meggie that he actually didn't exist. After I thought I had gotten the message across the first year, she went right back to believing, for one more year. Little did I realize the power of her magical thinking phase was stronger than the important information I was trying to impart.

But my favorite story was the one that upset her the most. I was around ten and she was seven. This was a two-part story. The first part was about my having a twin named Seth whose name conveniently rhymed with mine. We were *completely identical* in every way except that he was a boy. The famous *Institute for Geniuses* came to town and Seth and I were both taken for interviews. We, of course, tied for the honor of leaving our family and joining the Institute. Only because they had an opening for a boy did they accept Seth instead of me.

Now the second part of the story I told Meg involved her having a twin brother named Egg, who, of course, she did not remember. Around the same time that the Genius Institute came to town, a well-known circus also arrived announcing they needed a new freak for their sideshows. Meg and Egg both qualified to go, but Egg was accepted only because, once again, there was only an opening for a boy.

I told Meg I was genuinely happy that we both got to stay while Seth and Egg were sent away. This was accompanied by an unheeded warning to her not to talk to Mom and Dad about this because they were still upset about losing their boys. They pretended to be mad at me because of upsetting my little sister but I caught the quick smiles they gave each other and interpreted this as minor appreciation of my creativity.

Looking back, the tall tales seemed to dissipate much of my hidden anger and resentment at having to behave so well. And even better news, Meg and I are best friends today and have been for as far back as I can remember. And Meg's husband, who enjoys a good story like the rest of us, has a special pet name for his beloved wife, *Egg*.

PATRICIA BARONE

THE WINDOW BED
for Dan

The year you were four
Mom kept you in bed.
She made a cradle of her arms,
set you down and up again,
and wouldn't let you stand to pee
like other boys. She didn't speak
of the fever or your heart, too large
for your chest, only four years after
our brother died when he was four.

Your world, a bed by the window,
overlooked a playground,
the large toys of the real world.
Your cowboy hat on the bedpost,
you meshed your face to the screen.

Twelve years old and no where
        to be but there,
I read fairy tales to you.
Outside my window
boys and girls were touching
        as if in play.
When street lights lit, they scattered
but we stayed on.

One day we watched a tribe of children.
On the merry-go-round, they started slow,
tennis shoes down, then pulled their feet up,
not for safety, but to make it go faster, faster,
till the runner jumped on the only way—
    both legs at once.

This girl my age, her legs longer
than they'd ever be again,
pushed the others till dizzy
    then swung,
her hands tight on the bar,
her back arched concave,
her small round stomach
just grazing the ground.

I wanted to be that girl.
You'd laugh and hold on tight.

KATIE GLAUBER BUSH

QUEEN OF THE MAY

La querencia is a Spanish word that roughly translates as *home, hearth, nest,* or *sanctuary*. In bullfighting, it's the bull's favorite spot in the ring, where he goes when wounded to renew his strength and get ready to charge again.

My family moved to our home on Winchester Road in 1955. By the late 1950s, my *querencia* was the bedroom I shared with my sister, Ann, on the second floor. My two brothers slept in their room down the hall. A large storage closet and a yellow-tiled bathroom were the only other rooms in the upstairs of our suburban Louisville home.

Twin beds dominated our space. The headboards were built with a shelf for our books on either side. In the middle of the headboard, a sliding door supported my pillow and head or slid to either side to reveal a spot for hiding treasures. My headboard bookshelf housed *The Bobbsey Twins* and *The Bobbsey Twins in the Country*, both by Laura Lee Hope. Louisa May Alcott's *Little Women* held an honored spot. I loved to read stories about Bert, Nan, Freddie and Flossie. They make me think of my own family—Pete, Ann, Katie, and Joe. I identified with Beth in *Little Women* because I had been sick so much of my soon-to-be eight years on this planet. I also noticed that the authors I adored had three names, and I often tried to think of a third name to give myself.

Ann was three years older and the right side of her headboard stored a record player. The left side was filled with her 45 rpm record collection including Brenda Lee's *Dynamite* and *Catch a Falling Star* by Perry Como. We liked to lie in bed and listen to music before we went to sleep each night. I learned all the words to *Dynamite* and could tremble my voice like Brenda Lee.

The walls sloped down from the ceiling and we had to duck in some places or stand with our heads and necks bent. I didn't mind being tall because Ann was tall. But there were days when I yearned to be shorter.

One day in early May, I walked home from school and ran straight up to our bedroom. Ann was already home.

"Today, they picked the girl who will crown Mary," I said.

"Who did they pick?" Ann asked.

Tears welled up in my eyes. "Mary Denise Hudson," I sobbed.

One of the big traditions in our parish school was the annual May procession. It culminated in the crowning of Mary. The statue stood in the grotto at Our Lady of Lourdes, directly in front of the church. I had been so good all year because I knew a second-grade girl would be chosen to crown Mary and I wanted to be the one.

"She was chosen because she was little, Katie."

I knew Ann was right. Every year of my childhood, the smallest girl in the second grade was chosen to do the crowning. Perhaps the nuns wanted to symbolize, most vividly, the innocence of childhood. It was no different than kindergarten rhythm band. I was told to stand with the boys in the top row of the risers, handed a pair of wooden sticks, and instructed to keep time with them as our teacher played the piano. The medium-size kids played the jingle sticks or handheld shakers. Mary Denise got the triangle and tiny Bernadette McDevitt was handed the tambourine. I was crushed. Was there no place for a chubby young girl, taller than the second-grade boys, to play a special instrument or climb up the steps to do the crowning?

My relationship with my older sister was something I never questioned. Ann liked to play with me as long as I let her tell me what to do. I didn't mind. We played going on the train out west to see Grandma. Ann got to be the nurse on the train and I was the sick passenger. We played jail. Ann was the sheriff and fed me, the prisoner, dry saltine crackers in my jail cell beneath a small desk and a chair turned upside down. I made potholders while Ann plotted ways we could become rich selling them to neighbors.

This was a young woman of great imagination. Ann, my refuge, knew what to do. "We'll just have our own May procession right here in our room," she announced.

We got busy setting our small statue of Mary on the top of Ann's headboard, over the record player. The walls of our room were painted Circus Pink. Mother allowed Ann and me to pick out the color. When we turned on the overhead light, late that special afternoon, the room glowed. Aunt Irene had sewn layered café curtains for the window. The crisp starched cotton was striped in pink and teal. Black stripes separated the colored stripes and made them behave. The dust ruffles on our beds were made of the same striped fabric. We each had a quilted teal bedspread, short enough on either side to allow the dust ruffle to peek through. A loopy pink rug on the hardwood floor in front of the dresser was nubby and dug into my bare feet when I walked across it. We worked together to roll it up and get it out of our way for the May procession.

"Run down and get Mom's aluminum foil," Ann ordered. "While you do that, I'll go cut some flowers." Off we ran. When we got back to our room, Ann told me to crimp a small piece of foil into a makeshift crown. At the top, Ann stuck a small bloom from Virginia Perkins' spirea bridal wreath bush. We were ready. We closed the door and I waited for Ann to give the signal to start.

"OK," Ann ordered. "Walk like you're in a wedding. Step. Stop. Step. Stop."

How does she know all of this, I wondered. But I never questioned where Ann got her information. She just knew things.

"Oh Mary we crown thee with blossoms today," we began to sing. Solemnly, Ann stepped forward to start the ceremony around our small room. "Queen of the angels. Queen of the May." We slowly and reverently processed down the far left side of my bed, up the narrow space between the two beds, then down the aisle again and up the far right side of her bed. We traversed the room again and again until the song was ending.

Ann stopped, turned to me, and motioned me to go forward. To my amazement, she handed me the crown. This day, this one time, I was not to be the patient on the train or the prisoner in the jail. I was going to be the one who got to crown Mary. With all the dignity I could muster, I reached up and placed the regal floral headgear on the little statue.

We crowned Mary seven times that afternoon. Then we went downstairs to a dinner of fried pork chops.

By nightfall, I had long forgotten my hurt feelings and was just ready to go to bed. I loved sleeping in my cotton seersucker pajamas on a warm spring night. They were hand-me-downs from Ann and soft from countless washings. Ann and I lay with our heads at the foot of our beds in front of the open window. The attic fan pulled in tepid air to wash over our sweaty bodies. The scent of pussy willows and Virginia's spirea bush rode in with the wind. In this bedroom, this safe haven, the hum of the fan blade, turning round and round, sent us to sleep.

ROSE HAMILTON-GOTTLIEB

FAVORITE SON

Usually Willie's sister made sure Stefan got on the school bus, but today she'd gone home with a friend who lived on a different bus route, so Willie was stuck with their little brother. At the door to the kindergarten room, he heard Stefan's voice.

"And we have seven cows," his brother was saying. "One's named Beulah. And then there's Bossy . . . she's mean . . . and Tildy and . . . " Willie peered around the edge of the door and saw Stefan sitting on Miss Reynolds' lap, looking up at her from under those long black eyelashes women always went nuts over. Willie had spent first and second grades in old lady Reynolds' classroom, and as far as he could see the only kid she ever held on her bony lap was the superintendent's measly little girl. Now here was Stefan, and telling her some long-winded story.

Now, Stefan held one hand in the air and counted on his fingers until he came to the last cow's name. Then he slapped his hands down on his knees and gave his head a jerk.

That was Stefan's latest habit, shaking his head, like a period at the end of his sentences. It drove Dad crazy. Mom said it just made Stefan worse when Dad yelled at him for it, and Dad said if she had her way he'd be a baby all his life. Then Mom would accuse him of taking his troubles out on a little boy. They had a big argument about it last week when Dad came home upset on account of Frank Morgan's dying.

Frank Morgan had not only been Dad's old friend, but he had held his note, and now Dad had to come up with a lot of money all at once. This morning he left for Des Moines to borrow from a finance company that advertised on the radio. Willie knew all about it because he'd heard his folks talk about how the banker in town wouldn't loan his dad the money to settle up with the Morgan family.

It was a mystery why Miss Reynolds liked Stefan. She made kids stay in at recess for what she called "annoying nervous habits," like sitting at a desk all by himself would make a kid stop biting his nails. But the teacher didn't seem to notice Stefan's tics.

"And do you help milk the cows?" she said.

"No." Stefan jerked his head again. "But I will now I'm in school. Sometimes the cows kick though, and I worry some about that."

Willie supposed he shouldn't be surprised at the teacher's sweet tone of voice, after the way Sunday school teachers and the other ladies from church carried on about Stefan. He could understand them making a big deal over a baby, but Stefan's cuteness didn't show any signs of going away. Willie was eleven, and as far as he knew, nobody had ever called him cute. His three sisters teased him about his big ears and his freckles and crooked front teeth, and he supposed Miss Reynolds would fall over dead before she smiled at him.

Willie stepped into the room and caught his brother's eye and Stefan slid off the teacher's lap.

"There's my big brother. Gotta go," he said. He picked up his lunch pail and followed Willie into the hall.

"Miss Reynolds is nice," Stefan said, as they went down the stairs. "She's not a bit mean like you said. Today she let me pick up the reading books and put them on the shelf."

"Yeah, I might've known you'd be teacher's pet," Willie said. "Come on, we're late." He had to run ahead to catch the school bus before it pulled away from the curb. He waited, one foot on the bottom step, until Stefan had climbed, puffing, onto the bus. The driver, who had given Willie a dirty look for being late, smiled at his brother.

"You sit here." Willie sat him down near the front and went to the back to sit with the big boys, then wished he hadn't left him alone because he had to spend the whole ride watching to make sure nobody teased him.

The bus drove through town and out into the country past oat fields turned to stubble and corn, stunted and yellow from a summer without rain. Almost every week, clouds would roll in and there'd be thunder and lightning and a few raindrops. Then it would stop and Mom would look out the window and mutter something about there not even being enough moisture to settle the dust. Dad was in a bad mood most of the time.

The bus ride was short, a mile and a half on the highway and a quarter of a mile on the gravel road leading to the Hartin mailbox. Last year, Willie and his sisters had had to walk from the highway, but when their little brother started school, Mom made the superintendent send the bus up the gravel road, because if Stefan walked very far in cold weather he got asthma. Even now, walking up the hill on the dirt road, Willie couldn't go as fast as he wanted or Stefan would get out of breath trying to keep up.

The boys' shoes kicked up dust, and two redwing blackbirds dove at them while others circled overhead and scolded. "Why do those birds do that, Willie?" Stefan said.

"I don't know," he said, although he did know that the birds were trying to scare them away from their territory.

"Willie, how old were you when you first milked a cow?"

"I don't know." Willie usually answered his brother's questions that way, just to get him to stop pestering him, but this time he really didn't know. He'd followed Dad around all his life, sitting on his lap on the tractor, handing him nails while he made fence. He couldn't remember the first time he'd watched a calf being born. He'd hung around the creamery and the tavern with Dad and listened to him talk politics with the other farmers. "This is Willie, my son," Dad would say when he met someone new. He'd feel his father's hand on his shoulder and it was like something came into him from that strong hand. But he was different with Stefan.

Willie did remember being too little to help milk. The cows had looked huge and scary, the way they stamped their feet and blew out their noses as they climbed the ramp into the barn. One by one, his dad had fastened their necks into the stanchions so their heads stuck out into the walkway that divided the milking area from the horses' stalls. Willie had to watch from there after the day he fell into the manure trough.

He remembered going up and down the length of the passage, as Stefan sometimes did now, listening to the milk splash into the pails and to the stirring of barn swallows in their nests overhead. His dad had still farmed with horses, then, and sometimes the plow horses hung their heads over the sides of the mangers, breathing on his neck. The cows followed him with their big eyes as he dared himself to get close, and sometimes they lowered their heads and sniffed at him. Their mouths worked, always chewing, bits of greenish foam on their lips.

More than anything, Willie remembered being surrounded by big animals but feeling safe with Dad nearby. Then one day his dad unlocked one of the empty stanchions and helped him step from the walkway to the other side and set him down on a three-legged milking stool.

"Do you think Daddy will teach me to milk now I'm in school?" Stefan asked.

"I don't know," Willie said. The truth was, he couldn't imagine his dad teaching Stefan anything. For the last year or so, about the only time he'd paid attention to the boy was to scold him. Most of the time Willie was happy to be the favorite, but sometimes, like now, he felt sorry for his brother.

Stefan began to wheeze, and Willie slowed to let him catch up. Then, surprising even himself, he put his hand on his brother's thin shoulder and said, "I'll teach you how to milk."

The car was still gone, which meant Dad wasn't back from Des Moines. Willie hurried to change his clothes and called Sparky to go with him to get the cows from the pasture. He drove the cows into the barn and locked their necks in the stanchions, then helped Stefan pass from the walkway through an empty stanchion to the milking area. He put him on a three-legged milking stool alongside Tildy. She was the gentlest of the cows and the least likely to lose patience and kick over the bucket or switch her tail in the boy's face.

Willie got down on his knees behind his brother, at eye level with Tildy's swollen udder. The day Dad taught him to milk came back in a rush, the cow's warm smell mixed with smells of manure and dried hay and pipe tobacco, the swallows in the rafters, Dad's whiskery chin on the back of his neck. Now, he reached around his brother the same way his dad had reached around him. "Lean in close," he said, "and put your head up against her."

"Will she kick?" Stefan asked.

"Not Tildy. Not unless you do something stupid. Just be ready to close your eyes if she decides to whack you with her tail. Watch, now." He took hold of a teat with each hand. Swollen with milk, they were velvet smooth and warm to the touch. "You squeeze the top with your thumb, like this, then pull down, first on one, then the other." Milk pinged against the side of the aluminum bucket. "Now you try it."

Stefan grabbed hold and after several tries, a thin stream of milk splashed into the bucket. Then another. He laughed. "Hey look, Willie. Look, I'm milking."

"When your hands get tired, I'll take over," Willie said. "It'll be awhile before you can milk a cow all by yourself."

"I can do it. I can do it." Stefan squirmed on the stool as if to shuck his brother off.

Willie was wondering whether or not to leave Stefan's side when he heard the car door slam. Dad might think it was careless to leave his little brother alone on the milking stool, so he stayed where he was, on one knee, his chest brushing against Stefan's back.

Dad appeared in the doorway, dressed in the dark blue pinstriped suit he wore to funerals, his gray hair slicked back. He stared at Stefan. "What the hell's going on here?" he said. "He's not big enough to milk. He might get kicked. He'll make the cows nervous."

Willie felt Stefan's body go stiff. "It's okay, Dad. He's doing good. I showed him how just like you showed me."

"See Daddy," Stefan said, his voice small and cracked. "I can do it." Willie felt Stefan's shoulders tremble as he pulled, first one teat, then another. But no milk came now, and from the way Tildy stamped her feet and switched her tail, he knew she was holding back because she was nervous. Sometimes he thought the cows knew when Dad had had a bad day.

"I said, he's not old enough," his dad said. "Anyway, we only got two milking stools. Now get him out of here."

Bossy, the most nervous and mean-tempered of the cows, rolled her eyes and bawled and pulled against the stanchions. Dad swore and swung an empty bucket and hit her on the back. She bawled again and kicked out at him, and the other cows began stamping and bawling.

Willie whispered in Stefan's ear, "Go on. We'll try again some other time."

Stefan sniffed and slid off the stool and ran out of the barn door.

Willie took his place and buried his head in the cow's soft flank and took hold of the warm teats. But the sound of milk splashing in the pail failed to drown the sound of his brother's sobs as he ran to the house.

That night, Willie lay awake for a long time. Beside him, Stefan sprawled on the lumpy mattress, the covers thrown off. He was wearing his new winter pajamas that had come that day from Sears and Roebuck. The nights were still too warm for the plaid flannel, but he'd wanted to wear them, and Mom had probably thought that having something new would take his mind off what had happened in the barn. She was always babying him to make up for the way his dad treated him. Stefan's face looked whiter than ever in the moonlight and he slept with his mouth slightly open, wheezing a little.

Willie listened to the sound of crickets from outside and stared at the patterns the moon made on the wall. There had been a full moon the night Stefan was born. Willie had been the same age his brother was now, and had lain in this same bed, so frightened by his mother's screams he was unable to move. No cow ever carried on like that when giving birth, and he'd been sure she was going to die.

Other images came and went in Willie's head. The baby curled against Mom's side, eyes squeezed shut like a newborn kitten's. Mom's face the color of cement. The bucket of bloody rags on the back porch. The Red Cross box on the dresser that had held the plasma that saved his mother's life. His dad holding Stefan on his lap, a look on his face that Willie hadn't seen before. Much later, Stefan sprawled across the foot of his parents' bed where he slept until he was three. And later, dragging his pillow upstairs after Willie, then running back down to Mom when the lights were put out. And crying up the steps after Dad finally yelled at him and told him not to come back. Waking in the middle of the night to his brother's wheezing, his lips blue, his eyes wide with fear. And waking again to see Dad watching by the bed. Now, when Stefan woke up without breath, it was their older sister who usually tended him.

Maybe when Dad saw that his little brother was old enough to help with the work, he'd treat him better. Willie decided that tomorrow he'd make Stefan his own milking stool.

After awhile, his parents' voices drifted up the open stairway. "Thirteen percent interest. Can you believe that? One or two good years and I would have had Frank paid off; now I'm in debt up to my ears all over again."

Willie lifted his head off the pillow to hear Mom's answer. "Did you ask Frank's son to carry the note?"

"He said he'd like to help me but the family needed the money to settle the estate. Did I tell you I went out there the day after the funeral to see what he wanted to do and the son didn't even know I owed the money? He looked all over for the note before he found it in Frank's toolbox. Good thing I had my cancelled checks to prove what I'd paid."

Willie couldn't hear Mom's reply, and Dad lowered his voice so it blended into the night sounds of insects and dogs barking in the distance. They talked for a long time, though, and he fell asleep listening to them, safe in the knowledge that his father was downstairs, standing between him and the world outside the farm.

The next day, the car was again gone from the driveway when Willie got home from school. "Come on," he said to Stefan. "We'll surprise Dad." He found some scrap lumber behind the machine shed and sawed off a piece the right length and nailed two smaller pieces on either end.

While he worked, Stefan stood on one foot and then the other, chattering away. "Bennie, he sits behind me in school, he helps milk. He even goes after the cows all by himself. He says next year maybe he can drive the tractor."

Willie only half listened, answering with "Oh?" whenever his brother wanted an answer.

It wasn't a three-legged stool like the ones he and Dad used, but it would do. "I'll paint it on Saturday," he said, "but you can use it like it is until then."

He put the stool alongside Tildy, and Stefan moved in close and put his cheek up against the cow's soft underbelly and took hold of the teats, like he'd been taught. Willie watched him for a few minutes. His feet didn't quite reach the ground so that the cow was keeping him from falling off the stool. He'd never seen Tildy stand that still. After a few tries, the milk started to come.

"That's good," Willie said. "Stop when you can't get any more milk or when your hands get tired."

"Okay." Stefan didn't jerk his head like he usually did when he talked.

Willie sat down before Beulah, who stood next to Tildy. He felt light and happy, like when he'd spent the day selling paper flowers to raise money for veterans on Poppy Day. He'd made something useful with his own hands. He'd taught his brother to milk and made him happy at the same time. And his dad would be proud when he saw that Stefan really could help. Maybe Stefan couldn't ever do much in the fields because of his asthma, but he could do some things. He hoped Dad would come home before his brother's hands got too tired.

He heard the car backfire to a stop in the driveway, then the clang of milk pails and the rusty creak of the barnyard gate as it opened and closed. He held back a grin, imagining Dad's face when he came to the door and saw the baby of the family on his own milking stool, his legs not even touching the floor, his eyes shut tight in case Tildy switched her tail. Short, thin streams of milk came faster into Stefan's bucket, and Willie almost laughed out loud, picturing his little brother squeezing and pulling as if his life depended on it.

The moment came and went and he knew Dad had to be standing in the doorway. Why didn't he say something? He stopped breathing and waited. Then a pail crashed against the concrete floor. Beulah pushed her head further into the stanchions as if trying to walk right through and out the other side. Willie patted her flank and pushed back his stool, glancing under Tildy. All he could see was Stefan's hands clenched on his knees and his feet swinging. He didn't have to see it to know that his brother's head was jerking like it was about to fall off, the very thing his dad hated most.

"What the hell is this?" his dad said. "Didn't I tell you he couldn't help?"

Willie stepped clear of Beulah's nervous feet. "But he's doing great, Dad. You should've seen him. Look at the milk in that pail. And I made him his own stool."

Dad looked at Stefan. "Go on now." His voice was hard but controlled.

Stefan tipped over his stool as he scrambled off it. He stood in the corner, his eyes afraid and his head jerking.

Willie looked from his brother to his dad. Didn't he see he was standing between Stefan and the door and that the boy was afraid to go past him?

His dad picked up the fallen stool and sent it crashing. Stefan's pail upset and his milk spilled into the manure trough. "Now look what you've done. Get up to the house where you belong." Dad's fists were clenched and he looked as if he hated Stefan. Willie felt helpless as he watched his brother cower in the corner.

It was clear that Stefan wanted to run, but there was no place to go except past his dad, who blocked the door. Finally, he squeezed into an empty stanchion. It was locked on top so there was barely room for him to pass through, and for a few seconds he was trapped, his body from the waist up sticking through the wood posts. Willie sucked in his own stomach, as if that would help his brother squeeze through. Then Stefan was free and running through the narrow walkway between the stanchions and the mangers. He tripped on the doorsill and fell to the ground outside the barn. Willie heard him crying all the way to the house.

Dad stared at the corner where Stefan had been trapped a moment before. His eyes, full of anger then, looked empty now, and a little sad, as if he wished he could take back what had happened. But he never took anything back, never said he was sorry. Their eyes met and Dad looked away, then pulled a milking stool up to Tildy, who stamped and swished her tail as if she didn't like what had happened.

Willie went back to Beulah. It was awhile before either cow was willing to give up her milk, so it was quiet in the barn except for swallows twittering and cows swishing their tails. Willie swallowed his sobs, but his tears fell freely and he was grateful when the sound of splashing milk covered his sniffles.

That night he lay awake while Stefan slept beside him. He felt ashamed when he remembered how just last week he'd teased his brother about the red and yellow flowers on his flour-sack pajama bottoms. He studied his brother's face in the moonlight and tried to imagine what it was like to be him. Stefan's breath was even tonight, and his face was still, long black lashes dusting white cheeks. One side of his face was scraped raw where he'd fallen on cracked corn that had been scattered outside the barn for the chickens. Below, on his bare ribs, the full moon revealed more skinned flesh where he'd squeezed through the tight stanchion.

From downstairs came the familiar murmur of his parents' voices, a sound that had always made Willie feel safe. He wondered what made Stefan feel safe. Was it their mother, who'd kept him in her bed until he was three? His sister, who got up with him at night? His teacher, who held him on her lap and talked to him after the other kids had gone home? What did Stefan think when he heard their dad's voice floating up the stairs at night? He thought of his brother sitting between his legs with his face up close to the cow he'd been afraid of, and how his body had stiffened when he heard his dad's voice. His look of fear when he was trapped in the corner of the barn, afraid to go past his own father to get out. And Willie knew. It was up to him to keep Stefan safe, to stand between his brother and the world.

CINDY STEWART-RINIER

SUPER 8 VOICEOVER

The churning blades of our arms cut each other
out of the picture as, in repeated succession,
each of the three youngest siblings pushes
to the center of the frame. Behind our antic
jockeying, the eldest two play it cool.

Bell-bottomed and cosmically bemused,
my brother looks on from the porch where he leans
against the iron rail, his eyes obscured
by the overhang of his auburn Beatles bangs
while my sister, angled slightly away,

feigns indifference. Her arms cross tight
over her chest where Dad's camera tends
to linger too long and her darkly lined eyes
burn against her frosted hair and lips—
a cross between sexual pout and shout.

It's always someone's birthday, and inside,
Grandma holds the lit cake while across town
Mom irons rich people's clothes or picks apples
from the orchard in Opportunity to make enough
to feed the five of us when we return from our starring

roles in Dad's weekend spectacles, in which we remain
forever voiceless, actual words mere implications
drawn from the shapes of our mouths chewing
their cuds of air, the inaudible soundtrack—
"All You Need is Love"—endangering us, saving us.

STOICHIOMETRY

In the hands of six post-divorce children, science
manifests first in a test of genetic provenance:
Belonging issued as the dare, *Bet you can't*
roll your tongue like this! Each of us stepping up,
one by one, to muscle our tongues
into the shape of a ship's empty hull.

Then, experiments in transmutation:
We fill two jars with white vinegar,
ply one with a drumstick picked clean,
the other with the orb of a raw egg,
which floats like an eye enlarged
behind a coke-bottle lens.

For a while, we follow the lazy sizzle
that scuttles up shell and bone, bubbling
dissolved calcium into a sludge at the top
like dishwater suds. Then we neglect them
for days until we discover the egg, bloated,
denuded of shell, its yolk like a depressed

sun trying to shine through vellum membrane.
And we withdraw the bone, marvel at its loss
of brittle, how it's bendable, less breakable.
But that day all six of us line up across the dirty kitchen floor
from oldest to youngest,
join at the hands like a paper doll chain,

and counting to three, Rob grabs the handle
of the shorted-out refrigerator zapping current
down the line through us, is it another test
of bonds and broken bonds, or simply
reenactment? First the jolt, then the wonder
at the way we're threaded—if briefly—together.

BRIAN BURNS

HALF HEARTED

I spent my twenty-first birthday travelling from one urine-soaked bus terminal to another. November 25th always falls within a few days of Thanksgiving and the death knell of family gatherings was calling me home from Boston to New Hampshire.

"Mom feels bad for you," Summer, my middle sister, texted to our sibling group message. "You don't have any plans for your twenty-first?"

"Honestly, Bubby," Katrina, the oldest, replied. "You have to do something! And did you really tell mom that you wanted pumpkin pie instead of a birthday cake? What the fuck?"

I could have stayed in Boston that night but my friends were all leaving the city before a snow storm the next day. I wouldn't admit it out loud but I was relieved. By night's end, I drank a bottle of wine, watched real housewives hash out childhood traumas and waxed poetic to my mother about my lust for a straight boy. If Katrina and Summer still lived at home, they would have demanded we go out: bringing me to whatever dive bar in New Hampshire posed the lowest risk of Hepatitis-C. And I would have had fun. If I let myself.

"So, how's Luke?" asked Summer, pulling onto I-93 the next day as we drove south for Thanksgiving in New Jersey. "The straight boy. That is his name, right? Mom filled me in."

"Jesus Christ."

Summer, all dimples and eye makeup, laughed.

"You think I like resorting to conversations with mom? Kristine wouldn't be telling me about your life if you told me and Kat yourself."

"I don't know," I said, shifting in my seat. "I figure that you guys don't care that much about what I'm doing."

"We're your sisters."

Half true. For my sisters and me, the same womb and Dutch Colonial was called home. But, every Saturday, their father would pick them up to spend the afternoon together. My sisters—from our mom's first marriage—have a different last name, darker eyes and Roman noses. Children of a different decade, Katrina was in college before my voice changed and Summer was engaged before I could drive a car. My balls have dropped and I can parallel park but the half remains.

Thanksgiving dinner was at two o'clock. Katrina and her husband showed up at three.

"What are we drinking?" Katrina asked, slapping my ass and grinning.

"How do you think bringing up police brutality will go over with Aunt Karen?" I asked, handing Katrina a glass of wine and pointing at a copy of Bill O'Reilly's memoir on a table nearby.

Katrina clinked my glass, "About as well as things are going with that straight boy of yours."

At my age, both of my sisters were already in relationships with the men they've married. When Aunt Karen told me that I should bring my boyfriend to Thanksgiving, I asked her if she knew about someone I didn't. My sisters both made it look easy. Katrina and Greg, teenaged camp counselors at the time, met on a field trip to Medieval Times. Hopelessly millennial, Summer met Cory through MySpace: bonding over Chris Farley movies and angst rock. Katrina and Greg—still as adolescent in spirit as when they first met—don't have much in common with Summer and Cory but their love is all the same. A love I can't say I've found.

If it weren't for my Nana and Aunt Patti—kindred turkey babies, born a day before and after me—I'd dread the annual rite of opening gifts in front of my family. But the attention is distributed as evenly as the presents and, for that, I give thanks. Claiming a couch in the corner of Aunt Karen's living room, I reaped checks and cash, a crocheted scarf and a card from both of my sisters bearing a photo of a guy at a DJ booth.

I looked up at my sisters, both drooling in my direction as I held up the picture, "Explain."

"You're coming to see Tiesto with us in Atlantic City next month!" they said in unison.

Though this gift—as tragic and comedic as Atlantic City itself—wasn't something I would have asked for, I didn't roll my eyes or scoff or tell them to bring someone else. Instead, I thanked them and let myself look forward to it.

✤ ✤ ✤

Ground zero of grooming, our Atlantic City hotel room held more Aqua Net than oxygen.

"I hate boys," Katrina yelled from the bathroom. "You put on deodorant, a T-shirt and you're ready to go. Meanwhile, us girls devote half our waking hours to not fucking up a cat-eye."

I smelled burning hair and I was eight years old again. As a kid, I watched Katrina and Summer get ready for weekend parties and found magic in their rituals. The music they played, the phone calls they answered, the perfumes that lingered in the curling iron steam. In their hand drawn ovals on the fogged bathroom mirror, I saw all the work it took to be a girl. I worshipped them, knowing them as my sisters but understanding them as women.

Applying lip gloss with her free hand, Summer passed us champagne flutes and toasted, "To Bubby's twenty-first!"

A few minutes later, Greg came back up to the room from the casino floor. Not long after, Katrina's friends joined us as well—all coked-up Long Island princesses tweaking their way into high heels and short dresses. Music was put on and the girls started to squawk. But the toast, while it lasted, was just for us. We were the oldest we've ever been as we sipped that six-dollar brut but we all still knew each other as kids.

"Bubby? Did you just call your brother Bubby?" asked my sister's friend, Lauren, a Staten Islander with a voice ravaged by Newports and post-nasal drip. "Rose, my Jewish grandmother, is Bubby."

"I am a Jewish grandmother," I assured her.

"I'm telling you right now," Summer said, her heart full and flute empty. "Whenever I have kids—and don't even let mom know I said those words out loud—you're getting called Uncle Bubby."

I was more satisfied with the idea than I cared to admit.

"Their gay Uncle Bubby," I said. "Guncle Bubby."

The final false eyelash was glued onto a shaded lid and we were ready to walk down to where Tiesto was playing. My sisters talked about how I ended up being called Bubby along the way but couldn't trace the history. There's something about it. I get called Bubby by my sisters and I hear what it means. Their middle school dates I ruined and the things they sheltered me from and the things they exposed me to. To them, and for them, I'm still Bubby.

"Here's a party favor," said Greg once we claimed our spots by the stage, a pill lying in his open palm. "It's E. Don't get any more drinks. And chew gum."

It hit me slowly but all at once. I could feel the beat pounding in the floor below my feet and pummeling through the air around my head. Beams of neon light and bits of white confetti kissed faces in the crowd. Dancing next to my two sisters, my heart beating from the outside in, I screamed in their ears, "This is so good!" They couldn't have heard what I said but that didn't matter. My pupils were dilated and every light in the room was being let in.

Katrina introduced me and Summer to one person after another, her fellow disciples of club kid church. This was their midnight mass and I was learning how to pray. There were moments I can't remember and there were moments I saw things clearer than ever. I was cruised in the bathroom and got a rave-glove light show from a shirtless guido. I grinded with middle-aged women and joined strangers to the bar. But my sisters and I kept finding each other.

Katrina and Summer, the sisters who I'd spent my whole life watching, looked different to me. They asked me if I was having a good time and I felt it when I said that I was. The pill in my blood was our blood and we danced in time to the same beat. It hit me slowly but all at once.

TIM J. MYERS

FOR MY BROTHER RAWLEY

While I lay dreaming in a dark back bedroom,
napping at my parents' house,
a voice came through my sleep
saying this or that, and woke me—
and seemed my own voice.
Once awake I understood.
It was my brother, looks and sounds like me,
playing with my son on the living-room floor.

I who have felt myself apart
knew in that quiet of just-waking
that our blood is the same blood,

and in that moment first understood
my mother and father,
the wide good planting
of which I am.

MICHELE WOLF

ASTIGMATISM

When I held smooth the satin to zip
Up your wedding dress, frosted with flounces
And pearl-beaded filigree, a rococo
Confection more sugary than the cake,
And watched as you swiveled slowly to face
Me—all floaty notes, pure flute—so still
As I situated the baby's breath and the veil,
How could I have told you, knowing
You'd learn it soon enough, my perfect doll,
How fuzzy the world is, how the clearest
Picture, frill-tipped gladioli in primary
Colors, can dissolve into darkness, how
The eye can fool you, presenting a straight
Or diagonal path when the earth is curved.

"It can be corrected," I tell you, a half-truth,
When you call me to say you can no longer
Focus, nothing is sharp. And I can hear
How the light is bent in your voice, the shadows
Behind what you say, while in my mind's
Eye you stare at me, blinking, a week old,
The day you were placed in my arms,
Able to distinguish little but two black
Moons, my eyes dancing in the fog.
That this was the most exquisite
Instance of my childhood never changes.
Nor does the decade between us
Or the way you looked up at my face
After racing out the front door

To greet me eight years later, almost
Toppling me over, ringing my waist.
Two sisters, so nearsighted
That upon my return to you, before
I resumed my groping tromp
Through the world, you held me like a reference
Point, a place you will always find,
The sheen of your eyes announcing
My bearings as much as your clear
Shout of my name, as your words: *"You're here."*

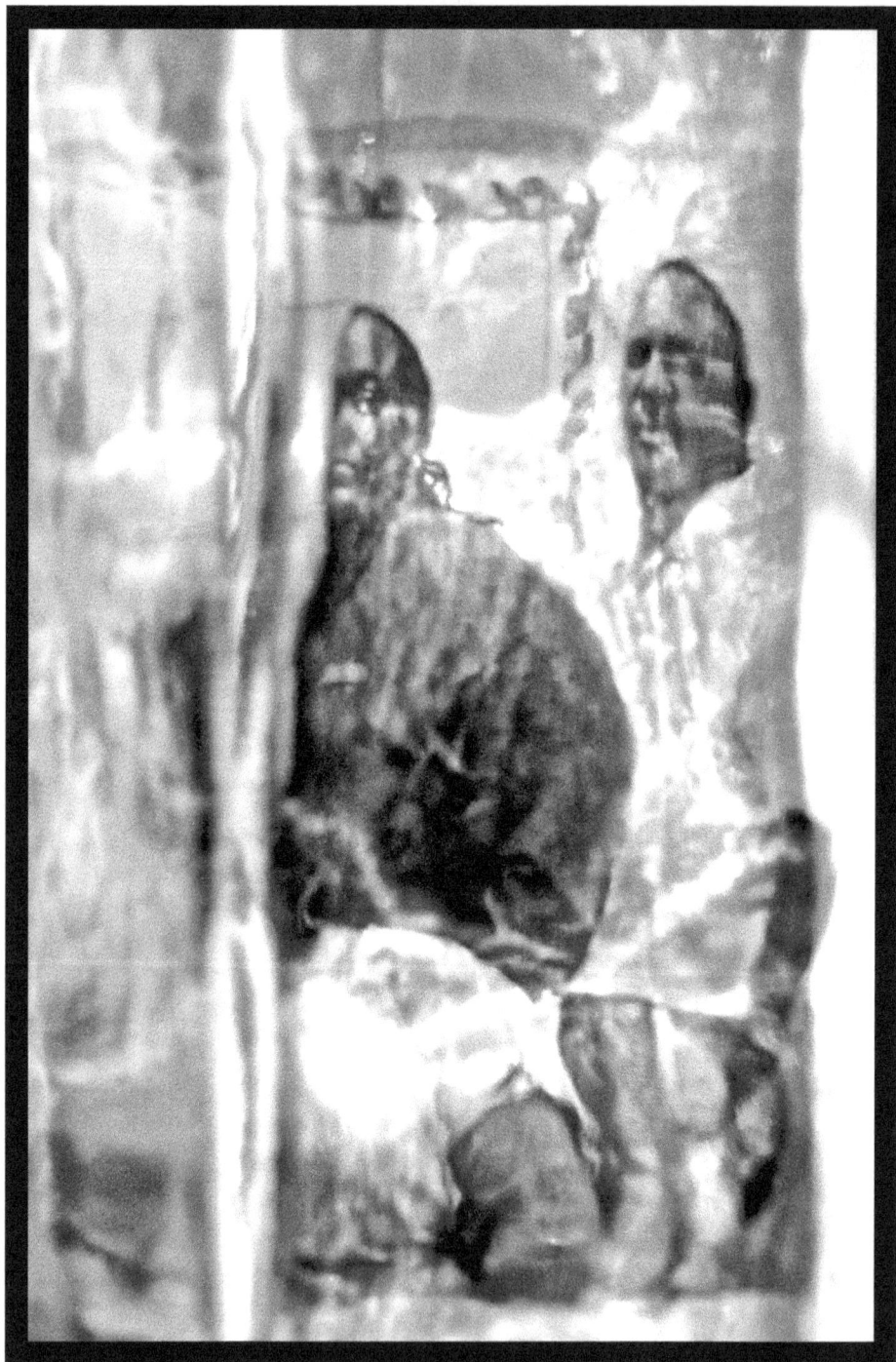

LORETTA DIANE WALKER

CANDIDATE FOR STATISTICS

He grows up black,
fatherless, poor
candidate for statistics.

Thirteen he cooks,
irons, rolls responsibilities
in a red rubber band, works
for the things we need.

His voice ripens to a
deep baritone.
He sings,
catches passes, runs
swiftly as a cheetah
candidate for a scholarship.

He can balance a world
of black and white,
peel disappointment
from skinned knees,
pray when others curse
his choices.

He grows
into the competent black man
statistics said he could not be,
the father he wished he had.
I sing his praises.
He is each of my brothers.

IN THE WAITING ROOM

Baa, baa, bare sheep, have you any wool?
No sir, no sir, no bags full!

The day is creased with anxiety.
The hospital's odorless walls
are framed with a dull quiet.
The sudden opening and closing
of a sliding glass door
is a monotone distraction.
We are a small flock of sheep
waiting in this brick pasture
for our mother to return from surgery.

Raymond, the first born, once rushed to fires
in his fireman's hat and big rubber boots.
When he was a teenager, he drove a fire red 65' Malibu.
Speed is not a luxury or an occupation now.
The Malibu is parked, the bunker gear retired
and a weakened back slows his pace.
He moves about with a sturdy folding metal walker
tricked-out with tennis balls on the rear legs.

James, the second born, paces—
rushing minutes that are stuck
in a slow pond of angst.
He is a soul seeking missile,
finds a couple sitting against a far wall.
Traces of concern rims his eyes
as he chats; he will know their story
before they leave.

As a boy, he was a gatherer—
collected history, friends, favor.

I am the third born, trying to find a poem
in the high white ceiling, worried expressions,
and humid air traipsing in and out of the glass doors.
Words are my crutch and solace, comforting
me as I flip through magazines.
A past conversation fills me
like this fertile field of fear we're grazing in.
I'm going to be a teacher's aide.
No, you're not. You're going to be a teacher.
Her words prevail.

Chris, the fourth born, is still on the road.
Trepidation is powerless,
cannot push his foot above the speed limit.
The staves of caution and law guide him
like Mama's stern voice.
Duty is the bell around his neck,
responsibility the cord that binds.
I cannot see him, but I know his heart
is racing.

Vince, the last-born male, sits composed.
Since childhood, he has known calm.
He is insulted by time, refuses to rush
even when his cell phone is flashing.
His demeanor is serene, body stilled,
save his fingers.
They manipulate keys, reveal his worry.
Numbers drive him;
their predictability keeps him anchored.

Kim, the youngest, rests her head
on her husband's shoulder.
Fatigue covers both of them like thick wool.

For six months they have nursed Mama back to health.
Their lives are connected like the plastic vein cycling
life through our mother's arm.

Mama was rolled in with two legs;
she will be rolled out with one.
And we are waiting
to see who can hold back tears the longest.

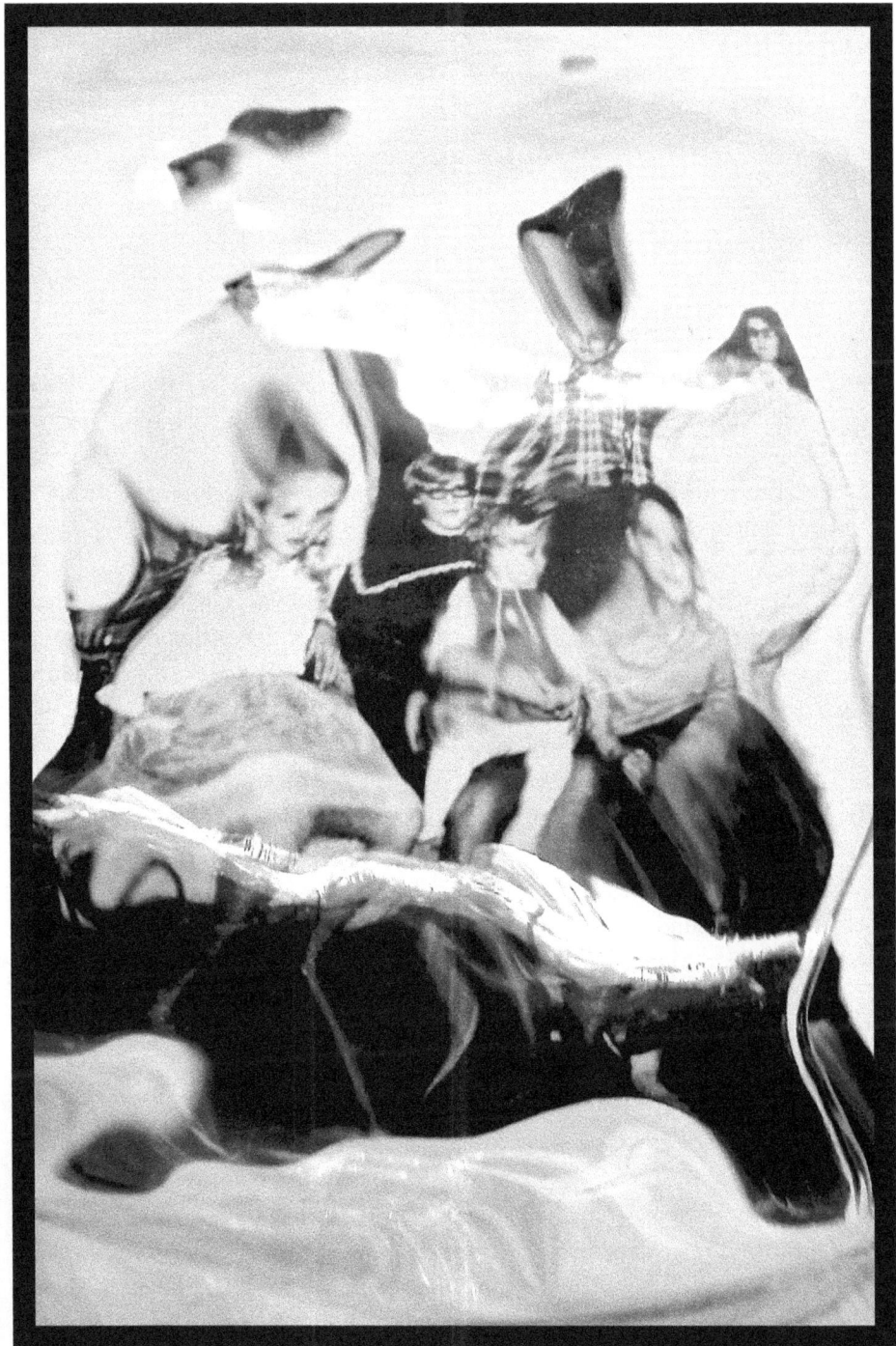

PATTI SEE

LIKE ME BEST

My mom's room at Golden Age Assisted Living is so tiny that it's impossible to be far away from her. I'm aware that I've got the best spot: I lean my elbows on her single mattress and smooth her hair.

"This is how I hope she dies," I say to my brother, "with lots of us sitting around telling stories, and Mom in the middle."

Joey nods.

We've had plenty of time to get used to her death. She's in her ninth year of Alzheimer's. I can't imagine getting through any of this without my seven siblings. Mom can no longer hold up her head or speak. She hasn't eaten in two days.

My whole life I've hogged Mom's attention because I was the youngest. In my defense, for much of my childhood I had both parents to myself simply because my much older siblings were gone.

I don't want to hog Mom today. I know Joey would never ask me to move over, so I say, "I'm going to the bathroom."

I walk around and talk to the other residents. When I come back, Joey's chair is close to Mom's bed, and he's stroking her face.

Joe Junior was the boy my parents longed for after four girls. The spring he was born—at almost eleven pounds, like giving birth to a four-month old—my mom came out of her drugged-up haze and checked his diaper to make sure she finally had a boy. When I was a kid and she told this story, I always giggled. At first I'm sure it was because of the checking-for-a-penis part, but also because of the possible foolery. My dad was a teaser, but certainly even he would not tease about something as important as having a son.

In the 1950's new mothers stayed in the hospital at least a week, and I suspect my mom cherished the time alone with her baby boy before going home to a house full of daughters—ages five and under. She spent hours gazing into his chubby face, and perhaps from the first moments after checking his diaper for the right equipment, she called him what she would never again call her husband: *my Joey.*

Now Joey talks gently to our mother, a soft voice and soothing words perhaps only reserved for his own baby daughters many years ago or for his beloved dog, Buddy. He tries to awaken her, tenderly rouse her from a deep place. Mom looks in Joey's direction, but her eyes are blank.

"At least I get to see your baby blues," he says to her.

Joey puts his face close to Mom's and kisses her full on the lips. She puckers up and kisses back, a real smack, more of response than any of us has seen in weeks.

"Did you see that?" Joey asks me.

✤   ✤   ✤

After visiting Mom, I decorate my parents' sixty-fourth anniversary cake with tiny plastic cows and pigs since their wedding reception took place on a farm. Dad doesn't want his picture taken with my "farm cake." I know his answer even before I ask: *Not without your mom.* She's too sick to visit home today.

Still, he's having a good time at his party, sitting at the backyard picnic table with my husband, brothers, and brothers-in-law. Family parties are often segregated like this: in the summer men tend to stay outside, women and children inside. He's telling stories, all of which begin, "So any-way—."

After lunch, Dad sits in the living room with most of the women. I tease a sister-in-law about something she told me when her youngest went away to college: now she could have sex on the kitchen table anytime.

I say, "I'm never eating at your house again."

Sister-in-law-in-question laughs and laughs and the rest of the women do too. She's been in the family for over thirty years. No reason to blush anymore, but today I find her red face so charming.

I say, "Then come to find out last night, her husband never even knew about it!" This gets her off the hook. She didn't really have *table sex.*

My dad shakes his head and laughs. He says to me, "How the hell does your husband put up with you?"

"He encourages me," I say. What I mean is that my husband loves my stories and wants me to not only tell them but write them down.

My sister, Jackie, says, "Don't forget to say in your blog that *Mom likes*

Jackie best."

All of us have played "Mom or Dad likes me best" for most of my adult life. It's funny to my sibs and me every time, via "reply to all" emails or on the phone or in person. Our dad taught us that teasing is love, and we all took to it.

When I was a little girl my two older brothers—Joey and David—often teased me till I cried, and of course I went running to my mom. She'd pull me up onto the wide expanse of her lap where I was sure I was going to get some comfort and the boys would get a tongue-lashing or Mom's worst punishment: make them kneel on the metal heat runs on the floor till their knees throbbed. Instead she'd hug me close and say, "You need to toughen up."

Now I say to my sisters, "You can have Mom, but Dad likes me best." He's sitting beside me, dozing. Even as a younger man, he had the ability to be an active part of a conversation one moment and asleep twenty seconds later.

Each sister one-ups another with evidence we've surely used before. Dad rouses himself and retreats to the *guy table* in the kitchen. You wouldn't think a parent could get tired of kids fawning over him, but at eighty-six perhaps he's more than sick of this (which means sick of us). I don't know if all of us kept him young, or we've worn him down.

Sometimes I wonder how my son, an only child, would have reacted if he'd had to compete with even one sibling for attention: if once in his twenty-one years he had to think *Like me best.*

My sister, Geralynn, comes back to the livingroom and says, "Dad likes me best. He meant to say your name just now, but he said *Geralynn* because it's his favorite name."

"Or he's having a stroke," I say. We laugh and laugh.

Our mother is too frail to come to her own anniversary party; no one says so, but we all know she's dying. A week from now she will not be in this world. Still, we're almost giddy. My frazzled nerves mean I'm quick to laugh or to cry.

Jokes about "table sex" go on for an hour. *Change the tablecloth before company comes*, one sister says. *Hope it's a plastic tablecloth*, says another.

We discuss what to get a niece for her bridal shower. *How about a kitchen table*, someone says. *What every young couple needs.* We laugh until we cry. We agree to give her a plastic tablecloth with step by step instructions for use.

"A tablecloth with watermelons on it," Geralynn says.

"Why?" I ask. Not the most sexual fruit, after all.

"Cause I love watermelon," she says. We laugh harder.

If Mom were here with us today, and healthy, she would be wiping her laughing eyes with a Kleenex pulled from the waist band of her pants. My sisters and I may not be aware that we're laughing Mom's share today.

As I start to leave the party, a brother-in-law asks me, "Are you putting that kitchen table story in your blog?"

"Yeah," I say, "but I'm not saying which brother and sister-in-law. Is it Joey and Tami? Or is it David and Lauri?"

Joey says, "Don't forget to write that Mom kissed me today."

Her kiss was a sweet, sweet surprise—a gift Mom gave him—one I may remember for the rest of my life. I won't tell my brother any of this just yet.

"Yeah," I say to him, "But she thought you were David—her favorite son."

·

II
BONDS & BOUNDS.

JILL WILBUR SMITH

PLAY, PLAYING, PLAYED

It was a Saturday morning like most in my sun-dappled childhood. My siblings and I had eaten our fill of Lucky Charms. The Road Runner was over and the Schoolhouse Rock gang had no more lessons to impart from the RCA console TV that was the centerpiece of our living room. So I imagine the five of us did what most kids did in those days before iPads and video games. We start a game of make believe.

My brother, Greg, seven years older than me, doesn't retreat to his bedroom, but stays to play with my three sisters and me. Dad is puttering in his workshop. Mom is out buying fresh eggs from the farmer just outside of town.

I am the Road Runner. Greg is Wile E. Coyote. I run circles through the living room into the dining room and around the drop-leaf table. He hides in the corners or under the table to try to stop me in my tracks. Shelly, the baby, giggles from the corner of the davenport where she hunkers to stay out of the way. Terri cheers me on. Patty, the oldest, reads her book in the corner, ignoring our antics.

I have the sugar-induced energy of a six-year-old. The activity escalates into one of near hysteria for which I have much more stamina than my brother. He wants to stop the game. But in that way of little sisters who know just where to poke, exactly the right way to aggravate and tease until someone breaks, I don't give up.

"Let's play. Let's play," I taunt, running circles around him. "Beep, beep."

"You are getting crazy, Jill," my brother states.

"Am not. Am not. Beep, beep."

"You need to calm down now."

"Do not. Do not. Beep, beep."

"This isn't fun anymore."

"Is too. Is too. Beep, beep."

"I'm going to call the loony bin on you if you don't stop."

"Will not. Will not. Beep, beep."

Greg doesn't say any more. He saunters to the rotary-dial telephone hanging on the wall in the dining room. He pulls the phone book off the shelf and thumbs through the Yellow Pages in the back, runs his finger down the columns until he finds the entry he needs. He lifts the receiver off the hook and dials.

"Hello? Is this the loony bin?" he says. "I think you'd better send someone over here right away. My little sister has gone off the deep end." He nods and listens. "Certifiable." He gives them our address and says, "See you soon."

He hangs up the phone and turns to me with a grin. "You might want to pack your suitcase. They'll be here in an hour."

"Liar, liar!" I screech. "Greg, you big fat liar. You did not call the loony bin." I look to Patty for reassurance. She shrugs her shoulders and goes back to reading her book.

"You'll know in an hour," says Greg.

This is the 1960s. Political correctness isn't a part of our vernacular. The "loony bin" is a stark institution where "crazies" wait in straitjackets until they can get their lobotomies. I hug my chest, wonder how it would feel to not be able to move my arms.

We return to the living room, but the mood is ruined. "Let's play Tinker Toys," Terri suggests. She goes to the closet tucked under the stairway of our one-hundred-year-old Colonial. The closet is the perfect fort, the ideal hiding spot. A bar near the front holds our winter coats. Behind the bar, the ceiling slants until it stops just above the deep drawers my father has built to hold our toys and games. Terri tugs open one of the heavy bins and finds the Tinker Toys buried under the board games, dolls and our Etch A Sketch.

We build Flintstone-looking cars, houses with see-through walls. The ominous clock in the dining room marks the time, which my brother announces in fifteen-minute intervals. "Forty-five more minutes," he says to me, eyebrows raised in that you'd-better-get-ready kind of way.

"Only half an hour more," he announces. I struggle to stay focused on my building enterprise.

"Fifteen minutes. Do you want me to get your bag?" he taunts.

At the top of the hour, he gets out of his chair and walks toward the door in the next room. "I'll go see if they're out there yet," he says. "I hope they remembered the straitjacket."

As he crosses the threshold to the dining room, the doorbell rings.

This is the moment that, nearly fifty years later, I remember as if it were last week. It is in this moment that, for the first time in my life, I believe my brother has betrayed me.

I scream. Patty puts down her book. Shelly starts to cry. I run to the closet, pull the door behind me, burrow through the coats and huddle in the corner.

The doorbell rings again.

Muffled voices drift through the wall. My brother laughs. Someone runs from the living room to the door. More voices as I cower, contemplating my fate. Footsteps approach and the closet door creaks open. Greg's face appears through the coats. "They're h-e-e-e-re," he says.

"Tell them to go away," I sob. "I won't be crazy again, I promise."

His face softens and he crawls in beside me. He puts his arm around my shoulders.

"Oh you big goof," he says. "It's only Uncle Harold and Aunt Lorraine. Mom told me they were coming."

"Greg, you big bully!" I yell at him, pummeling his chest with my fists.

He laughs, swats away my hands and stands. "Come on. Aunt Lorraine brought a cherry pie."

He is my brother once again, but the relationship is forever altered.

Greg leaves the closet and closes the door behind him. I sit in the dark and take deep breaths. I wipe my face on my sleeve and try to stop myself from snuffling. Finally, I pull myself together and open the door.

I walk into the light to face my family. They tease me for being gullible and I try to laugh along. But that kernel of doubt has burrowed its way into my being. The innocence of a child's game has turned my idyllic world into something less than perfect. I have tasted fear, felt the sucker punch of recognition that someone is other than he seems. I have learned that trust is conditional.

ELIZABETH STOESSL

PLAY THERAPY

> *For the error bred in the bone*
> *Of each woman and each man*
> *Craves what it cannot have,*
> *Not universal love*
> *But to be loved alone.*
> —*W. H. Auden*

On her dollhouse rooftop
a cradle rocks untended,
its contents dumped in headfirst.
She who banished it
predicts killing rain—
    Days of it.
    No survivors.

Below, in warmth and safety,
underneath the eaves
she tucks the favored girl-doll
snug between her parents,
loved, and loved alone.
    Here, only here
    all as before.

She spies a plastic dragon—
jagged fangs in monster mouth—
lifts her shirt, suckles it
at small flat dry nipple
then swaddles it
    smothers it
    beneath a lacy pillow.

CUT

Because she lived just across the street and I could watch her as she kneeled on her wet lawn to cut her giant peonies and when the grass dried and she pounded spindly wickets to play croquet with her daughter and I'd run over and sometimes they let me use the blue mallet and ball even though it was Alice's favorite and because when I brought her gassed butterflies in jam jars and she showed me how to soften them and pin them into the bottom of a cigar box so they wouldn't curl and once she even rode bicycles with me to Cox's farm after I learned to keep up on my blue birthday Schwinn—

Because of all this I knew Mrs. Winter the best at the start of fourth grade but she pretended I was the same as all the other kids so I had to start all over and wash blackboards and help the slow kids with their multiplication and the ones left behind on Catechism days with their reading and because I did all this I thought she finally liked me again like before—

But because one afternoon when our mother was late coming home from the Susan B. Anthony club, we had to stay inside and I had to watch my brother and he was misbehaving and flinging my dolls around so I told him I'd throw the butterfly-death stuff in his face but I knew there wasn't enough to do the job so instead I went after him with a butcher knife that was in the sink after our mother had cut liver for dinner. I only held the knife up once and it didn't even touch him but he ran outside and I was glad and didn't look for him. When our mother came home dragging him in she sent me to bed but it was worth it because I didn't know where he had gone, but the next morning at school when Mrs. Winter told the whole class about the little boy who banged on her door and asked her to keep him safe from his sister who was going to stab him, then I knew. And she laughed and the class laughed but I did not laugh because it was too late to start all over again.

RACHEL SQUIRES BLOOM

RUTABAGA

Driving to church one post-Vatican II
Saturday, I look at Deb and splutter,
ru-ta-ba-ga. She instantly replies,
ru-ta-ba-ga. Our eyes lock as tightly
as our seatbelts across the wide bench seat
of the Plymouth Fury. I echo her echo,
syllables gaining momentum, consuming
us with hilarity and racket. Despite
tight seatbelts, we fall toward one another
like praying hands, a toppled steeple,
managing between laugh-breaths to repeat:

ru-ta-ba-ga. We don't hear *shush, quiet,
shut the hell up,* until Dad veers the ark
of a car wildly, left hand on the wheel, right
wrenching behind his oh-my-bad-back
to smack at us yelling, *If I have to pull over . . .*
Deb and I are deaf to all but four sounds,
an amazing change in meaning as the word
is blurted anew, each reassemblance
of the multi-syllabic *ru-ta-ba-ga.*

Filterless, my dad bellows, *why do I have*
these stupid kids? No one knows,
or tries to read what Mom thinks,
eyes turned toward the window, ringed
pink-tipped fingers fondling a Viceroy.
She's thinking if the whole goddamn
car crashes the kids and I will be scooped
up to heaven, the bastard beside me dragged
down to where he belongs.

Oblivious to all that, Deb and I discern nothing
but the next round of hilarity, the chug and roar
of syllables rushing over tongues, let loose
beyond our teeth in gasps of joy in language
beyond word, beyond meaning.

KEEPING OUT OF TROUBLE

Watch those geese fly North
my father says, although, age nine,
I know they're headed South.
Geese spell out words in the sky-
see if you can read what they're trying
to tell us. I quietly question what message
is so vital, so imperative as to warrant
an entire winged species learning
our letters and language to transmit it.
I watch V merge to C then to cursive A,
maybe.

Shake these creamers until
they turn into butter.
In Howard Johnson's garish orange
Dad hands us plastic thimblesful of cream.
Hope momentarily interrupts
a sisterly argument; maybe
this time we'll actually make butter!
We shake, stay busy.
We keep out of trouble.

CHRISTA CHAMPION

THE SUN IS THE CENTER OF THE UNIVERSE

1—Little Twins

When I was a little kid, my big sister was my best friend and more—she was my trusty leader, my light in the darkness, my guide to the world. She was the most important person in the world to me. I thought she hung the moon. I couldn't imagine doing anything that didn't include her. From my point of view, we belonged together, like salt-and-pepper shakers, or Batman and Robin. I followed her everywhere; we came as a pair.

How she viewed me at the time, I have no idea. It never occurred to me to think about it from her perspective. When the sun shines on us, do we think about how the sun feels? No. We simply enjoy the light, and the warmth on our skin.

Back then, we spent the entire day together, every day. We woke within minutes of each other. We ate our meals at the same time and at the same table. We played with each other exclusively, shared the same toys, bathed in the same tub of soapy water, and heard our good night stories sitting side-by-side on our father's lap. Our mother dressed us in matching outfits, but crisscrossed colors: if my Keds were blue that year, and my sister's red, Mom would sew my play clothes of red material, and my sister's of blue. That way we knew whose was whose. We were adorable. Everybody said.

Not even school came between us. When my sister started kindergarten a year ahead of me, she came home every day and showed me what she'd learned. Right after lunch, we'd go into the family room and lie down on the floor with scratch paper and crayons. She taught me about numbers, and the alphabet, and how to draw out all the letters of my name. It was the secret code of the world of books, and she shared it with me. For that, and for everything else she taught me about the world around us, I loved her unconditionally.

Although we were nearly eighteen months apart in age, we were the same height growing up, which I always attributed to the difference in our gestation times. My big sister had been born seven weeks premature, and I imagined that she was still catching up. At that time, seven weeks early was serious business: at a birth weight of just above four pounds, she was considered to be on the borderline of viability. The doctors were surprised that they only had to keep her in the incubator for a few days. When they sent her home, they told my parents, watch out, this one's a fighter. That's my big sister—always taking everything as a personal challenge. She treats every situation like she's fighting for her life.

Whereas my sister came early, I was nearly three weeks late. Guess I liked to take my time about things, even then. Check out all the options, y'know? Be sure I'm making a good decision. Look before you leap and all that. Nowadays the doc would order drugs to induce labor, or talk the expecting mother into an elective C-section. None of that modern-day medicine for my old-school mom; she just put her feet up, asked Dad to make an ice pack for her back, and waited 'til I was good and ready to face the world. I was a big baby when I finally debuted, almost nine pounds, ninety-sixth percentile. By the time I was crawling I was as tall as my sister, and we stayed pretty much the same height into our early teens.

Two little girls, same height, dressed every day in matching outfits. Naturally, people would ask if we were twins, right? Which is kind of ridiculous, since other than our height and the color-coordinated clothes, everything else about our physical appearance was completely opposite. She was strong-limbed and olive-skinned, her straight blonde hair in its neat pageboy perfectly framing her soft brown eyes. I was skinny-limbed and pale-skinned, my freckles and green eyes half-hidden behind dark tangled bangs that I refused to let my mother trim. That people could honestly think we were twins just goes to show you how quick people are to look only at the surface of things, their glances so superficial they can't get past the clothes. The matching outfits screamed "twins" so loud that some people couldn't see anything else.

So there we were, twinned in our clothes and together in our daily lives. From my perspective, life was perfect. We were a perfect pair. I had no reason to think our relationship wouldn't be that way forever. It never occurred to me that my big sister might want her own life, separate from mine.

2—Divergence

Moving vans. Bigger town, smaller house. New baby brother, so the sisters will have to share a room, but I didn't mind—does Mercury mind having the closest orbit to the sun? It would be fun, I thought, picturing late nights, lights out, whispering secrets to each other across the darkness.

I didn't picture cold shoulders, clothes flung in my face, me afraid to stand in the wrong place.

My home life was suddenly full of rules, most of them delivered in bitten-off words from a mouth so tight and hard it looked like it pained her to even talk to me.

Get out of my way. Get your stuff off my bed. Leave my things alone. Don't touch the radio. No, you can't use my colored pencils. No, you can't borrow my sweatshirt. No. No. No.

I decided I didn't like our new town. I sat in the upstairs window seat, arms crossed, not even offering to help as my mother folded sheets.

This place is creepy, I said. I don't like it here. I hate my new room. I want to go back home.

My mother didn't say anything, just kept spreading her arms wider, snapping and shaking the sheets out without me.

I don't get why moving here had to change everything—what in the world did *I* do?

Nothing, my mother said. You didn't do anything. Just go out and play. Make your own friends.

I didn't budge.

Go on, she said. If you go out and play, you'll feel better, I promise.

I uncrossed my arms and re-crossed them the other way.

My mother stopped folding and tried again. What your sister is going through, she said slowly, is about her. It has nothing at all to do with you.

My eyes filled up. I immediately tipped my head back and stared at the ceiling, lifting my eyebrows to make more room, trying to keep the tears right where they were. I tried to believe I hadn't heard what she said, but the words repeated over again in my head. *"Nothing at all to do with you."*

My mother folded two more sheets, patiently, letting me cry on my own for a bit. But when it was clear I wasn't going to stop easily, she moved to the window seat and put her arm around my shoulders, pulling me close. I cried and cried and cried, my mother wiping my face with a bleach-clean pillowcase. It's okay, she said, over and over. It's okay. Everything's going to be all right.

3—Obscuration

As we got older, I realized the best way to avoid our one-sided fights was to stay out of her way. I tried to become invisible, lose myself in the background. Things got easier in middle school with after-school activities to join. When she and her friends decided to take gymnastics at the Y, I walked to the other end of town and joined a junior bowling league.

Turns out, I loved bowling. I liked the potential of the first ball, of course; everyone does. The clean slate, and the chance you might hit the pocket just right for a strike. But to me, the second ball was even better. The challenge of trying to imagine how the pins will fall and spin; how to get the most out of each situation. I started hanging out on Saturdays to watch the adult leagues, pick up some tips, maybe even bowl a string or two by myself on an open lane.

Upstairs from the bowling alley was a roller skating rink, and occasionally I would poke my head in for a few minutes to watch. It was mostly older teenagers, whizzing around the dusty wooden floor, some in pairs, some in groups, some even skating backwards. One Saturday I went up to take a break from the bowling action and saw my sister out there in the middle of the floor, wheeling around at the end of a long chain of girls holding hands. The Whip, they called it. They make the skater on the end go faster and faster until eventually she either lets go or falls, then they do it all over again with the new end person, until the song is over. The Whip was like a big group game of chicken.

I knew my sister would not be one of those girls who let go early, skating over to the side breathless and giddy at having avoided the disaster of a public fall. No way; not my sister. I watched her hang on tight, laughing as the Whip snapped her around. The girl who was second-to-last was laughing, too, but barely staying upright on her skates. Around and around, faster and faster. The song was almost over when the third-to-last girl suddenly lost her balance and fell, letting go of the last two who flung off like a shooting star, headed straight for the railing. A crash seemed inevitable, but somehow my sister turned around and skated backward for a stride or two, then pulled the other girl into a tight spin like Olympic figure skaters on TV. The spin didn't last very long, but it slowed their momentum and they tumbled to the ground harmlessly in a tangle of limbs and dusty jeans. Everyone cheered, even the boys—it was a spectacular wipeout.

I had been watching from over by the jukebox, next to the wide doorway that led to the lobby and to the bathrooms. That's where my sister and her friends always go to talk about stuff, which they have to do after almost anything that happens. This clearly was a time for the girls' room, and when they turned and skated toward me, I realized I was right in their path. It was too late to retreat, and I was suddenly hyper-conscious of my feet. My red and green bowling shoes seemed to be screaming out for attention. Everyone else was on roller skates; I was a shrimp in a land of giants. I shrank back beside the jukebox and tried to blend into the wall.

I don't know what I thought would happen if she saw me. Would the carriage turn back into a pumpkin? Would the coachmen all become mice? Which one of us was Cinderella, anyway? I guess I expected to be punished in some way for invading her space. But I needn't have worried. Nobody was going to disappear in a puff of mist. Nothing was going to evaporate or be shown to be only a dream. In fact, nothing was going to happen at all. When my sister went by with her friends, she couldn't help but see me, pressed into the corner next to the jukebox. She looked right at me and just skated on by, without missing a beat or a single word in the story she was telling. It was as if I did not exist.

4—Separate Spheres

When I got up to the high school last year I immediately looked for places to fit in, spaces my sister hadn't already staked out. Her two big things were the school newspaper, for which she wrote a weekly advice column, and the yearbook, where she was the photo editor. Both groups had their offices in the English wing, so I headed the other way, toward wood shop, drafting, and home economics. I like to eat, so I signed up for cooking class, and before long the teacher had talked me into taking sewing too.

At first it was just goofy stuff, learning to cut patterns and use the machine, making things I didn't really care about like potholders and napkins. But then we took a field trip to a fabric shop in Lowell, and I found this bolt of cloth from Guatemala, woven through with purples and greens and blues. I hadn't planned on spending any money but I couldn't resist. I ripped up an old peasant blouse for a basic pattern, used some cheap cotton for my prototypes, and started learning how to make comfortable shirts that looked good on me.

When I wore that first Guatemalan shirt home my mother was so proud of me. Her mother had worked in the garment district for years, so Mom decided that sewing talent must run in the family. I didn't want to make a big deal out of it, but I knew the shirt looked good. Mom wanted me to make one for her, so I asked my big sister did she want one too. She said no thanks, nobody wears those hippie clothes anymore. What are you trying to do, single-handedly bring back the seventies?

✣   ✣   ✣

In English class this term we are reading Shakespeare, and the teacher is always trying to show us how the characters are like updated versions of famous Greek myths or something. What a joke. As if I would kill my father for a crown, or stab out my own eyes, or sell my child into slavery. They're all so serious, so "life-or-death" all the time. Where do they get these ideas?

I am in danger of flunking this English class, because I just can't take all that crap seriously. And Mr. So-and-So just doesn't understand why I'm not more brilliant, why I'm not like my sister, editor of the school paper, whipping off advice and opinion columns like they're nothing, always tying everything in to some grand theme of life. Whatever. I'm not her. I try to make that clear. I'm not her; I'm *me*. And the me that I am right now is a me that simply cannot stand Shakespeare, or Greek myths, or any other stupid soap opera stuff. I slouch down in my seat at the back of the class and wait for the bell.

Thank god, math class is next. Calculus is a stretch for my brain too, but in a good way. I can see in my mind's eye the shapes of the functions: waves, curves, ellipses. And with three variables, you can get cones, cylinders, spheres. Math is real, and it's fun. The equations don't fight, gossip, or betray each other—and they never kill their siblings.

✣   ✣   ✣

Luckily I have a friend who actually likes all that Shakespeare stuff, all the history and myths. If it wasn't for Mary Caroline, I'd either flunk or go crazy. She's the one who gets me through the tough spots.

Mary Caroline has been my best friend for more than a year now, but it seems like forever. We met on the first day of ninth grade because our lockers were next to each other, and right away we realized we had three big things in common: we both love the Beatles, mystery novels, and tramping around in the woods. We have a pact with each other that someday we'll start a rock band, hike the Appalachian trail, and become private eyes together, although not necessarily all at the same time.

Until then, she helps me with my English papers, I help her with her math and science homework, and together we try to figure out how to get invited to parties where there might be beer. This week, we are practically in heaven, because we have finally hit the jackpot. Harriet, one of the seniors on the Math Team, is throwing a party to celebrate our Bi-County Cup win. Because Mary Caroline tagged along with me to the last few meets and helped keep score, they've decided she's our manager, so she got invited too.

It's kind of funny to me, Mary Caroline being part of the Math Team. She tells me I better watch out, or she'll have me trying out for a part in a play, maybe even Shakespeare. I say, right. Fat chance.

But she's oh-so-happy to be a member of the nerdy Math Team this week, now that it's getting her invited to upper-class parties. The two of us can hardly wait for Friday to get here. Harriet's party is going to be awesome. It'll have practically everything that we love, except for trees. There will be beer, and munchies, and music, lots of it. Harriet's family is full of artists and musicians, and she told us that they have a kick-ass stereo system and tons of albums, everything from jazz and blues and rockabilly, right up to the latest New Wave stuff. There's sure to be a couple Beatles albums in there somewhere. And the best thing about this party is, we won't have to worry about having to pass muster with our parents at the end of the night, because everyone's staying over. There's a partial lunar eclipse this weekend, so we've sold our parents on the idea that this Math Team party just *has* to be an all-nighter. We're all gonna stay up until three in the morning to stargaze and see the eclipse. Harriet's older brother, the one who's buying the beer, even has a telescope. Music, beer, munchies, telescopes, and eclipses—plus no parents, and no worries. It's gonna be a great party. I can't wait.

5—Dissonance

It's a funny thing, sibling rivalry. That's what people call it anyway. But it never feels like I'm her rival. Not from my perspective. I never feel like we're in a competition at all. If we were, she'd be winning. She has tons of friends, and interest from all kinds of boys. She has style, class, and good looks. Long brown hair, pearl-white teeth, a curvy build, the right kind of clothes. She fits in *and* stands out.

Me? Bad hair, wrong clothes, and only one close friend, besides the small group of nerds that I hang out with in the math office. Sibling rivalry, my eye. Seems more like "sibling survival-ry" to me. Just trying to make it through another school day without some teacher comparing me to her. Or right now, me trying to make it through one more Friday night dinner without getting dragged into an argument.

I can't believe you're making me follow that *stupid* curfew, Big Sister is saying to my parents. Just because some boys I *don't* even know had a couple beers you don't have to treat me like a *criminal!*

My brother and I keep our eyes on our plates and just keep eating.

She's going to a party tonight, too; why aren't you giving *her* a curfew? She is glaring at me.

Rats! I say in my head. It's a sleepover, I say aloud.

Omigod, a sleepover party of math nerds, she says. Save me. What are you going to do, stay up all night solving word problems?

Leave your sister alone, our mother says. And you just make sure you're home by midnight.

6—Harmonic Convergence

Two best friends meet on the corner and head downtown, nearly skipping the whole way, hearts full of adrenalin, heads full of adventure. The early arrivals to the party help with preparations—brownie batter to mix, cupcakes to frost. Somebody gets the idea to draw mathematical symbols in the frosting with multi-colored jimmies. Eventually the older brother appears with whiskey and beer, and everyone drinks a few toasts. To the Math Team! To the Bi-County Cup! To the lunar eclipse! To freedom from parental eyes!

Every time the front door opens, the early spring breeze plays on three sets of hand-made ceramic windchimes hanging in the front hall. Some chimes are animals painted in reds and browns, others are geometric shapes in primary colors, and one set is made of stars and planets in muted blues and purples. Together, the chimes are beautiful and sound like a musical composition, constantly changing and evolving, as the door opens and closes and people arrive and are greeted and the party begins slowly to gather its hum.

The Celtics are playing on the television at one end of the huge living room, with the sound turned all the way down and the stereo turned way up loud. At the other end of the room, a card game gets underway at a large oaken table. In the kitchen the pot brownies come out of the oven, and soon the philosophical hypothesizing begins in earnest. People discover the art supplies in the dining room and start drawing caricatures of each other in bright pastels. The exchange student from Germany is showing people how to fold paper cranes.

The party may have started slow, but, as most high school parties do, it continues to grow. A friend of a friend, and so on. People peripherally connected to the invited guests show up, and are welcomed in, especially if arriving with more beer. The clique boundaries that seem so set in stone in the school hallways start to melt and slide, people talk and collide, inhibitions dissolve.

7—Syzygy

As it turns out, neither Mary Caroline nor I saw the eclipse after all. I fell asleep a little after one in the morning, and Mary Caroline, well, she didn't even make it to midnight. I feel bad that I got separated from her so early on in the party. We just got caught up doing different things. She told me later she had skipped dinner, not realizing how much faster the beer would affect her on an empty stomach, how hard it would hit her. If I had been with her, I would have noticed it happening. I could have explained it to her, the chemistry of it, the math. I could have convinced her to eat something more than brownies and beer. She would have listened to me.

But I was off in a corner, lost in my thoughts. I ended up over by the record collection, happily reading liner notes, when I realized that the party was really humming. There were tons of people there who were definitely *not* on the Math Team. A whole group of older kids from the "in" crowd were playing cards at the big table, and I practically fell over when I realized who was dealing the next hand—my sister! I couldn't believe it. What the heck was she doing here? She wasn't friends with anyone on the Math Team, was she? I glanced around the huge living room, disoriented by the sudden crowd.

When I looked back at my sister, I got surprised all over again—she was wearing the Guatemalan shirt, the one I made for my mother. The hippie shirt my sister said was totally out of style.

Part of me wanted to walk right over there and act normal, say hello and compliment her on her cool shirt—why shouldn't I?—but another part held me back. And a third part of me wanted to run and hide in the back room, like a little kid. I was busy refereeing this inner debate, hiding behind a Stevie Wonder double album, when my ruminations were interrupted by a crash and a clatter from the other room, followed by a small cry, like a dreaming dog's whimper.

There was a split-second of near-silence, a hiccup in the party sound track, and then the deep hum resumed, and everybody went back to whatever they'd been doing.

Almost everybody, that is. I slid the album back into place on the shelf and started in the direction of the crash. My sister was just ahead of me, and Harriet got there first.

It was Mary Caroline. Somehow she had tripped on the threshold of the foyer and knocked some kind of plaster statue over. The thing was in pieces on the floor, and Harriet was furious.

You're *sorry*? Harriet was yelling at Mary Caroline, who was on the floor, trying to push herself up into a seated position. Sorry won't fix my sculpture!

I didn't mean to, Mary Caroline said. She set her back against the wall, and put her hands up in front of her face as if to ward off blows.

Get out! Get out of my house right now! Harriet jabbed her finger at the door, her arm shaking with anger.

My sister stepped into the foyer, right between the two of them, like a boxing referee. You can't send this girl home in her condition, she said.

Well she's *not* staying here! our host said.

That's not how it works, Harriet Latham, and you know it. My sister had one hand on her hip, and with the other she punctuated her points with the deck of playing cards. You invited these kids here, she said. You let them drink beer, told them they could sleep over—you can't just turn around now and send Mary Caroline home, drunk, to face her parents.

But I spent *weeks* on that piece, Harriet said, and *SHE!* The accusing finger was now pointing at my friend. *SHE* got drunk and ruined weeks of work in two seconds!

I went over and put my arm around Mary Caroline, and started to edge out of the foyer and down the hall.

It stinks that she busted your statue, I could hear my sister saying, but you will *not* throw her out of this house unless you throw me out too. And I'm not leaving.

✦   ✦   ✦

Mary Caroline and I took refuge in the downstairs bathroom. She got sick a couple times, and after she had puked up all her beer and brownies, I found her a place to lie down in a small study off the back hall. Once she had settled in on the old leather sofa, I said good night and turned out the light. I stood in the doorway for a while, listening close to make sure I could hear that she was breathing okay.

Hey, you know something? Mary Caroline called to me from the darkness, her voice soft and scratchy.

What's that, I said.

You're my best friend, she said. I love you.

I love you back, you loser. I started to close the door.

You know something else? Mary Caroline said.

What.

Your sister.

I waited.

She's a super hero.

Yeah, I said. She is.

❧   ❧   ❧

By the time I came back to the party, it was as if nothing had happened. Someone had cleaned up the foyer, the Celtics were still ahead, the music was blasting, people were starting to dance. And my sister, practically glowing in my beautiful Guatemalan shirt, was sitting at the head of the big oak table with everyone turned slightly toward her. She was dealing again, and winning at Hearts.

GREY HELD

AT LA PETITE FRANCE

Pass the salt, I say.
    My brother is salt, and I—pepper,
    second born, second best.
S'il vous plaît, my brother says,
    so he'll be praised.
Pass the salt, I say.
    I help my father crack his *crabe.*
    The baby in her high chair unclips her bib.
Will someone pass the salt?
    My mother is complaining:
I'm cold.
    To endure I start eating.
My sweater's in the car, my mother says
    to my father, but he passes
    the keys to me, Mister Dependable.

ON OUR ROAD TRIP WEST

Huge explosion of tire.
        The black treads hobbling into
our lane. You swerving. Almost
        catapulted over the guardrail.
Ended up facing the wrong
        way in the breakdown lane. Then
you asked me to take the wheel.
        I adjusted the rear view
and for a hundred miles loved
        life, loved you singing *Fire and Rain*
off-key. I didn't mind your brotherly
        grumbling about the muffler clunking
or the knocking of a box
        of metal tent pegs in the trunk,
or the old smell of mildew
        on the carpet. And who left
that sun roof open? *You did,*
        I insisted. *I didn't do it.*
Yes you did. And so we argued
        for four exits, as we drove that goddamn
Conestoga across the Sonoran Desert.
        The windows down. Air rampaging
both ways so hair-slapping fast,
        we had to shout to shove
our words across the bucket seats.

THE BESTED AND THE BEST

My brother always made me
sit in front of him
in our dinghy, so he could
poke me in the back
with his fishing pole.

Sometimes he'd clamp his hand
around my neck, hold me,
so he could peel off
the ragged coast of my sunburn,
until I screamed.

Now it's my kids flaunting
words at each other—
hell, shit,
and stomping and pinching.

It's a full fledged fight.
And they stand there
in Star Market, proving
one apple is always better than another.

And isn't it always the older boy
telling the younger what he has to wear
to play King of Condiments,
who gets to stand on a footstool by the stove,
stirring the pot: Quaker oats,
the confetti from a hole punch,
mustard, spit.

When he shouts *Tabasco!*
Grenadine! Ginger Ale!
guess who has to bring it?
He dips a ladle in
and holds it up,
so his younger brother must drink.

And even if I could
love them equally,
all the time, would they
ever see it that way?

LORI DESANTI

RISKS
For Joey

My brother had called to tell me
that the craps tables at his hotel bled
chips into his pockets the night before;

I listened to the television
warning me that down the street,
there was a research student at Yale
who had been quarantined
locked in a cell, I imagined.

He went on and on
about how he hit the fire bet,
five dollars and burning,
which was the same night

that student's skin was heating
up with fever,
Ebola cells bursting,

the same time I called our sister
to make sure *today*
wasn't the day she was doing
her rounds at Yale—but

she was on the other side
of town, filling in at a rehab center,
while my brother was across
the country counting his
winnings, telling me

how fun it was,
to gamble.

DIANE D. GILLETTE

BALLOONS ADRIFT

When Jeanie arrived at the park, she realized it was actually possible to be seventeen and glad she didn't have her own car. Over a thousand people gathered to see the balloons every Labor Day Weekend. She knew this, but still, seeing it firsthand was completely different. There wasn't a single place left to park. She had a hard enough time finding a spot to lock up her bike.

Jeanie had seen the balloons rise year after year, but this was the first time she'd ventured to the park to see the magic up close. Whenever Labor Day weekend rolled around, she and Rick and their father had always climbed up on their roof and watched the balloons rise while they munched on powdered sugar doughnut holes and cheered for their favorite balloons. Jeanie's favorite was the blue balloon with the Colorado flag symbol. Rick tended to cheer for the shaped balloons, like the T-Rex or the cow, though those balloons usually proved themselves undependable, and often sank to the ground early on, if they ever got up in the first place. There was nothing more breathtaking than a clear blue Colorado sky filled with over a hundred hot air balloons. Balloons drifting around against the Rocky Mountain backdrop was the perfect combination of man-made objects and natural wonders.

The year Rick ran away, Jeanie couldn't bring herself to climb up on the roof and watch the balloons alone. Her father never even mentioned the balloons that year. Neither one had picked up the tradition since. They found less and less to talk about without her brother around.

Jeanie chained her bike to an empty length of fence and began to pick her way through the crowd. People stood around and shivered in their sweatshirts and sipped coffee from one of the many vendor carts that had set up shop especially for this weekend. Children sleepily awaited the promised balloons. The plush green carpet of grass was heavy with morning dew, making Jeanie's sneakers damp and socks soggy. The sky was a clear blue; no clouds littered the unblemished azure canvas.

Unsure of where to go, Jeanie pulled a folded postcard out of the back pocket of her jeans and studied it, looking for a clue, though she'd already memorized the few scrawled lines. Without any direction, she wandered around aimlessly for a little until she heard a man with a bullhorn. The test balloon was up and conditions were perfect for ballooning. The first phase of balloons would begin to set up. She watched as people who appeared completely ordinary suddenly separated themselves from the crowd and flew into action. They pulled bright pink T-shirts with CREW printed on them in block letters over their sweatshirts. They began to motion the crowd out of the way as balloons unrolled, slowly inflated, and lifted gracefully into the sky.

Mesmerized by the colors and sounds around her, Jeanie wandered with no particular purpose until she spotted her old favorite, the Colorado flag. The crew unrolled the balloon into their designated area. It started as a lifeless piece of cloth, but began to grow quickly. By the time it had reached the halfway point, Jeanie had to suppress her irresistible desire to run inside of the balloon like she did in the inflatable playhouses she had played in at the state fair when she was ten years old.

The crew started to pull on the ropes in order to upright the balloon. Jeanie cheered with the crowd when the Colorado balloon lifted off of the ground and began to drift southwest. She ran along below it to see it touch down on the lake. She held her breath as it slowly descended onto the lake and lingered for a few seconds before they lifted off again. It drifted lazily into the sky before she turned back to the rest of the balloons and noticed her rumbling stomach.

She fumbled in her pocket for a couple of dollars to buy some orange juice and a doughnut. As she counted her money in front of a doughnut vendor, she heard her name through the crowd. She turned, stomach clenched in hope and fear. Before she could fully comprehend what was happening, she was swept up in a pair of masculine arms and was being spun around. When her feet were finally placed firmly on the ground again, Jeanie tried to focus on the man in front of her and reconcile him with the boy she grew up with, but everything was still spinning. Rick had gained weight and the nose ring was gone. He still wore his hair long. It was pulled back into a tight ponytail.

"I didn't know if you'd come," he finally said. "If you even got my postcard."

Jeanie pulled it out and showed him. "Of course I came. But what're you even doing here?"

Rick pointed to the bright pink T-shirt he wore.

"I'm crew for one of the balloons."

He pointed out a green and white balloon, which had taken its place in the patchwork quilt in the sky.

Overcome with the moment, Jeanie laughed and threw her arms around her brother. "I can't believe it," she murmured into his shoulder.

"So where's Dad?" he asked as he stroked her hair.

Jeanie pulled back, and felt her cheeks heat. "I was afraid to tell him."

Rick pulled back a step and studied her face.

"But won't he wonder why you're not there for the balloons?"

"No. He hasn't taken much interest since you left."

Rick's forehead crinkled and he shook his head slightly. "That was always such a big deal for us."

Jeanie shrugged and turned her attention back to the balloons. Most of them had lifted off by now, and the second phase of balloons was rolled out for its turn. "You know how stubborn he is. Might as well try to move a mountain."

"How about breakfast? My treat," Rick offered.

"Don't you have to chase the balloon now?"

"Trust me, they can survive without me."

They walked several blocks down from the park to a diner that looked like it came out of a 50's movie. The waitresses wore roller skates and name tags that said Midge or Flo. They had pencils stuck behind their ears and blew pink bubbles with gum while they took orders. The place was already mobbed with breakfast-minded tourists, so they put their name on the waiting list and sat outside on the curb.

"So senior year, huh? What're your big plans, brainiac?"

Jeanie shrugged. "Don't know. Just going to graduate, get a job and move out, I guess."

Rick put his arm around her.

"Dad must be pissed. You were always his shining star. His little college-bound genius."

The hint of resentment startled Jeanie. "Hard to tell these days. He's not exactly a great conversationalist anymore."

"You guys never used to have problems."

"Yeah, well, I never used to be pissed at him for kicking out my only brother."

Jeanie felt Rick pull her around to face him.

"So what? You just don't talk to him now?"

She looked out across the parking lot. "We've done it for three years now."

Before Rick could respond, a waitress stepped outside and called his name. They followed her in silence and slid into a booth in the back. A picture of Marilyn Monroe stared down at them from the wall, and Jeanie became very interested in the menu before Rick could try and pick up their conversation.

But he seemed content to let it go. Instead, he reached across the table and brushed Jeanie's bangs out of her eyes and smiled at her. "You were always the tough one. You'll be okay. Cut Dad some slack, okay?"

Jeanie turned away from him and watched a scrawny waitress with a beehive hairdo and a one enormous tray serve a table of six without a single hash brown hitting the floor.

Rick evidently decided it was time to change the subject and started telling her about his girlfriend back on the east coast.

"Lucy helped me figure a lot of things out. If it wasn't for her, I'd probably be dead now, but she was with me every step of the way when I decided to get clean. You probably had no idea of some of the stuff I was involved in when I left."

Jeanie shook her head. She knew more than he thought, but there was no need to bring it up. It would only make him feel guilty.

"Anyway, Lucy was volunteering at a shelter I ended up in. She'd been there herself just a couple years before. She was pretty good motivation. I relapsed more than once, but Lucy never gave up on me. I've been clean for seven months now."

Tears came to Jeanie's eyes.

Their food arrived, and while they ate, Rick told Jeanie about how Lucy spent most of her time working with teens in trouble, and how her parents gave him a job in one of their restaurants. The pay wasn't great, but he couldn't afford to be picky.

After Rick paid the check, they headed back to the park. They continued on safe topics until they reached Jeanie's bike. As she unchained it, she heard him clear his throat, and she turned to meet his gaze.

"Don't be so hard on Dad. He did what he had to do."

"To force you to leave?"

"He gave me my choice, and I made it. Clean up my act or leave. It all worked out for the best."

Jeanie nodded and then hugged Rick. She backed up and started to ask him why he couldn't have cleaned up his act here, with his family. But as she got on her bike, she asked him to visit home before he left town instead.

"I don't know. Sounds like Dad might not be ready to see me."

Jeanie wasn't sure about that herself, but she didn't want to let Rick go again yet.

"I'm sure it'll be fine. Come see him."

Rick kind of jerked his shoulder and stared past Jeanie into the sky.

"You don't know why Dad asked me to leave, do you?"

Jeanie rolled her bike back and forth slightly as she wrinkled her forehead. "Wasn't it the drugs?"

Rick leaned back against the fence and crossed his arms over his chest.

"Partly. I just don't think it would be such a good idea to come home right now."

She followed his gaze up to the sky in search for the balloons that were no longer there.

"Why not?"

"Dad kicked me out when I stole Mom's wedding ring and pawned it."

Jeanie stopped moving her bike and stared at him. She shook her head and searched for a response. Rick wouldn't meet her stare and gently kicked her bike's front wheel.

"He won't forgive me for that."

When he looked up, Jeanie saw the tears in his eyes. She got off of her bike and hugged him.

"You might be surprised. Why don't you at least think about coming home? Things are more screwed up without you."

He slowly nodded.

"I'll think about it. I mean, Lucy's parents are kind of hoping I won't be back anyway. They pretty much just tolerate me for her sake."

"Whenever you're ready."

He smiled a weak smile and waved good-bye.

On her ride home, Jeanie noticed a few random balloons in various places around town, though most had disappeared. One or two were in the various stages of being taken down in some empty fields she passed. Several were still in the air. As she glanced westward, she took in a sharp breath as she saw four perfectly arranged balloons against the mountain backdrop. The scene would probably end up on a postcard in a gift shop somewhere, but that still didn't mar the beauty of the sight.

She stopped by a bakery on her way home and bought a box of powdered sugar doughnut holes. The ride home was slow as she attempted to balance the box on her handlebars with two fingers and steer with the rest. As she attempted to digest her reunion with Rick, she walked her bike around to the backyard and entered the house through the kitchen. Her dad was seated at the table with the newspaper in front of him.

He glanced up, surprised.

"Where've you been?"

"Out. I got us some doughnut holes."

She set them on the table and opened the refrigerator to look for some orange juice. Her father reached for the box, but she placed her hand on top of his.

"I thought we could save them for tomorrow. There's still two days of balloons left, if you're interested."

Her father looked up sharply.

She sat at the table and drank her orange juice. Her father stared at her over the top of his newspaper.

"I . . . uh, got a postcard from Rick the other day."

She pulled the crumpled postcard out of her back pocket and slid it across the table.

He read it in silence.

Jeanie sipped her orange juice and waited for a response. When none came, she shifted uneasily in her chair.

"We could go tomorrow," Jeanie paused, "if you want."

Her father nodded and pretended to go back to his newspaper, but his eyes stared past the paper. Jeanie didn't know how to interpret the nod and tried something more.

"I saw him. He looked good."

He father sort of grunted a little.

Jeanie swallowed hard and bit her lower lip.

"Look, he told me why you made him leave."

Her father nodded again.

"Maybe I didn't have to. Maybe I wouldn't have, if I knew how things would be after."

He picked up the postcard and stared at it for a long moment.

"You know, in all the years I've lived here, I've never been to the park to see the balloons up close."

"It's pretty amazing," Jeanie said.

"I bet," he said, tucking the postcard into his shirt pocket and turning his gaze back to the newspaper.

KATHARYN HOWD MACHAN

VIRGIN POEM

If we lived in the South Sea long ago,
brother, you might have been husband
or lover, taking me in the flowered tent
in ritual, at the festival.
My friends would have brought me shells
and coral, combed my fine brown hair
back from my face, giggling
to think of kisses there. To think
of you, older brother, striding into the tent
to find me there on the sweet soft cloth
stretched upon the sand, my breasts
years from blossom, my hips
straight and narrow as a young palm.
Oh, your manroot there. Your hands
tender and gentle with knowledge
taught you by the village fathers,
tradition, protecting me from evil
spirits that would gather to my hymen.
You would hurt me, yes, but you
would recognize my pain, acknowledge
tears, go on loving me as clean
little sister, and I would know
the pain would end and leave me whole.
How different, brother, in this northern land
where you tore my flesh and left me broken,
dirty secret, shameful sister
knowing eight years into life
love is a jagged island of ice
where flowers never grow.

MY BROTHER

My brother lives in a box of cigars.
Each day every day
he lifts the lid to peek at the world
and hopes the world won't notice.
Bristles grow on his face and throat.
He smells, fears soap.
He never throws his loose hairs away
but carefully keeps them, dirty and dark,
in the teeth of a green plastic comb.

Long ago he spent years committing incest.
I survived but we never mention it.
He's thirty-five now and still lives with our mother.
My favorite joke when I visit is to talk
of the time I stabbed his thigh with a fork
and sent him screeching around the table
for ruining my first perfect crayoned picture.
We pretend to laugh and the scar
does not go away. Migraine headaches
take me back to the fork, to the fort
he built under cool pines
where he wouldn't let me visit
unless I would . . . and I did.

Now he does his best to repel.
He rots his teeth, sucks his cigars,
growls and belches and grows fat.
Each night every night
he grows a little smaller inside.

One morning my mother, weeping,
may find he's flickered out at last,
a small gray heap in an ashtray.
I'll visit, leave the jokes behind,
bring instead a perfect crayoned picture
to wrap around his coffin.

CHRISTMAS EVE, AND I SEE

him, in the flesh, not his ghost,
my brother, his hand shutting
my bedroom door so he won't see
my nakedness after a hot shower
as I dress in bright holiday velvet
for him, this visit, sweet cookies
fresh from the stove, cinnamon
lingering in thin air: he's there,
his voice, his smile, quick wit,
my need pulling him from death
as though suicide were Santa's sleigh,
a time-free ride through cold and dark
a body can take back and forth forever,
fire in ashes, a snowflake's breath.

TANIA MOORE

THE MESSENGER

Snug beneath the pulse of living breath, in a protected and watery nest, I grew and learned to suck my thumb. Like other gardens I would come to know, though, this secret place was filled with strife. My mother had carried and born her first child, my older sister Delilah, just three months before the cluster of cells that would be me found refuge in her womb. My arrival, then, was neither intended nor wanted.

My mother was not the only one less than ecstatic at my appearance in the world. I was a usurper, an interloper who stole, if not my mother's love, then at least her time. Delilah was only eleven months old when I was born. At a year and a half, her flaxen hair haloed in sunlight, she sits beside me on the grass in Walden, Vermont, where we were born and would spend our first few years. In the snapshot I squint sleepily over at Delilah as she lifts her finger towards my eye, perhaps to see if this is really happening, if I am, in fact, real. Someone, however, was watching, capturing Delilah's suspended finger, her expression curious and perturbed. And what, meanwhile, was I thinking as I gazed into the dappled branches and watched the shifting pattern of sunlight through the trees? Did I understand, even then, in that time before words, that this was a sacred place, and I was bathed in love?

✤   ✤   ✤

My mother's devotion to Delilah was all-consuming, but I snatched comfort where I could, and when I was old enough, I would often remain at the dinner table with my father after my mother and sister had gone upstairs. He would share with me his theories about ancient civilization or astronomy, or why he preferred Swift to Shelley, and while I did not understand everything he told me, I discovered that if I bided my time, I might learn all manner of tantalizing details, like that my name came from Titania, Queen of the Fairies in *A Midsummer Night's Dream.* Or that in Shakespeare's *Antony and Cleopatra,* sometimes the messenger has to get flogged.

"When you were born," my father told me in one such nocturnal conversation, "your mother was unable to care for you. She did not have the natural feelings that one might expect for one's child." His manner was nonchalant as he twirled his spaghetti onto his spoon, the kitchen dim and drafty.

"Was that because Delilah and I were born so close together?" I asked.

My father considered for a moment. "Yes, probably." He reached for the jug of wine behind him, and while he re-topped his glass I mulled over this word, *probably.*

"You were a few weeks old," he continued, "when I realized that you just might need my protection."

✤ ✤ ✤

The idea of having my father to look out for me was thrilling in an abstract kind of way, especially since, in reality, he was rarely around, and although Delilah was my mother's favorite, this did not seem to dispose my sister any more favorably towards me.

Would another child have been as consumed by jealousy as she? Who knows what combination of factors—genes, perhaps, or chance—conspired to fill her so with rage. She was not, however, envious all the time. We played together often, and Delilah ruled our games with creative, even benevolent, zeal.

When she was six or seven we were both given baby dolls with molded plastic heads, arms and legs, and cloth bodies. Mine was called Pumpkin Pie because of her thatch of orange hair, and Delilah's, with ringlets, dimples, and eyes that opened and shut, was named Crissy Doll. Delilah, however, did not like Crissy Doll; she wanted Pumpkin Pie.

My mother brought Crissy Doll back to the store and exchanged her for Sweetie Pie, who was identical to Pumpkin Pie in every respect except that the new doll's hair was glossy brown. Enraged, Delilah grabbed my arm and twisted it as hard as she could before lifting Sweetie Pie up by her ankles and slamming her down onto the grass over and over until the doll's head separated from her body and lay staring up at the sky.

I hastily retreated to my house of pillows behind the nubby wool of the living room couch. No sooner had I settled into my nest, however, than Delilah was storming the barricades, kicking and stomping away the pillows, picture books and stuffed animals. A second later our mother appeared. She dragged Delilah out by her arm and slapped her across the face.

"That's enough!" she cried, her nails gripping Delilah's arms as she shook and shook. "You stop it *right now!*"

"I hate you!" Delilah yelled, wrenching free. "You're the worst mother in the whole world!" She charged upstairs, our mother's footsteps close behind. When I went to the bottom of the stairs I could hear my mother chiding and cajoling until Delilah forgave her, and the cycle could begin again.

✤   ✤   ✤

One autumn evening after dinner my father was peeling his nightly orange with the knife he had made by attaching a piece of wood to a blade sharpened to a dull gleam. I sat across from him and watched as the peel unfurled in one long spiral.

"The days are getting shorter," he said. "Soon Helios will be driving his chariot across the sky earlier and earlier." I nodded; we were learning about Greek myths in fifth grade.

"I was going for my walk before dinner," he continued, "and out of the corner of my eye I saw the moon. But when I turned I realized that what I had seen was not the moon, but a streetlight that had just been turned on. For an instant, though, the light was the moon in my mind. Who knows what is delusion, and what is truth?"

A single candle flickered in the center of the table, the drips from a myriad tapers layered and covered in dust.

"And maybe," I said, coiling the orange peel back into a hollow globe, "this is the sun."

My father broke into peals of laughter. "Wonderful," he said. "Wonderful."

✤   ✤   ✤

The times when my father would laugh from deep in his belly, delighted with something I had said, were rare, and when I left him to his ruminations I would often hear him muttering or reciting poetry in a loud, florid voice to the blank panes of glass.

One evening I woke after having gone to bed to find his backlit figure standing in my doorway.

"Another report card with straight A's," he said. "Are you pleased with yourself?" I struggled to orient myself as I stammered my reply.

"So you got all the right answers," he continued. "Crossed your t's and dotted your i's. Bravo. But what do you really *care* about?"

"What time is it?" I tried to make out the hands of the clock in the dark.

"What time is it?!" he cried. "You really are a superficial little twit, aren't you?" Turning on his heel, he stormed out of the room.

❧   ❧   ❧

Meanwhile, from one day to the next, Delilah and I were growing up. While I discovered the changes in my body with queasy excitement, Delilah seemed less than pleased. When she turned twelve she took to wearing OshKosh overalls every day to school, but the baggy clothing could not stop her own shape from changing, underneath. One Sunday afternoon she cut her hair in chunks, the bathroom scissors backward-sliding and blunt.

She was the fastest runner in school, and in tenth grade she was state finalist in the long jump. She wore sneakers with cleats, her legs strong and muscular, her hips slim. Everyone said that she was beautiful, but Delilah did not think so. She decided that she wanted to be like me. She took the pillowcase off my bed, the one with the silk-screened picture of a ballet dancer on it. She slid the case onto her own pillow and sewed it closed with a scar of black thread. She also started copying what I ate—an apple or a slice of bread spread with peanut butter, tomato pulp squishing over the counter as I attempted to slice the fruit with a bread knife. I tried to ignore her, and I didn't notice how thin she had become until she bent down and I could see the knobs of her spine like smooth, round stones rimming the shore of her back. She did not look like me.

That spring Delilah ate a handful of our father's blue sleeping pills, but when she started to nod off she stumbled into our mother's room. My father came running, and he walked Delilah up and down the hallway until the ambulance arrived.

Delilah did not come home right away, and her absence was like an echo, a pale beating of wings that I would listen for in the stairwell or in the hallway outside my room. Perhaps I believed that like a spider, if I could snatch the ache of her out of the air, I could wrap and bind it and make it disappear.

Every few days I would construct a miniature terrarium for my mother to bring when she visited Delilah. I would wash out a Gray Poupon mustard, or a Smuckers jam jar and fill it with leaves, clover, tiny pine cones or smooth stones that I had found under the lilac. Delilah refused to see me, but she did accept these silent missives. One August afternoon I was outside gathering items for my gift, and after snapping a twig off the hawthorn tree I wandered over to a copse of oaks. The grass beneath the canopy was a downy, emerald green, and as I lowered myself against the tree I was surrounded by sounds of life— the cawing and trilling of birds, a scuffle in the underbrush, a white butterfly drifting soundlessly by. I sat until my back became uncomfortable against the rough bark, but when I rose I was momentarily disoriented until I realized that what was missing was my constant, gnawing worry that had drained away, leaving me strangely empty. As I walked back to the house it was as though I was being sustained by a pulse far vaster than my own beating heart.

❧   ❧   ❧

Delilah went off to Bates College as planned, and I left for Princeton the following fall. When I returned after my freshman year, though, I was surprised to find that Delilah was already home. My mother, her voice strained, her mouth drawn into a thin, straight line, explained only that Delilah was transferring to NYU in the fall.

I waited until later that evening when I would have the opportunity to talk with my father alone and ask why Delilah had really returned early. We were sitting in our usual places, a different candle dripping over the same layers of wax in the wine bottle holder.

"The school felt they couldn't handle her," my father said. "Delilah has always had a flair for the dramatic, but apparently they felt that taking rat poison was going too far." His words floated, tiny black specs, but when I tried to gather them into phrases that made sense, they kept breaking apart. I watched as he sifted through his collection of spices—turmeric, coriander, basil, and when he unscrewed the cap of the red pepper, I rose from my chair.

How can you sit there, I wanted to scream, *sprinkling cayenne pepper on your food while you tell me that my sister ate rat poison?*

He didn't look up as the kitchen door swung shut with a shudder.

❧   ❧   ❧

I continued upstairs to Delilah's room, where I found her sitting on her bed clipping her nails and smoking. She had cut her hair short and dyed it L'Oréal Baby Doll Blonde, and with her aquiline nose and rosebud mouth she looked like a picture in a fashion magazine, *Details* or *Elle*.

"Hi," I said.

"What do you want?"

"Daddy told me what happened," I said softly. "Why? I thought things were going well."

She glanced up sharply. "Stay out of it. There are things you'll never understand."

The walls of her room were covered in her intricate drawings in pen and ink with watercolor washes; they, too, were beautiful and inaccessible, and I struggled against the urge to slip away.

"Could you try?" I asked.

She took a drag on her cigarette. "Why would I tell you anything? Daddy's little darling."

"Because I care about you."

Her mouth twitched, but otherwise she sat perfectly still.

"What else did he tell you?" she asked.

"Nothing. Just that."

"Funny that he neglected to mention the part about molesting me."

"What?" My voice came out in a whisper.

"It stopped when I was twelve. Now he can't stand to look at me."

I pressed myself against the doorjamb, as if it could keep me from falling. "When did it—?"

"Begin? I didn't mark the date on my calendar." She stared at a point along the floor. "I was eight, maybe nine."

"I'm so sorry," I murmured. "Is there anything—"

"You can do? Sure. Take my place." She flicked her ash in the general direction of the ashtray, and in the halo of light from her bedside table lamp I noticed a smattering of pockmarks traveling up her arm. They were perfectly round, like raindrops on sand. When she saw me looking she flinched, then held up her cigarette.

"I did it with this," she said. "Now go."

❧   ❧   ❧

Delilah made me promise never to tell our father what she had told me, and if I asked her about what had happened she would angrily change the subject. The rules were clear; I was to ask no questions, and no details were to be revealed. If my own world had been torn apart, well, what was this compared to the horror of what Delilah had endured? As time passed, though, I became confused. I would watch my father, looking for clues, and if I thought that his expression looked haunted, I would pounce on this as evidence. Most of the time, though, he was the same as he had always been, and in my worst moments I wondered if there wasn't even a part of Delilah that wanted to drive a wedge between me and my father, inserting herself between us.

✤   ✤   ✤

Throughout the summer I kept Delilah's secret. My father and I fought whenever we saw one another, his expression perplexed and preoccupied. Then Delilah left for New York in the middle of August, and one evening I once again remained at the kitchen table after the dinner dishes had been cleared.

"Yes?" He glanced at me warily.

"I know we've been fighting a lot," I began, "and I wanted to tell you why." I took a deep breath, but if I thought his defenses might be softened with wine, I was wrong.

"She's a liar!" he roared almost before I could finish speaking. "Who does she think she is, making vile accusations against her own father, the person who has nurtured her, put food on her table and a roof over her head!?"

"She didn't want to tell me. I kept asking, and she made me promise not to say anything—"

"It was your *obligation* to tell me! Who else have you spoken to? Have you told your mother?"

"No."

He glanced at me quickly, then carefully lowered his wine glass to the table.

"Do you believe her?"

"I—don't know who to believe."

"Your sister is evil, *and you don't know who to believe!?*" His hair rose wild from his head, his pupils two pinpricks in ice.

"I—don't know who—"

"Is lying?" Neither of us moved.

"Get out of here," he said with disgust. "You are no longer my daughter."

❧   ❧   ❧

When Delilah found out that I had told him, she refused to speak to me. Six months later she dropped out of NYU. She left the Lower East Side studio she had been renting, leaving no forwarding address. Months went by, until finally a note arrived in the mail saying only that she was okay. The return of address was a post office box in New York City, but when my mother and I wrote, neither of us got a reply. I sent Delilah money for Christmas, and I only knew that she had received it when the check cleared. Her message was clear; she wanted nothing to do with me. No matter how much time passed, though, I kept telling myself that things would change, and we would be sisters again. When she didn't come to my wedding, or acknowledge the pictures I sent when my children were born, it still didn't sink in. If I was walking down the street in New York City, in the back of my mind I believed that she would appear—a shadow, a reflection in a plate glass window—if I turned my head fast enough, she would be there. Only she never was.

❧   ❧   ❧

Eventually the time came when my father was dying. Although we had remained estranged over the years, and my parents had long since divorced, I didn't hesitate as I drove back to the house I had grown up in, and where my father now lived alone.

When I approached his bed his eyes opened, a startling, crystalline blue, as if all of his life was now concentrated in his gaze. He reached out for my hand, and I held it as he drifted in and out of sleep.

"Why was it so difficult between us for all these years?" he asked when he awakened, his hair a wisp of sea spray. "Was it because of Delilah?"

"Yes," I said. "I think so."

He nodded, too spent to say more. I sat beside him, dust motes twirling down like petals or snow, and I mulled over my father's words. For so long Delilah's name had remained unspoken between us, and his acknowledgement, his claiming of this travesty, felt like a confession. As the late afternoon sun drained from the sky, though, I realized that this was not what he had actually said. He died that night.

✤   ✤   ✤

Occasionally, now, I stop by my father's home, although it isn't his anymore, and was sold to a family with two young children years ago. I park my car on the street, climb over the stone wall, and ease myself down against the gnarled gray bark of one of the oak trees. The lilac has grown unruly over the years, and it screens me from the house, so even if someone were to look out their window, they would not see me sitting on this mossy patch of grass. I am surrounded by stillness, and I bide my time, waiting for the chatter in my mind to subside. I might put my head in my hands and cry. Other times I ask for forgiveness, even if I'm not quite sure why. Perhaps for not knowing who to believe, or for the acceptance that I never will. Often I raise my arms and offer my father and my sister to the light filtering down from above. I turn them over again and again, and sometimes they are lifted.

PATRICIA BARONE

SUNDAY DINNER

Before your voice comes down
like a fist on the table
Mother and I are still
setting casseroles
on trivets on
our good tablecloth
over the felt
silencer

What are you yelling to
make me and my brother cry
Did I spill the milk
Did he drop the ball
Did I wear lipstick
Did he shave his chin
Did I talk back
Did he look sullen
Did I love a Socialist
Did he drive a bus
Did I leave home
Did he send his laundry
Did I have noisy children
Did he never marry
Did I Did he Did I Did he

Between the red wine and the white
I say, "You drink too much!"

"Your mother is so loud," you say,
"my heart, my age, my depression . . ."

It's your silence   you've hired
the booze to make you dumb.
You sit at the head of our table—
an empty bottle that the wind
howls over moans over passes on.
Do I feel   fill me up
so I won't   feel any more.
Do you feel   Shut up and don't
     tell me any more.
Remember once when you were sober,
and Mom poured water in the stemware.
Then we dipped our fingers
racing round each rim—

a dissonant harmony,
and you listened, Dad, to us.

IRA SCHAEFFER

DODGE CITY THEME PARK, FAMILY PHOTO, 1959

There we were, my sister,
caught in the crossfire
of a wild west shootout,
me with a toy gun ready
to pick off a black hat or two, you
the defenseless maiden
protecting your ears
from gunshots.
We were already typecasts
in our family's knockdown
highrise, serial drama.

Down the apartment corridor
I'd hear you screaming
in frenzied terror,
beseeching the townsfolk
to call the law on our jangled,
pistol-whipping Mother.
But those doors never opened;
our father, the sheriff
had abandoned his star
for saloon dreams
in a bottle of red-eye.

I was never the hero
who could stop with a slug
our deranged Mother;
my toy gun was loaded with fear.

I stayed the bystander, and watched
her slap your face, smash
your lavender radio,
trying to break
your delicate beauty.

Even now, dear sister,
when our Western façade
has gone the way of Gunsmoke,
we're both stuck in Dodge
still nursing flesh wounds
and a darkness lodged deep—
too late to remove.
Madness fixed our places
in this snapshot.
Can't you see?—our childhood
was taken at gunpoint.

EVER AFTER SISTER

Our calls are mostly strained and sunny,
a scripted conspiracy
of chirpy notes and emptiness,
breathless, we hang up
running from the chill ghost
of childhood still relentless
in pressing its claim.

But last night your voice softened,
quieted, the way it did long ago
telling me stories that bridged the darkness
as we traveled to the far land of sleep.

Remember, we were always *Hansel and Gretel*,
abandoned, starved, our innocence cannibalized
by mother's promise of gingerbread. Victims,
allies, we doubled our chances
to walk away, as our straw house smoldered
and the ugly witch went up in smoke.

We thought it was her fire
we had to fear, but wasn't it ice?
How pretty the light glinting—
the pure, pure white of it—
soothing hurt as it froze
our lives in place. Even apart
we stayed in the old house
believing we'd escaped
its terror heart. We grew numb,
deriding the thaw of love.

Arctic, bleak, your new story's built
from blocks of ice. You tell me
your plans to sleep death away
in a cryogenic deep freeze.
I almost laugh but your voice
becomes so solemn, so prayerful
that I want to cry as I listen,
picturing a wrinkled Snow White
reposed in an ice cathedral—the apple's
slush in her veins—waiting
for some prince in a lab coat
to kiss her awake.
Fairest one, you're gone.

It's near the end of winter
and I'm exhausted from our paralyzing tales
of breadcrumbs and chicken bones
and evil that resides only in witches.
I want to hear a tale of happiness:
how two snow angels regain their hearts
by taking in the sun—feeling
the cut of blood, the channel
that opens to the brutal, tender world.
I want to live.

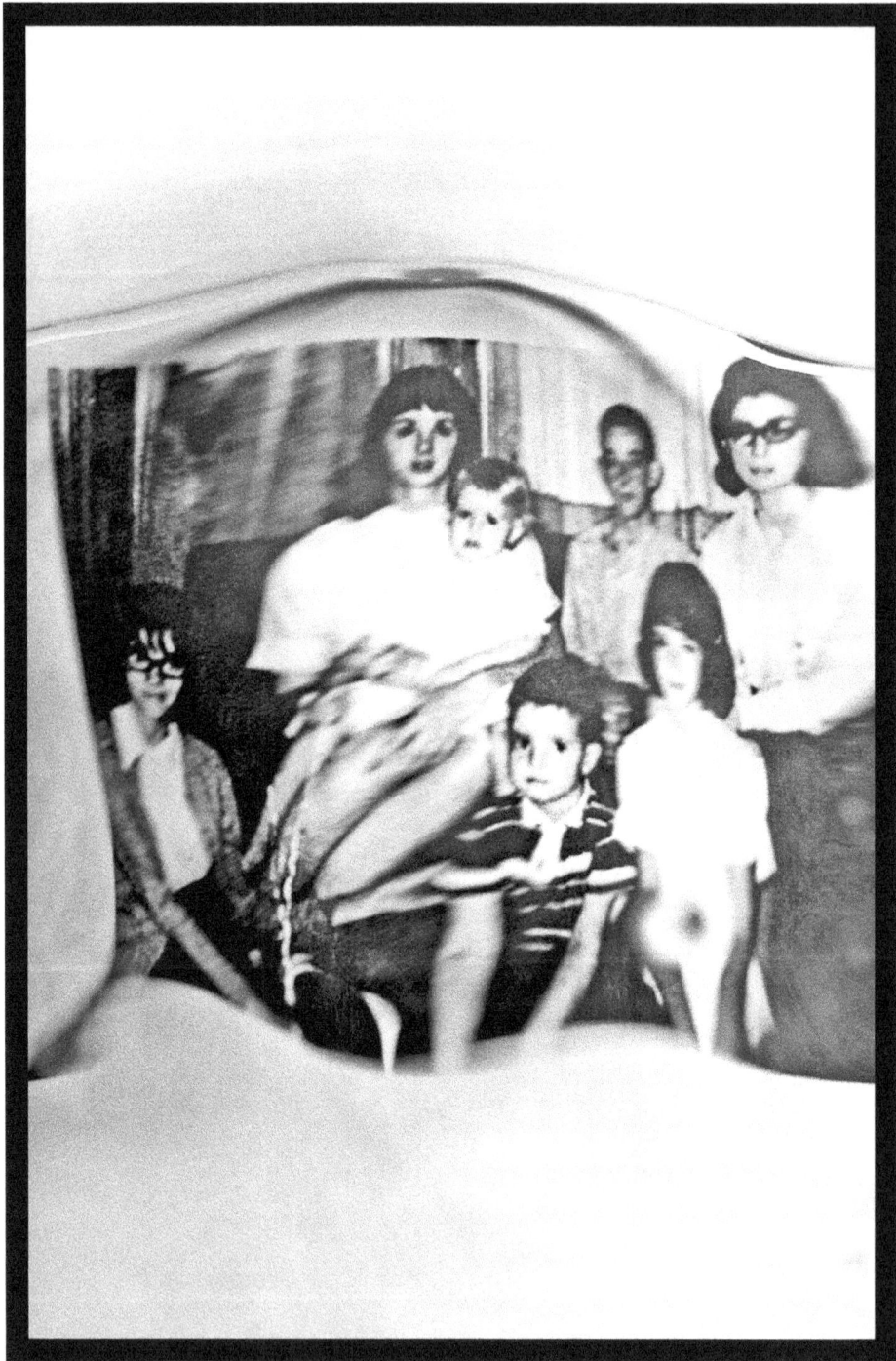

SARLA S. NICHOLS

MOTHER, SISTER, FRIEND

"I can't go to sleep. Stop that damn rocking. Jesus, Carrie, why can't you just lie down and go to sleep?" I hear her sobbing. My sister Carrie is ten years younger than me. She is the fourth of five children born to my stepmother, Elaine. Three boys, Scott, Mark and Kirk, preceded Carrie. I remember little of Carrie's arrival . . . only that Elaine was emotionally and physically spent. A frail woman, not 5'4" tall, with thinning brown hair and a stooped carriage, she worked full time to feed our family of eight. Like so many women of her era, the 1950's and 1960's, Elaine survived on Valium, "Mother's Little Helper," and alcohol, mostly beer.

Why Elaine and Carl, my father, had so many children is a mystery to me. Our two-bedroom, one-bath house barely accommodated the seven of us before Carrie came along. None of us wanted or needed another child, but there she was, an innocent tow-headed bundle of joy, another mouth to feed, a nuisance to her brothers, and an added responsibility for me.

As her designated baby sitter, I treated baby Carrie like a life-sized doll. I ran the neighborhood, house to house, with her tucked under my arm. I abandoned her in the middle of our concrete alley to shoot hoops with the boys. I dragged her over to my best friend Jill's house where I dumped her in the living room to fend for herself.

"Carrie, shut up. Will you please stop whining? Jill and I are dancing. I can't hear the music. You are such a pain in the ass. God I wish you'd grow up." My best friend Jill and I were spinning 45's and dancing in her living room with her sister, Patti. They didn't mind Carrie being around, but I hated it.

An indelible snapshot of her as a toddler, sitting, wide-eyed, tears rolling down her cherry red cheeks hangs in the recesses of my mind. Day after day, year after year, I tormented, ignored and abused her. She was the bane of my existence.

"Grandma, please watch Carrie. I have somewhere I need to go."

"You know I can't do that." Grandma said, glaring at me. "I'll be up and down the basement steps, doing laundry all day long. She needs constant supervision."

"Well then, just put her in the playpen and let her cry."

Grandma's expression said it all. I knew arguing would not help. Once Grandma made up her mind, she was immutable. I threw Carrie into the wire basket on the front of my red Schwinn bicycle. Scared, she tried to climb out. "It's okay," I snapped. "Just hold on. I'll get you a treat when we get to Bushbaum's." She smiled.

I loved to ride my bike, the feeling of the wind blowing through my unkempt hair, the feeling of the sidewalk flying by under my tires. The world was mine for the taking. Looking back over my shoulder, I hollered to my friend, Debbie, "Hey, did you bring any money with you? I found a couple bucks in my dad's suit pocket but that won't be enough to buy my Coke float and get a treat for Carrie. Gotta keep the little brat quiet or old Mr. Bushbaum will throw us out of the pharmacy."

"Look out!" Debbie screamed.

I turned just in time to see the side of a car pulling out of an alley right in front of me.

Brakes squealed as I slammed into the car.

Stunned, I picked myself up off the street and looked down at my banged up knees.

Debbie was freaking out. "Oh my God, Sarla, Carrie is bleeding. Look at her. I think her head is cracked open."

Lifeless, Carrie lay crumpled on the sidewalk. A red gusher spewed from the center of her forehead.

I yelled for someone, anyone to help me. "Is she dead? Someone call an ambulance."

A voice in the crowd answered. "We did. We used the phone at Bushbaum's."

I felt nauseous. "My mom is going to kill me. Oh what have I done?" I mumbled.

As I leaned over Carrie, I heard a voice warning, "Don't touch her. She might have a spinal injury. "

I heard the sirens. "Dear God Please let her be okay. Please." *Shit, what if she is permanently crippled or brain dead? What have I done?*

Carrie turned her head and smiled up at me.

"She's alive. She's alive." I sobbed.

A broad-shouldered man jumped out of the back of the ambulance and kneeled down beside me. "Where are your mother and father? I need to speak to one of them."

Another man checked my sister's head. "She's going to be fine," he assured me. "It's just a bad bump with a slight cut."

"Why is there so much blood?" I asked.

"Head wounds produce more blood than cuts or lacerations on any other part of the body."

Whew. She's going to be okay.

✤   ✤   ✤

Who knew then that Carrie would have such a rough go of it? Once my brother Scott left her at the A&P grocery, getting all the way home before he remembered where she was. Mark, another brother, cut off her hair. Kirk, a third brother, stole the birthday money Grandma Elmore had given her. And I made it my mission to stay as far away from her as possible.

When she was seven, the axle of a wooden cart fell on her ankle and almost crushed it. She still cannot walk long distances without pain.

A few years later, an electrical fire in the attic forced the family to split up and move out, finding shelter with various relatives and friends. Twelve-year-old Carrie and the three older boys lived by themselves for six months in a trailer parked in their driveway while our father, Carl, stayed in the one room at the house that was not damaged by fire or water. It took almost a year to settle the insurance claim and get the family back together.

✤   ✤   ✤

At fourteen, traumatized by a pregnancy terminated with an abortion, Carrie came to live with me in Memphis. I was only twenty-four at the time, barely an adult myself, and ill equipped to care for a dysfunctional teenager. That's why I was so happy when Aunt Jackie called from South Bend to tell Carrie, "You need to come home, now. Your mother is at St. Joseph Hospital in a coma." Elaine, a new convert to Christian Science, had severe hepatitis and refused to get treatment. Carrie was distraught and I could not comfort her. I was glad Elaine was sick because it meant I could ship Carrie out on the next bus for South Bend. Jeff and I celebrated by going to our favorite bar.

❦   ❦   ❦

Motherless, Carrie and my other siblings did the best they could to survive. My dad talked the kids into signing over their share of Elaine's Social Security money, claiming that he would be the one to support them now. He did not. God only knows what he used the money for, but they never saw a penny of it. Mark managed to graduate from high school. The others dropped out or just quit going.

Grief does not explain why Carrie married Danny, a misogynistic crack head and the father of her only child, Crystal. I could not believe that my twenty-year-old sister was a mother living with a no-good, unemployed drug dealer. She was living the nightmare I had left South Bend to avoid.

Little did I know that having a child would give Carrie the courage she needed to leave Danny. When Crystal was four, she and Carrie moved back home to live with Dad and her brothers Mark and Duff. Carrie took a job waiting tables at Shoney's Big Boy and did her best to raise her daughter.

I do not know how she lived in that filthy house with those helpless men. She assumed the role of maid, cook and laundress. Duff, the youngest, did help out by walking Crystal to and from the school bus stop, and caring for her when Carrie picked up an extra night shift.

It must have been hard on Duff when Carrie met and married Kevin, a chemical engineer. They moved into Kevin's parents' house until they could find a place in Indianapolis. Kevin eventually adopted Crystal. He encouraged Carrie to get her GED. She did that, and then went on to get a sociology degree. I was very proud of my sister, the ex-high school dropout, when she graduated from college.

Whenever I called to check in, she gushed news of her work. She loved helping young, unwed mothers learn how to care for their babies. And when these same women were ready to work, she talked them through the interview process, found them appropriate clothing, and adequate childcare. The hardest part of her job was removing children from abusive homes.

I can only imagine what she might have thought going into those homes. Whatever the circumstances, she quit. She told me, "It makes me too sad."

We are so different. I would have sought help, gone to therapy and tried to overcome the fear and sadness.

She explains our differences this way. "My journey through this life has

been different than yours. My way of dealing with the past is gratitude for the
present. And believe it or not, I am happy. I wake each morning thankful for a
new day and the journey before me."

❧   ❧   ❧

Our reunions, maybe six in the past thirty-five years, were born out of
necessity, two weddings, Crystal's and my daughter Katie's, two Thanksgiving
dinners and a few family birthdays. I felt the closest I ever have to Carrie on my
visit home just before my father's death.

This house should be condemned. That's what I was thinking as I walked up
the outside steps of the house I never lived in but which my father, brothers and
grandmother called "home." My brother had put a chain link fence around the
entire property. The front gate had a padlock hanging on the latch. The message
to visitors was loud and clear.

Carrie was with me. "Do you think there is anyone home?" I asked her.
"The place looks deserted."

I knocked, but no one answered. "Dad? Dad?" I called out as we moved
into the house. Whole walls were missing. The fireplace mantel was leaning
against the dinning room table. To the left of the living room I saw exposed
beadboard with a big hole that opened to the outside yard. The stairs leading
to the second level looked as if they were suspended in air—no railing and
no walls—-just the risers remained. Huge, stringy cobwebs hung from naked
crossbeams. Pieces of ceiling sheetrock hung like stalactites waiting to impale
me. One caught my sleeve and left a permanent stain on my white sweatshirt. I
smelled the stench of rotting garbage, cigar and pipe smoke, dog poop, decaying
wood, stale air, old fireplace smoke, and molded, musty furniture.

Turning to Carrie I said, "This is reminiscent of a Flannery O'Connor
story. Have you ever read her work? She describes rooms like these filled with
old useless things; rooms in houses where nobody lives, just the ghosts of the
past." Carrie shook her head and looked around.

I was thinking of turning back, of leaving when I saw him standing in
the hallway leading from the living room into the kitchen. His beautiful wavy
hair was thin and graying around the temples, and his receding hairline was
more pronounced. Frail, gaunt and pale, he managed a smile revealing perfectly
straight teeth streaked brown from years of smoking and drinking black coffee.
At three o'clock in the afternoon, my father was still in his tattered, blue, terry

cloth robe. He was so short——even shorter than I remembered. Our eyes met. The last time we had talked, seven years ago, I told him I hated him and never wanted to see him again. Now all I felt was love and sadness. It was as if we were seeing each other for the very first time.

Carrie and I walked with him toward the kitchen. The stove, an old brown, four-burner gas one with a glass-windowed oven door, was covered with blackened food residue. In the sink, I saw a pile of dirty dishes covered in gray grime, which seemingly spread outward to every visible surface. He lit the gas burner and set a teapot on to boil. "Dad, how can you live like this? Why don't you go move into Aunt Honey's house?" I asked. "At least it's clean. You're sick."

"No, no," he said, pouring himself a cup of tea. "This is fine. Really, honey, I'm fine. Don't you worry about me." He kept talking as we walked back to the living room where he gingerly sat down in his favorite chair. It was draped in an old blanket that covered exposed foam cushions. I watched, incredulous, as he picked up and relit a discarded cigar. Smoking had caused his cancer, but it was too late to worry about that now. His death was imminent. He showed me a can of Ensure, which he had left sitting on the end table next to his chair. "This is all I can eat now. I don't have much of an appetite anyway."

I stood next to him smiling, still trying to take it all in . . . his old tobacco pipes, the ones I remembered from childhood, hanging in his circular pipe stand, the bald spot on the top of his head, his raspy, compromised breath, and the utter chaos around him. I tried to speak, "Dad? Dad, I . . ."

"Everything is fine, honey. I'm fine. Really, don't worry about me."

I felt myself melting, the hard edges of my armor slipping away. I wanted to hold him like a child in my arms. This man, whom I had hated for so long, was now at death's door. I could not bear to stay any longer. I leaned over his chair and hugged him. "I love you Dad. I love you so much."

He stood up turning to hold me. "I love you too, honey. It's okay. It's all okay now."

Carrie and I looked silently at one another. She nodded. I touched my dad on the shoulder. She took my hand as we left.

❦   ❦   ❦

My last visit with Carrie was in July of 2011. My husband and I drove to Bloomington, Indiana for her husband Kevin's fiftieth birthday bash.

Carrie and Kevin's house abuts a run-down cemetery. In order to escape their two barking dogs and the clutter of their tiny bungalow, I spent hours sitting on their raised backyard deck. Their quiet yard, dotted with an odd assemblage of birdhouses and exotic plants, offered a reprieve from the memories that haunted me. Looking out at the graveyard, I noticed names, now indistinguishable, that were once carefully carved into the fallen gravestones.

Maybe it was all the wine we drank. Or perhaps it was the suitcase of pictures my niece Crystal brought with her. She found them going through her Uncle Duff's belongings. I am sure that is how Duff, our youngest brother, later came up in conversation. We were all sitting down to eat in their cramped dining room. Kevin's brother, his wife and their child; Carrie, Kevin, and Crystal; my husband, Jimmy, and I; and my brother Mark crowded around a lace covered mahogany pedestal table.

We were sharing our memories of Duff and expressing openly our regret about his passing when I said, "Duff was destined to die young. His body just gave out."

Carrie exploded. "What do you mean? Duff never had a chance. You left before things got really bad. You can't imagine what it was like after Mom died. We didn't have anyone. Carl talked us all into signing our Social Security benefits over to him. I don't know what he did with all that money, but I do know he didn't give any of it to us."

Red faced, she went on. "Duff never went to school. He stayed home all day and smoked pot. Nobody cared."

"I'm sorry Carrie. What do you want me to do? I had a way out, and I took it. You would have too. When things got hard for you, what did you do? You came to Memphis to live with Jeff and me. Is it my fault you went back to South Bend?"

She lit into me again. "You don't understand. Everything was so much worse after you left. We didn't have parents. There was no one to look out for us."

"Oh and I did have parents? I'm so tired of being the bad guy."

Carrie stared at her half-eaten food. "I know. I'm sorry. It's just that I miss Duff so much."

"Yeah, Duff is dead, but what did you expect?" I then listed his litany of mistakes, telling Carrie what we both already knew . . . that Duff smoked four packs of cigarettes a day from the time he was ten, that he got so many DUIs he had to give up driving completely, that he had two children, neither of whom he cared for financially or emotionally. "I know you miss him. You and Duff were closer than all the rest of us, but he's dead and you need to move on."

"That's easy for you to say. You moved away. We had nowhere to go. Duff couldn't . . ."

"Stop. I'm here now. I love being here. I'm so glad we came." I looked at Jimmy for support. "But as far as Duffy not being able to help it . . . how do you explain that? He could have quit smoking."

"Sarla, when he found out he had cancer, it was already stage IV. Stage IV. What was he supposed to do? Quit smoking? What good would that have done?"

"Did Duff ever do anything to take care of himself? You could have been a high school drop out like him, but you wanted to make something of your life. Duff is dead, and we're not. Is that my fault?"

"I'm a sociologist and I know more about these things than you do. I've seen this over and over again. Duff was part of a system that destroyed him."

"Oh, so you're some fucking sociologist. Just what does that mean? If you were so good at what you did, why aren't you working now? Sis, I have had years and years of therapy, and I can tell you right now that a person can make anything they want to of their lives, but they have to try."

"He did try. You just don't understand. You weren't there."

Here we go again. I know this dance, hopping from one position to another only to come back to the same hurtful spot. I LEFT. There is no changing that.

"I'm leaving the table now. This conversation is going nowhere."

I stormed into the bedroom. Slamming the door behind, I threw myself down on the bed.

I wanted to run. I wanted to pack the car and leave. I did not want to be there. I felt like the frightened child I had fought so hard to protect. The rough bedspread irritated my skin. The room was so small and the only door led right back out to the people I had just so rudely left behind.

My husband Jimmy sneaked in and attempted to console me. I pushed him aside, but he stayed close and waited. In no time, I curled up next to him. Engulfed in his strong, loving arms, my sobbing subsided. We lay still.

Just as I was calming down, there was a knock on the door. It was Carrie. "Sarla, I'm so sorry. Please don't leave. We have a great day planned for tomorrow. Crystal is making her famous paella for Kevin's birthday dinner."

"No, I won't leave."

"Good. That would be awful. I mean we are all here together. I miss Duffy so much and he was so sick for so long. I just wish he'd had a chance for a better life."

We managed to patch things up enough to spend the next day celebrating Kevin's fiftieth. There was plenty of beer and wine to ease the pain.

Jimmy and I made an early night of it. Using Jimmy's migraine as an excuse, we left the next morning ahead of schedule.

I have spoken with my sister a few times since then. A flurry of conversations ensued around the birth of my daughter's first child, Amelia, but the fragile connection soon shattered.

Finally I wrote this in a letter:

> *Carrie, I am sorry that we are estranged, but I cannot continue to wallow in the past. I do not want to die blaming Elaine and Carl or my mother for my fate. I believe we each have the power to overcome, to move beyond, and to be more than our past. Not to forget, but to heal by looking honestly at what happened to us and using our experience as fodder for creativity. I miss you, sis. I hope you are well. Wish you would return my calls.*

Carrie does speak to me now. She and Kevin moved to Atlanta in October, just a six-hour drive from my home in Memphis. She knows that I am writing a memoir and has even been willing to read some of my stories. This was her response:

> *Thoughts . . . I did not know you were so responsible for my care when I was little. This explains why I have felt abandoned by you so many times in my life. I must have looked to you for my mother figure. I remember when you would come for visits to South Bend. When you returned to Memphis I would feel physically sick from you leaving, as if you had abandoned me.*

J.S. KIERLAND

A QUICK KILL

Three in the morning in the Hollywood Hills feels like five in the morning anywhere else. The coyotes and owls have crossed the northern boundaries and strayed down under the big HOLLYWOOD sign that glistens in the moonlight at the top of Beachwood Canyon. Field mice, possum, snakes, and house cats become fair game for the wild intruders that prowl the narrow winding streets and canyons for a quick kill and a quiet meal with the family.

I nursed my bourbon, waited for the big owl to land on the roof, and listened to the ice tumble in Nicky's glass as he downed his third quick scotch. He'd come in from New York to record some background jazz for a new Steven Spielberg film, and it wasn't going well. The improvised score wasn't working like it had in other films and Nicky seemed more out of place than usual. He was a true New Yorker, born and bred, and remained that way for better or for worse. Hollywood was just the suburbs to Nicky.

We managed to avoid talking about the family until he opened one of my dusty liquor bottles and eased into some hard comments about his ex-wife and their three kids. I was Nicky's older brother and knew him a lot longer than anyone else but had always been as confused about his ex-wife and kids as he was. In fact, it was because I knew Nicky so well that I'd decided to stop being his brother. It'd become too dangerous, and getting a quiet divorce was the best thing I could do for the both of us.

"I can't begin to tell you how much money she's cost me," he said in that raspy voice that suddenly had an edge of aggression in it. He assumed I knew who *she* was, and I did. "And my goddamn kids. They don't know what they want. Wouldn't know how to get it even if they did know," he said, looking up with that intense stare that showed up after his second or third scotch.

His kids were having a difficult time adjusting to what we both called, "the dear, dear, modern world." His and his ex-wife's constant tongue-lashing and bare-knuckled brawls hadn't helped their kids' situation either. I could see the defeat and confusion in his eyes. My mind raced through convoluted back roads looking for a way out of the conversation, but it was too late. "Your kid's doing all right, isn't she?" he asked.

"She's certainly way ahead of me at her age," I mumbled, hoping the subject would pass.

"I always liked her," he said, taking another hit of the scotch. "What's she up to these days?"

He knew "what she was up to" but I just shrugged, and said, "She's working for some movie producer."

"I don't know where *my* daughter is. She won't give me her phone number."

"That right?" I said in a faked surprise. I had sworn not to tell anyone that his daughter was staying with my daughter.

"I don't know what the hell she's doing," he mumbled, taking another gulp of the scotch. I felt it coming as soon as he lowered the glass. "We never went through this shit, did we?"

The "*we*" was a reference to a time long gone when I was still Nicky's brother and we were growing up, sharing an odd-shaped bend in the hallway of a Bronx railroad flat. It was a memory that seemed to hang on our lives like a cursed family jewel.

"Things were tough, but we got through it, didn't we?"

I'd heard this question, that Nicky never wanted answered, many times before. The question would always lead to the usual anecdotes about the cramped apartment and exaggerated incidents that had lost any true meaning years ago. I waited for one of these Bronx tales to begin but his dark eyes were deeper and sadder than I'd ever seen them. He slumped over his scotch like a beaten fighter. Then he did something he'd never done before. He looked straight at me, waiting for an answer to his question. It was absolutely terrifying.

"No," I said. "I don't think we ever did get through those years in the Bronx. We only thought we did, but never quite made it. Graduating from movie matinees at the Paradise Theatre to concerts at Carnegie Hall and then working in Hollywood is a progression, but we never quite put the Bronx behind us."

To my surprise, he smiled and nodded as if it'd been the answer he'd expected and wanted. I heard a scraping sound on the roof and knew the owl had taken off to catch a silent dinner somewhere below on the hill.

"I always think of the Bronx as the good years, but you don't, do you?"

he asked.

"My memories of the Bronx aren't exactly good ones."

"What do you remember?"

I avoided his eyes and said, "I remember the old man charging down that long hallway, half asleep and half naked, coming to beat the shit out of me. Probably giving you a few licks too."

Nicky didn't move for a long agonizing moment. He finally nodded and took another sip of the scotch. "Yeah, I remember that too," he said. "The old man had one hell of a temper."

"He had more than a temper. He was one frustrated son-of-a-bitch that beat us for being what we were. Kids."

He hardly breathed when he said, "But we grew up."

"Sort of," I answered. "We grew up and he died, then turned into one of those ghosts that won't leave you alone. He insists on hanging on for the whole trip, so I have to fight him off every morning just to get out of bed." The owl landed on the roof again, and I said, "The only real difference is that I live with it—"

"And I don't."

"You sidestep it."

He poured more scotch and we watched the family ghosts dance around us in the eerie silence. "You never liked him," he said.

Him was the old man, my lingering ghost. "No," I answered, letting the subject hang.

"They had it tough. A lot tougher than we did."

They included our long-suffering Irish mother. "Maybe," I said, "but having it tough shouldn't be a reason to take it out on your kids. They don't come with demands. If you eat your children then they'll probably eat theirs. It can keep going like that for generations."

He didn't say anything for a long time, and then growled, "That's what I did. I ate my kids."

It wasn't a question, more a statement of fact, so I didn't say anything. We just sat there and listened to the owl's mocking hoot and the distant yap of a coyote.

"How did you get around it?"

"Around what?"

"Not eating your kid."

"I don't know," I said. "It's not easy keeping your neuroses to yourself.

The hard part is admitting there's something wrong with you and working at it from there."

"But they end up being just like us anyway."

"I tried keeping that to a minimum," I said, finishing my watered down bourbon and wondering why we both had avoided this subject for most of our lives. The coyote yelped again and the sound was much closer.

"What the hell was that?" Nicky asked.

"Just a coyote."

"You're kidding," he said, going to the window.

"I doubt if you'll see him in the dark but whole families of them hunt in the Hollywood Hills every night."

I watched as the New Yorker stood at the window and tried to catch a glimpse of the coyote in the darkness. "They don't eat their kids, do they?" he asked.

"No, they don't," I said.

"I didn't think so," he mumbled.

At that moment, when he was still looking for the coyote, I wanted to tell him why I wasn't his brother anymore and that I knew how much he wanted to hurt me, but I never said a word. The night just passed in a silent, soundless, brotherly divorce. No lawyers, no courts, no visiting rights, no tears. It was the last time I ever saw Nicky. The next day he flew back to New York, leaving me out in Hollywood with the owls and the coyotes.

DONALD R. VOGEL

ESAU AND THE LAODICEAN

In my slide into the valley of misanthropy, I can thank a brother for the ride and a stepbrother for the brakes. Part of the decline has involved watching my youngest sibling devolve from a teenage social drinker to a drunk, who now lives with his family in my mother's trailer in Pennsylvania. What has provided some hope is my stepbrother who has shown restraint and toleration in the face of being cast out. Meanwhile, I strive to reconcile belief with reality from the dust of the created and the misbegotten. The ghosts of Cain and Abel, Esau and Jacob, fratricide and stolen birthrights, all haunt the perimeters of a family joined more like Siamese twins than the Brady Bunch.

Before I moralize on anyone else's sins, I must confess my own. I too indulged in booze and myriad other substances as a teenager growing up in the 1970s. It was about a five-year period, from the age of fifteen until about twenty when I became an evangelical while serving in the Navy. My brother, Steve the drunk, was about five and my parents were divorcing, so I may have had an influence on him without a consistent father figure present.

This wasn't remedied when my stepfather Jason appeared with his three kids, Sharon, the oldest, Bill the middle, and Melissa the youngest. On our side there were my sister, Lisa, me, Derrick next, and then Steve. Our parents married within one year of the ink drying on their divorce papers. My stepfather Jason was the epitome of the nerdy postman. He recently died, after thirty-four years of marriage. The funeral proved to be the demarcation between the brothers of blood and choice.

❖   ❖   ❖

Here's what was beyond my control. Like any of us, my brother was the victim of fate and his own choices. Dyslexia was compounded by youngest child syndrome. Steve was shoved into special education from which my parents could never extract him, even when experts said he was ready to be mainstreamed. That stigma didn't end with the school bell. He was also coddled by Mom. Whenever he's fallen, she's been his safety net so that over the last thirty years, he has never had to face the consequences of his actions. This was epitomized by his trying to build a house, a few months after moving into his first one and selling it before getting the new one up to code. He lost both. My mother got a second mortgage to buy my brother a house in her development in Pennsylvania. He lost that too, unable to hold a job. Because of all this, Mom and Jason lost their home as well, and with their credit wrecked, were reduced to living in a trailer.

My stepbrother, Bill, closest in age to my middle brother, Derrick, joined the family with his sisters. I was seventeen and he was twelve. He was never my mother's favorite and when Sharon fled to her own mother's home soon after the wedding, my mom constantly accused Bill of trying to get Derrick in trouble. But Bill was a straight arrow. Somehow I, the long-haired, stoner remained my mother's favorite, until she threw me out in my senior year because of the drugs, three months before her marriage to Jason. Since I was on the delayed entry program to join the Navy that September and she missed me after a month (I lived at a friend's), I was allowed back home. Not long after I returned, Bill joined Sharon at their mother's home. The youngest, Melissa, followed in her time. Today all of us are scattered across five states.

I carry a certain amount of guilt for having gotten stoned and left. However, I also understand that my influence was severely limited by age and immaturity. How much would it have helped had I been a perfect role model? It is somehow comforting that the guilt is the product of values instilled within me from my upbringing. My later adopted biblical beliefs are now literary, rather than literal. I can't see how one can interpret scripture or life any other way. Fundamentalism is like a flashlight in a fog illuminating immediacy but not distance.

Though not welcoming to Jason's brood, Mom did her best to keep a roof over our heads. I will always wonder if her marriage to Jason was one of utility. He tried to defend his own, but Mom was just too willful, and the guy had nowhere else to go with his kids estranged. I too was distant, especially from family, preoccupied by friends and getting high. After graduation, I was onto life with four years at sea and college thereafter.

Like me, my stepbrother Bill joined the military—the Army as an MP in Germany for his tour—and became a cop after his discharge. He stayed with his mother when home on leave. I was away at a Christian college, immersed in God and academics, and dreaming of being a writer. I was not only learning to be a critical thinker, but also learning the Christian tenets of selflessness and forgiveness. The irony is that in learning to be Christ-like, I was driven ever more inward, deeper than various substances had ever taken me. Otherwise, I might have played a larger role in the amelioration of my family's dysfunction.

Today I am the father of one son, Dylan, who is fourteen. He has a cousin and a step-cousin who were both born within six months of him. One, Grace, is the opposite of her father, my youngest brother Steve, and the other, Bobby, still soils himself. Grace is bright, pretty, and dating a boy who is four years her senior who stays with her at Mom's to babysit her dogs overnight. Bobby, who is Bill's second son, is severely autistic and when I last saw him a few years ago, he could only utter "dit-did-it-dit." When Bill is not training cadets at the county police academy, he is spelling his stay-at-home wife. Somehow he still finds time to go boating, mountain biking, and motorcycling. With Steve, it's pretty simple: he drinks, can't hold a job, gripes about how he never knew his real father, and gets counseled by my niece's boyfriend, whose own father died from alcoholism. My son Dylan would get gift cards for Christmas from my mom, while Steve's daughter Grace got trips to Build-A-Bear. Bill's son Bobby got nothing, not even a visit.

My stepfather died in November 2014, after wasting away in a veterans' home for two years with Alzheimer's and Parkinson's. He was in the early stages of the former, but it was the latter that killed him. Toward the end, he was in and out of the hospital with my mom rushing there and screaming on the phone for Bill to race four hours from New Jersey whenever the end was predicted, which seemed perpetual. Steve was living with her by then, having lost his apartment and job, yet again. Mom claimed Steve and his family provided moral support, but all they did was leave her kitchen cluttered with dirty dishes and trash. Whenever I called for news on Jason, Steve would answer, slurring as he told me how he had everything under control. This continued, until my stepfather's tortuous downward spiral.

Jason's death was, to me, an interruption of the stasis I've come to cherish in life. And perhaps it is the rude awakening I needed to become, if not a better Christian, at least a decent human being. Read the book of Revelation about the seven churches, and you'll encounter the Laodiceans, the lukewarm church Christ wishes was either hot or cold and, because it is neither, spews it from his mouth. I worship there. Translated to my personal life, stasis is an excuse not to engage in the work of relationships. Maybe in all of this there is a path to resolution, if not redemption.

Parkinson's robbed Jason of his ability to swallow. Had he not had a DNR, the option would have been to have him intubated. Mom was tempted to supercede the order. She called me one night in tears saying she didn't have the strength to watch him die of starvation. In my response, I alluded to quality of life and what it meant for her, shuttling in and out of the hospital only to watch him die anyway. The question that persuaded her was "do you really want to preserve him until he doesn't recognize you anymore?" After that the volley of calls intensified, as the step family descended. Sharon, my stepfather's oldest daughter, was the first to arrive and with her arrival, thirty years of suppressed resentment and guilt came to a head.

Among the calls I received was Mom detailing her conflicts with Sharon, who surreptitiously tried to overturn the DNR. Mom protested that if Sharon succeeded, she would gallivant back to California, leaving her with the burden of watching Jason waste away. I wondered where Steve, a forty-two-year-old man, was in all of this. The trailer park where my mom lived was full of his ilk. The few times I visited with my family while Steve was living with her, he guzzled cheap beer with these 'friends' rather than spend time with us. I figured that's where he was.

Bill made it in time to watch his father die. I can't imagine his internal efforts to cope with Jason's death, while his sister and stepmother each vied for his loyalty. He coordinated with me via cell phone to get Jason's body from Pennsylvania to the veterans' cemetery in New Jersey. I was ambassador for my mother's wishes. If it were up to her, Bill and his family would have had no say in the funeral planning.

At the wake, the viewing room was the DMZ between blood relations and steps. Derrick, Steve, and I sat with my mom the first hour. No one from the other side approached for condolences or even to pray at Jason's casket, except for Bill. When I first arrived, I hugged my stepsister Sharon, and expressed sorrow for her loss, and that was it. I did approach my stepsister Melissa, Bill's youngest sister in from California, and shared my fondest moments of her father. She said "I'm happy *you* have those memories."

Bill, when he wasn't hanging with his cop buddies who he'd arranged to provide a color guard and escort for the funeral, would sometimes sit with my mother or would take her arm to walk her around. My brother Steve slunk away whenever he could to slug from a bottle he'd hidden in Mom's car, drinking even when he was chauffeuring her and the rest of his family. She was paying for their motels and meals as well, while in debt to the veterans' and the funeral homes. I tried to cover what I could. Knowledge of the imposition on Mom and me is what angered me more than Steve's actual drinking. I seethed from years of this.

Partly because of Steve, I am weary and intolerant of people I perceive to lack the skills or common sense to deal with life. Christ says somewhere that one must forgive one's brother seventy times seven, yet it seems like my forgiveness for my brother has only empowered him to persist in adverse behavior and fueled the ticking time bomb that is my chronic passivity. As Paul Simon once sang, "I might do some damage one fine day." At this funeral, I finally did.

Between afternoon and evening services, we had gone with my mom to get pizza. After dropping her off, Steve drove away with my niece and her boyfriend in the car. He was gone about twenty minutes to get another bottle of alcohol, we learned later from my niece. He rejoined us for dinner and went to the bar. Derrick followed and returned without him a few minutes later. I then went and found Steve with a beer, which I grabbed from him and ordered him to desist from his drinking. I left and he still took several minutes to return.

Derrick and I and our wives were rolling our eyes as Steve reverted to his tropes, whining about how Jason was the only father he ever knew because our own father (dead fifteen years at that time) left when he was young. In unison, we told him to shut up, at which he stormed out of the restaurant. My mother began to cry prompting my sister-in-law to follow Steve. The rest of us consoled Mom who shared her own worries and weariness with my brother, who was at that moment screaming at his wife just outside the restaurant. That was my breaking point. I gritted my teeth so hard my ears rang. I was going to hit him.

The rest of the family pleaded with me not to go. I think my niece was crying as I huffed out the door. I called him the most selfish prick on earth. Had he no concern for his mother or the family he jeopardized when he drove? I grabbed his upper left arm, fingers biting flesh, with the idea of ripping it from the joint. That grip, by remaining the epicenter of my fury, was his and my salvation. I only yelled.

I still boil thinking about that moment and regret not hitting him. I don't know if that makes me a coward, prudent, or something else. Everyone seemed relieved when I got back to the table. It was my niece's seventeen-year-old boyfriend who went out to counsel the blubbering slob. Mom lit into Steve when he returned and that's where we left it.

The larger crowd at the evening service prevented any further confrontations. While we engaged friends and family, I would occasionally see Steve schlepping around and yammering with some childhood friends. I had nothing else to say to him for the rest of the funeral and burial. Bill also noticed Steve's condition and came over to commiserate. It opened a floodgate of catharsis between us. I apologized when he later told me that my bipolar sister Lisa had called him at home during Jason's week of decline to curse him for not supporting my mother. When his sister Sharon shunned my mother's attempt at reconciliation after the memorial service at the cemetery, Mom thought Bill should have intervened, and also belittled him in our limousine, in which he had chosen to travel instead of the one with his sisters.

Several weeks later, Bill and I went to see the tombstone on Jason's grave. A wreath for the grave lent no warmth to the scene on that drizzly December Sunday. At the grave, Bill wept little, but admitted he was more overwhelmed when he'd come the week before with his older son, Mike. Bill scrounged for memories and found only one: golfing with Jason before my mother had whisked him off to Scranton in 2003. Bill seemed resentful of that more than anything else. Afterward we had lunch, more catharsis, and promises to stay in touch. We haven't.

I'm left with myriad emotions, none greater than humility and gratitude. I am humbled by self-realizations I hope will prepare me for the additional damage Steve is destined to cause, as well as grateful that my stepbrother is a model of tolerance. Do I feel some sense of resolution or closure? No. Death is the only finality and resolution is just a period at the end of a sentence that requires similar dots on a page to define its place in a narrative. Faith is what will carry me, and I will have to find it in myself, God, or people. I think I need to re-visit the book of Revelation to choose the next church at which I will worship, if I don't talk myself out of it beforehand.

RUTH LATTA

THE FAMILY TOGETHER

Frank always phones his younger brothers, Oliver and Jack, on alternate Sunday afternoons. Sylvia, his wife of forty years, points out that both of his brothers could press Frank's button on their speed dials and call him for a change, but he just shrugs.

"They call only when they want something," she says, "like when one of their kids gets married and would like an expensive present."

Frank nods. "I know, but they're family."

Though he's sixty-five, he still honors his promise, at twenty, to his dying mother, to "keep the family together." Sylvia, however, defines "family" as their two sons, both prospering in faraway cities.

Now, as Frank in Ottawa dials Jack in Fredericton, he wishes it were the Sunday for calling Oliver. He likes Oliver, a genial retired teacher in Toronto. Brusque Jack is harder to love, as he prides himself on speaking his mind. He owned a hardware store for years and always considered himself superior to Frank, who did not have a business of his own, but had been a stockroom manager for an automotive parts company. You would think Jack had founded the store and built it up from scratch, but in fact, he became the owner, eventually, because he'd married the boss's daughter. Now he has sold the store and is fond of saying that he's enjoying "freedom fifty-five."

Today, Jack picks up on the second ring.

"Hey, there, Frank. I was going to call you," he says.

"Beat you to it," Frank says pleasantly. "What's new?"

"Well, our black sheep is embarking on a new adventure." Jack's tone is rueful.

"Black sheep?"

"My elder son. Dustin, of course. Who else? The girls are happily married and doing well, and Chad is winning scholarships and doesn't owe me a dime. Dustin's another story."

"Has he borrowed more money from you and Peg?" inquired Frank.

"No, indeedy! He knows better than to ask, because he hasn't repaid a cent of what he already owes us."

Apparently, Dustin partied his way through a college business course and flunked out. Then he borrowed $5,000 from his indulgent mother, Peg, to buy into a classmate's restaurant venture. Dustin was to be manager; his friend, the cook. The business went belly-up within a year, leaving Dustin jobless, broke and in debt. The last Frank has heard, Dustin is a janitor in an elementary school, and couch-surfing among his friends because Jack wouldn't let him move back home.

It has been a while since Frank last saw his nephew. He remembers Dustin as a fifteen year old, nervous and eager-to-please. The lad must be twenty-five now.

"Is he in some kind of trouble?" Frank asks.

Jack snorts. "*He* doesn't think so. He's on Cloud Nine, because he's engaged to be married."

"Well! Congratulations are in order. Who is the lucky girl?"

"Her name is Kathie-Lee Staghorn and she's a teacher's aide at the school where he pushes a broom. I never thought of my screw-up son as a catch, but he's a step up in the world for Kathie-Lee."

"Oh? Do tell."

Jack sighs. "This girl is a real hillbilly. Not the voluptuous Moonbeam McSwine kind, either. Kathie-Lee is skinny, and parts her hair in the middle and scrapes it back with an elastic like some backwoods granny. Her father runs a sawmill in the back of beyond. He looks just like Jed Clampett of *The Beverly Hillbillies*, except that Jed Clampett had teeth. Her pappy says, 'I seen' and 'ain't.' Kathie-Lee's the oldest of five. They're a bunch of breeders. I wouldn't be surprised if she has a bun in the oven."

Frank winces. Who does Jack think he is? Their own father was an ordinary railway section hand, their mother a homemaker who sewed for extra cash. Their ancestors, whom Frank has traced, lived pretty close to the bone when they first came to Canada from the States in the late 1700s. Possibly Kathie-Lee's family has the same heritage.

"Kathie-Lee is the first of her family to go to beyond high school," Jack continues. "Incidentally, a teacher's aide isn't a real teacher. She's a graduate of some babysitting course from a community college."

Then she'll fit right in with you and Peg, thinks Frank. *You two barely got your high school diplomas.*

"You'll receive some kind of half-assed wedding invitation one of these days, but we understand if you decide to send your regrets," Jack continues. "The ceremony will be in some gospel hall, followed by a picnic and barbecue on the Staghorns' dog-patch farm near their sawmill. I won't have to get out my tux for this wedding." He chuckles.

Jack looked dapper in a tuxedo at his daughters' weddings to a forestry biologist and a veterinarian, and at the marriage of Oliver's daughter in Toronto to a professor of medieval history.

"I wish we could attend Dustin's wedding, but Sylvia has her heart set on visiting the boys and their families. San Diego and Seattle are both on the west coast, but the cost of going there will be considerable, and we can't afford two trips. We'll send Dustin and Kathie-Lee a check."

"That will be much appreciated, since the two of them don't have a pot to . . . well, you know."

Frank doesn't like Jack's smutty language. Their parents taught them better than that.

"Where are the young people living?" he asks.

"They're in her tiny apartment. Their only asset is Dustin's old beater of a car."

"Well, Sylvia and I didn't start out with much," Frank says.

"Peg and I are convinced that Kathie-Lee is knocked up, because why else would they get married when their prospects are so poor? But I'm not asking any questions because Peg forbids me to. She says my relationship with Dustin is tenuous at best."

Frank's neck is prickling. Should he remind Jack of the informality of his own marriage to Peg? Peg's father never actually got out his shotgun, but Peg was pregnant—a scandal in those days. No, to mention it would be unkind.

"You never know how things will turn out, Jack," he says. "Getting married may be the making of Dustin. It may turn his life around."

Jack laughs shortly.

"The best predictor of future behavior is past behavior, as your psychologist-in-residence will tell you." He's referring to Sylvia, who is a psychologist. "It's a heartbreak, having a son who's such a loser. Your two boys are real achievers. I suppose I should be thankful that my girls and their husbands are happy and prospering—and did I tell you about Chad? He won the award at the robotics show?"

"Terrific!" Frank exclaims.

Chad, Jack and Peg's youngest, was a sullen, uncommunicative child and hasn't changed much. It seems that he has always been preoccupied by deep scientific thoughts. Sylvia suspects that Chad has a touch of Asperger's Syndrome. She and Frank have never understood why Jack prefers this younger son to the elder one.

Frank wonders if he should advise Jack to look on this marriage as a new beginning for Dustin, an opportunity to extend a friendly hand to the prodigal. Then he reminds himself that nobody likes advice. He cuts short the conversation with Jack, saying there's someone at the door.

✤   ✤   ✤

One sultry July evening, Frank is wakened from his nap on the sofa by the sharp peal of the telephone. Sylvia, in white shorts that he particularly likes, puts down her book and answers it.

"Dustin. What a pleasant surprise! And congratulations!"

She beckons to Frank, who sits up groggily. Why is Dustin calling? To thank them for their check? Maybe. They never got a written thank-you in the mail. Another thought strikes him. Is Dustin calling to ask for a loan? Perhaps their generous wedding check gave him the impression that his old Uncle Frank and Aunt Sylvia are loaded.

"Yes, we'll definitely be here," says Sylvia. "Yes, do put Kathie-Lee on. Hello, Kathie-Lee. How nice to meet you!"

Another pause.

"That's wonderful! Frank and I went to Niagara Falls on our honeymoon. I didn't know it was still the fashion for newlyweds nowadays. Yes, we'd love to have you stay with us next weekend on your way there. No, it's no imposition at all. Now that our boys have left we have empty rooms."

She picks up a pen and notes the date and time of arrival.

"I'll put Frank on and he can give you instructions as to the best exit off the 401 and to our place in Parkwood Hills."

As she hands the phone to him, Frank notices that she is energized, in organizing mode, as she is when their sons and their families come to visit.

"I'll have to go to Loblaws," she says, after he gets off the line. "Will you make some of your chili? That would do for one dinner while they're here."

🌢   🌢   🌢

The following week, Frank checks his email regularly to see if Jack has sent wedding pictures. It would be helpful to know what the bride and groom look like, since he hasn't seen Dustin for years, but no photos appear. As he chops onion and tomatoes he thinks about the kid.

Not everyone is cut out for a business career. Frank's boys are not entrepreneurial, but professional—Stu a zoologist; Frank Jr. a psychologist like Sylvia. But Dustin, raised by Jack, probably saw a business career as his only option in life, whether or not his talents lay in that direction. Jack's attitude to his elder son has always been oddly adversarial. Why?

Jack can't blame Dustin for trapping him in an early marriage; the child who forced his wedding to Peg was their beloved, successful elder daughter. Besides, Jack has always seemed happy to be married and a father.

Was Jack so insecure as a man that he felt threatened simply because his first son was another male in the household? Frank wonders if he and Oliver, ten and five years Jack's senior, dwarfed and intimidated him when he was young. He doesn't think so. Both he and Ollie tried to be good brothers. He sighs and stirs the meat in the frying pan.

🌢   🌢   🌢

The young couple take Frank by surprise. He is dozing on the sofa when they pull into his yard in a rusty Chevrolet Celebrity. Dustin is no longer a lanky awkward kid, but a tall man who has grown into his looks. He is bursting with pride over Kathie-Lee, who reminds Frank of Rory on *The Gilmore Girls*. She seems younger than twenty-five, with her long brown hair tied back and her air of innocence. She's delighted to be embraced and to show off her rings, explaining that her widowed grandmother gave them to Dustin.

"Granny knows how it is when you're young and starting out," she says.

As Sylvia admires the old-fashioned setting, Frank feels a wave of sadness. Poor Dustin couldn't even afford to buy her engagement and wedding rings.

Over dinner, the honeymooners show pictures of their wedding. Jack, Peg and their adult children are elegant and fit compared to Kathie-Lee's kinfolk. Her family members are either rail-thin or thick-built, sagging in the middle. They're all prematurely grey and have teeth missing.

"It looks as if you were having fun." Sylvia bends her head over the wedding photos, all candid amateur shots, probably because the bride couldn't afford a professional photographer. Frank peers at the wedding buffet, served on a plank table mounted on saw-horses, and at the wedding guests, in motley attire, kicking up their feet on the dance floor—some planks laid down in the front yard of a grey farmhouse. The string quartet, if you can call it that, consists of four Willie Nelson look-alikes who played piano accordion, dobbro, a fiddle and guitar. Whenever Jack and Peg appear in a picture, they look wooden and pained. Yet Dustin, in a white shirt and dark trousers, and Kathie-Lee, in a white borrowed gown, seem to float among the guests like magical moths. In one photo they are dancing barefoot on the lawn, under a maple in new leaf.

Prompted by Sylvia, Kathie-Lee talks about her job. Each year she is assigned each semester to a student with a disability, often Attention Deficit Disorder, and it is her job to see that he (usually a "he") gets to classes, pays attention, and understands his homework. She's eager to hear Sylvia on the subjects of A.D.D. and Tourette's Syndrome. As the women talk, Dustin gazes lovingly at his bride.

Frank wonders why Jack implied that Kathie-Lee was stupid. Obviously, he and Peg have never had a conversation with her. Later, when Frank asks about Dustin's job, Dustin shrugs.

"It's no creative outlet but it helps keeps the bills paid," he says.

Kathie-Lee has never before visited central Canada. The previous night, she and Dustin stayed in a Quebec village on an air mattress in her cousin's living room. When she sees Frank and Sylvia's spare room, she gasps and says it's almost the size of her studio apartment back in Fredericton.

The following day, Frank and Sylvia play tour guides and take the newlyweds to Parliament Hill, the National Gallery and the Central Experimental Farm. That night, after dinner, Kathie-Lee asks if she can call "Uncle Oliver" in Toronto. It turns out that she and Dustin will be staying with Oliver and his wife for two nights after leaving Ottawa, and must confirm this plan and get directions.

While the young people are on the telephone, Sylvia and Frank watch the sunset from the deck. She draws close to him.

"What a resourceful girl!" she whispers. "Obviously they can't afford hotels, but she has found a way for them to go on a wedding trip anyway. I bet she has lined up friends and relatives to stay with every night for the two weeks of their travels."

"Jack would call her a freeloader," Frank mutters.

"Jack should applaud her initiative. She's so friendly and down-to-earth I know they'll be welcome at all their ports of call. I only wish the poor thing had something decent to wear if Oliver and June take them out to a fancy restaurant. She has worn the same jeans and cotton shirt with the sleeves rolled up ever since they got here. Remember the trousseau Mother made me when we got married?"

He nods. She looked as beautiful as Jackie Kennedy in the styles of the era.

"Frank, may I give her those two Alia shirts you gave me for my birthday? They're a bit too small for me but they'd fit her."

He puts his arm around her. "Go ahead. They're yours."

❧   ❧   ❧

The next morning when the young folks leave, Frank offers to help them load the car but they won't let him lift a thing. In addition to their suitcases, they have a picnic lunch that Sylvia has packed, and a large shopping bag from which a silvery grey fabric protrudes. Frank recalls Sylvia wearing a cocktail dress from similar cloth last New Years. He also notices that Kathie-Lee is wearing the pink Alia shirt.

"Come and stay with us on your return trip," Sylvia says, as she and Kathie-Lee embrace.

"You're too kind, but we can't impose again, not when you're preparing for a trip of your own," the young woman says. "Besides, my friend, Kim, in Brockville wants us to stay with her. Thank you so much for everything, especially the clothes."

"It's nice to meet another recycler," Sylvia says. "Dustin, you've chosen a wonderful girl."

"I'm lucky she chose me." He grins ear to ear as Sylvia plants a kiss on his cheek.

When Kathie-Lee hugs Frank, he blinks back tears. After the Chevrolet goes around the corner and disappears, he turns to Sylvia and puts his arm around her.

"When I phone Jack, I'm going to say a lot of nice things about those kids," he vows. "I predict they'll do just fine."

❧   ❧   ❧

The future, of course, is not Frank's to see. He has no idea that in five years he will be weeping by Jack's graveside. Who would have imagined that the youngest, his little brother, would be the first to go? Clutching Sylvia's hand, he will be thankful that he stilled his tongue and refrained from telling Jack off on the many occasions that he felt provoked.

Frank doesn't imagine that he and Sylvia will be the guests of Kathie-Lee and Dustin in their fixer-upper, nor that the young people will be such hard workers, with Dustin heading the school physical plant and Kathie-Lee taking night courses.

"Once I get my BA," she'll confide, "maybe we'll have a B-A-B-Y."

Frank and Sylvia will smile and some of the grief and fear inherent in old age will subside.

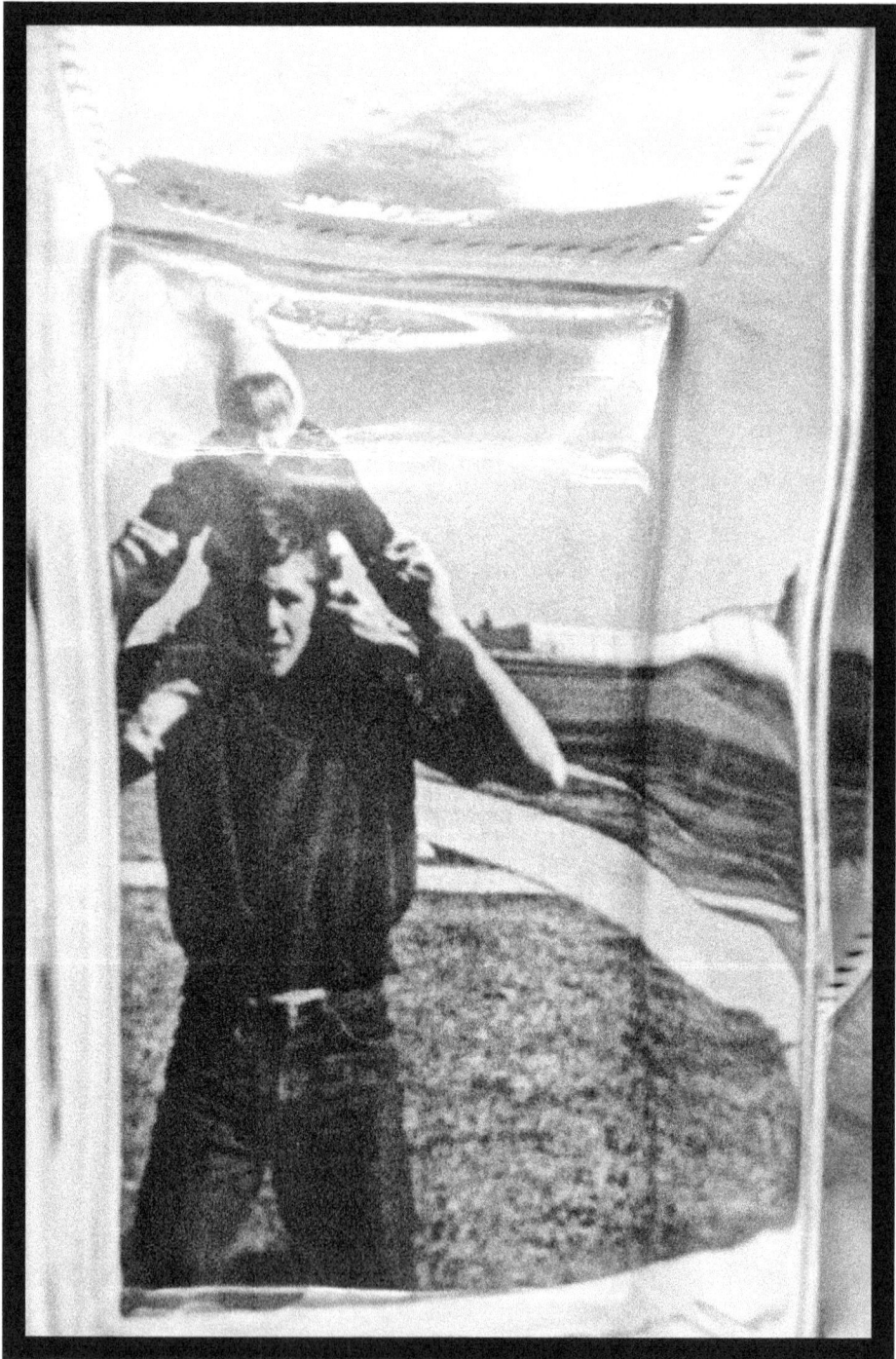

III
BROTHERS, SISTERS, KEEPERS

SUSAN MAHAN

GODDESS OF THE MOON

My sister Cynthia is two years older than I, and she has spent most of the last forty-five years in state mental hospitals because of schizophrenia. She was committed at the age of sixteen, on the first Sunday in January 1965, three months before our mother died of a brain tumor. Like they say, when it rains, it pours. After that day, I didn't see Cynthia again for about a year; though I heard Dad had brought her to the funeral parlor to see Mum the first afternoon before people got there. Living all these years behind locked wards and barred windows, Cynthia has been the only one of us free enough to talk about our mother. The irony of this has not escaped me, though that's a story for another day.

My mother's illness didn't cause Cynthia's to occur. Cynthia had always been different from the rest of us kids—quirky, emotional, and hyperactive before anyone used that term. She followed her own mind most of the time, neither heeding rules nor thinking out the consequences of her actions before she took them. She was always in trouble in one way or another at home and at school. We were close in age, and Cynthia was often the bane of my existence, but untouched as she was by the ordinary constraints in life, she sometimes served as my window on the world of possibilities.

Once before dawn when she was ten years old, Cynthia let a stray cat in the bedroom window of our first floor apartment. We weren't allowed to have pets because of a city housing ordinance, and there was no room for one, anyway. While we eventually moved to the suburbs, our family of eight then lived in a tiny five-room apartment. The cat leapt in the window and onto the bed I shared with Cynthia, waking me as it scratched my leg, and leaving dusty paw prints on our sheet. I was afraid of cats, but Cynthia loved them and I could see the unfettered joy on her face as she scooped the animal up in her arms. "I think I'll name him Shadow!" she exclaimed. Cynthia was inconsolable when my parents awoke and made her put the cat back outside.

Cynthia had been kept back a year in school and was in the same grade as me. School wasn't her forte, but in certain ways, Cynthia was smarter than me. She was, seemingly without effort, an excellent speller, while I had to pore diligently over each week's spelling list to get the same results. She had a phenomenal (although highly selective) memory and an affinity for learning then remembering the birth dates and middle names of everyone she ever knew.

She also knew the derivatives of many names and would use them interchangeably if she was addressing or referring to someone. She told me that her own name came from Greek mythology: Artemis, goddess of the moon. She often called me "Lily," the Hebrew derivative of my name. In fact, at home she usually called me "Li-ly, Li-ly, Li-ly," laughing and enunciating each syllable in a lilting teasing tone. This irked me to no end, but there was no stopping her.

As Cynthia entered her teen years, her hormones were well ahead of mine, and she fell in love with movie stars and pop singers. She wrote fan letters to the television actors on *Ben Casey* and *Dr. Kildare*, and to the singing group of Gary Lewis and the Playboys. At the same time, she entered a secret world and began to talk to herself. I was unnerved by this and a little afraid. She would go into our shared bedroom and carry on an animated conversation, smiling all the while, with her eyes rolling up into her head till only the whites showed. I couldn't make sense of what she was saying most of the time. *Who was she really talking to? Why did it seem that they were talking back?* I knew it wasn't right.

But she only did it at home, and my father usually yelled at her to stop. The more she was yelled at for doing it, the more secretive she became, eventually locking herself in the bathroom and lowering her voice to a whisper. The urgently whispered conversations became increasingly more frequent in the months following my mother's cancer diagnosis, and I was with sixteen-year-old Cynthia the day she lost her shaky grip on the rational world forever.

We had gone to the Rexall drugstore for donuts and hot chocolate following the nine o'clock Sunday mass. There were two stools left at the counter, and I sat down, placing my purse on the worn green Formica. I turned to ask Cynthia what kind of donut she wanted, but she hadn't followed me to the empty seat. She was sashaying to the opposite corner of the shop where a group of high school boys a year or two older than I were gathered. I knew she had a crush on one of them—a handsome, popular football player. She talked about him all the time at home. While my sisters and I teased her about him, I knew she didn't really have a chance with him. He was way out of her league. Cynthia was talking to the group, but I couldn't hear what she was saying. Three of the boys were facing me, and I could see that they were laughing at her.

I grabbed my purse and ran over to Cynthia in time to hear her tell them in a coy voice that wasn't hers that she was moving to Florida to get married. She was smiling to beat the band, thinking of the glorious days to come, I guess. My face flushed with shame, and I hurriedly pulled her arm to leave the store. *"Come on, we have to go!"* She began an incessant stream of babble that would become familiar to me over the years, but which on that day embarrassed me horribly. Indeed, for the rest of my teen years, I wanted to disassociate myself from her entirely. How could I possibly explain what had happened to her? How would I protect myself and my family from the publicly-held, privately-spoken, ridicule that was sure to follow?

Cynthia did not resist me as I dragged her out the door and down the street, the smart remarks of the boys echoing in my ears. As we headed toward home, two of our neighbors drove up and offered us a ride. I weighed the decision of letting them see her like that—I was mortified, and we were such a private family—but decided it was more important to get her home quickly. I pushed her into the back seat of their big gray car and slid in beside her.

As Cynthia repeated the story about moving to Florida, I shook my head quickly to let them know it wasn't true, but I didn't say a word. I just stared straight ahead as if there was something infinitely interesting in the distance through the windshield. It was the longest five-minute ride on earth. At home, my father made a series of hushed phone calls and that afternoon, Dad and Uncle John took Cynthia away, leaving Mum crying in their wake.

ALISON STONE

ASPERGER'S

As a girl I was awed by his ease
with algebra and actors' birthdays. Sage
of monster trivia, pariah among peers
who pushed him and tore pages
from his books. Terrified, I sucked grape
popsicles beside him on the grease-
stained couch as families fled Rodan's grasp
or Godzilla flattened cities and spare
characters. Dubbed voices misaligned as the gears
in his brain. Calm always pass-
ing. Childhood tasted like my brother's rage.

MY BROTHER'S COLLECTIONS

It started with the acorns
littering our lawn.
Capped or bald, nibbled or whole—

he wanted them all.
When the wind picked up and Mom
tried to end the collecting, he exploded.

He was still throwing rocks
when my father got home
and forced him into the house.

Things got worse with action
figures (bookcase overturned). Dragons
(phone torn from the wall).

Mostly he wanted monsters—horror movie models
painstakingly glued and painted, then shelved
away from my young, clumsy hands. Stuffed mummies

and King Kongs he'd sometimes share.
Inflatable Frankensteins Dad turned purple
trying to blow up. Swarms of glow-in-the-dark bats.

My brother heaped creatures
on his bed. Slept scrunched to the wall,
surrounded by plastic eyes and felt claws.

Dad patched kicked-in doors
and told me, *Some boys*
have a temper. Cracks

showed through the new paint.
Mom's fingers trembled on the steering
wheel. She scoured malls

to find the final members
of his latest set. He was a bomb
one missing Dracula could detonate.

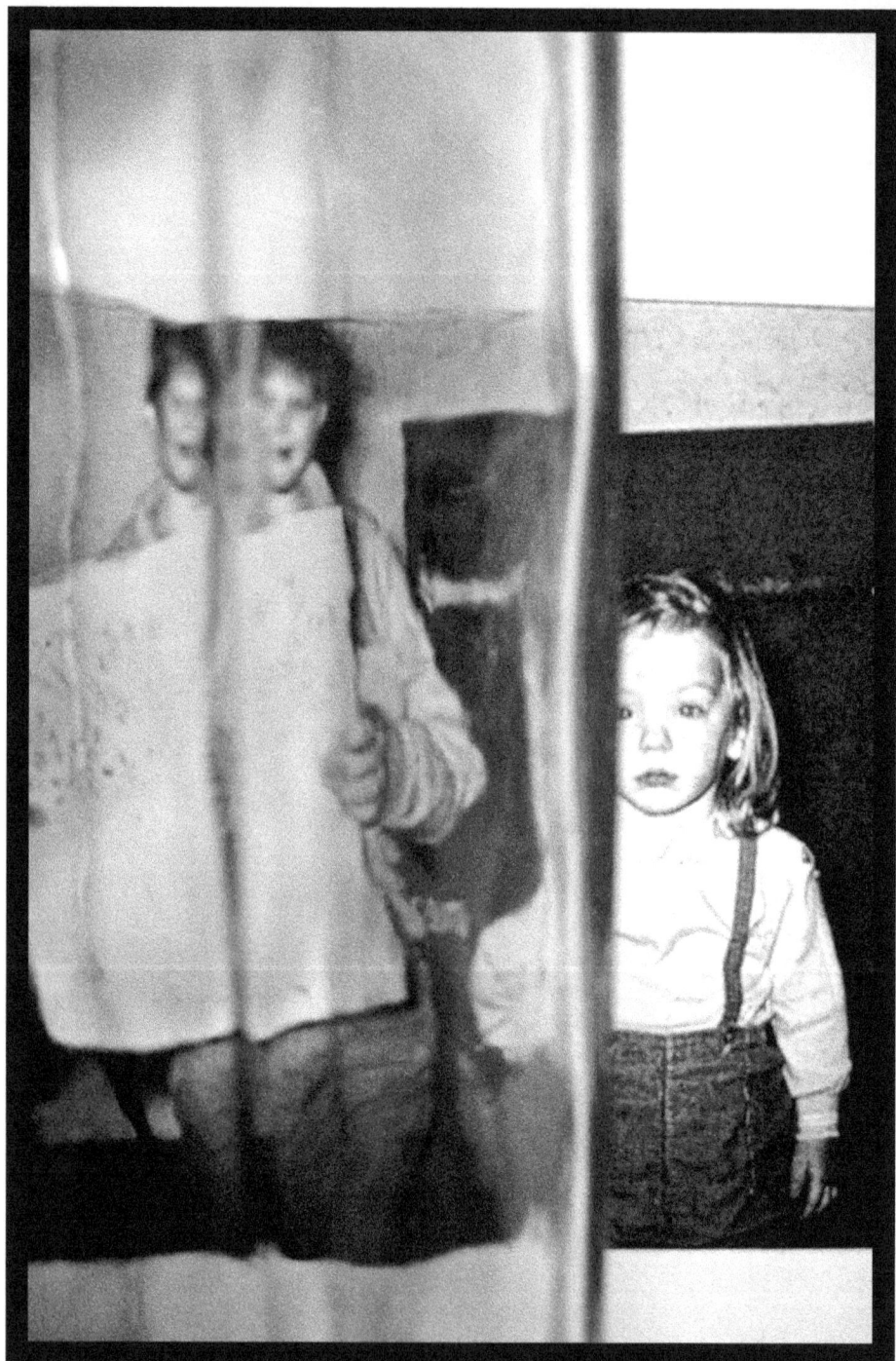

EMILY RUBIN

CRAZY

Here's a list of things my family can't do because of my older brother
Nelson:

Live in the same house
Go on vacation together
Have sharp scissors in the art supply drawer
Go to the movies as a family
Have matches in the house
Use steak knives when we have steak
Do anything spontaneous

My parents think because my brother has a mental illness, I'm the one
with the problem. The other day, my mom showed me a flyer for a support
group for siblings of kids with mental problems. The flyer had a picture of a girl
sitting by herself with a rain cloud over her head. So dumb! She said, "Harper,
it might be good for you to meet other kids who have a brother like Nelson."
Give me a break. It's bad enough that I have to see Dr. Knowles every Thursday,
when I could be hanging out with my best friend Zahara.

The first time I went to see Dr. Knowles, he stood up from his chair and
said, "Harper, I'm going to toss a ball to you. When you catch it, you name a
feeling. Ready?"

He said the word *feeling* like it was a precious heirloom, like he was going
to toss an antique necklace across the room to me. Inside I groaned but I stood
up and said, "Okay, I'm ready."

He threw the ball and I said, "Hungry."

"That's good, Harper," he said, winking at me, "let's do it again."

What a moron. Seriously. Is this what people go to medical school for? I
shut my eyes, wishing I was at home or even at school. Anywhere else. But this
is how I spend my Thursday afternoons.

✤   ✤   ✤

For the past year, I've been living with my grandparents, six houses down the street from my family because it's not safe for me to live at home with my brother. He's three years older than me, so he's fourteen, and he's been going to special schools and seeing psychiatrists since he was five. Sometimes he's the nicest brother in the world, and sometimes he's mean and violent. It all depends on his mood, and his medications, and if he's had enough to eat and drink, and if he's gotten enough sleep.

The weird thing is that when Nelson's not acting crazy, we have a lot of fun. For one thing, he's really good at accents. He can listen to an accent and then speak in that accent almost perfectly. He can sound like a British pirate or a French chef or a cowboy from the Wild West. Sometimes we act out scenes from cowboy westerns, setting up a saloon on the porch of my grandparents' house. We take juice or soda we find in the fridge and mix it together. Usually it's a combination of orange and cranberry juice, sometimes white grape juice. Then we take a funnel and pour it into grandpa's old army flasks and walk around with those tucked in our belts. Or else we pour the juice into shot glasses that we gulp down fast like they do in the movies.

But there always comes a point when my brother does something bad and then he has to go home. Back to what used to be my home. Like he'll pick up a big rock from the garden and almost smash me on the head with it. That's when grandpa comes over and holds his wrists so tight that he can't help but drop the rock. Lucky for me, grandpa is really strong. He likes to tell me that he's a military man, so nothing can get past him.

My brother's done all varieties of bad things. But he's not a bad person. It's just that sometimes he can't control himself. Like he's tempted to do things that he can't resist. I think it's like having a friend who's a bad influence and you end up getting in trouble because you go along with doing terrible stuff even though a part of you knows you shouldn't. For Nelson, that friend who's a bad influence is inside of him. So he can never get away.

Some of the bad things he's done: setting stuff on fire, including the piano, his bed and the bathmat. Jumping out of the car on the highway. Cutting himself. Trying to poison the hamster. And he's given me a lot of bruises.

When I first moved to my grandparents' house, it was great. Like having a sleepover that never ended. I got to watch whatever I wanted on TV, and have sugary cereals that my mom doesn't allow, and my grandparents drove me to school so I didn't have to take the bus anymore. That was my one condition for moving to my grandparents' house: not having to ride the bus.

The bus stop is right in front of my real house, and I knew all the neighborhood kids would see that I was walking from the other direction, and they'd ask why. What would I tell them? Even though my parents say it's not true, I feel like I can't tell the truth about my brother. For one thing, it's embarrassing. Nobody I know has a brother who acts all crazy and dangerous. Everyone I know has regular siblings, and they eat dinner like a regular family without all of the yelling and screaming that happens in my family. Another thing is that it's no one's business. That's what my grandparents tell me to say. But how stupid is that? As if an eleven-year-old kid is actually going to say, "It's none of your business," when one of my friends or even one of the bullies asks why I'm walking from the end of the street when the bus stops right in front of my house.

But the real truth is that I feel sad having a brother like Nelson, who can't be normal even after all of the pills and doctors and special schools. It gives me a stomach ache just thinking about it. That's probably the worst part about having a brother like Nelson: everyone has questions and I never know what to say.

✤   ✤   ✤

I'm in school. It's fourth period, and we're walking to art. My class sounds like a herd of horses when we stomp down the hallway because so many girls are wearing clogs this year. *Clop Clop Clop* as we head up the stairs to the art room. Today Mrs. Norton tells us we're going to use collage materials to make a picture of our family and our house. The sun is shining through the window, making her squint as she talks. Mrs. Norton holds up baskets one at a time, tilting them to the class so we can see the contents. First, a basket of brightly colored shredded tissue paper. Then one with small pieces of furry fabric. "Maybe these can be used for a roof?" Mrs. Norton asks as she holds up a basket of tiny metal squares and circles. And so on. My stomach starts to cramp, which Dr. Knowles says is from anxiety. Everything about my family is complicated. Especially the way we live.

Sheila raises one hand while twirling her braid with the other. Mrs. Norton calls on her. "What if my family is in two houses? I spend half the week with my mom and half the week with my dad. Which house should I make?"

Mrs. Norton nods her head. "Good question, Sheila. There's only space for one house, so you can choose either one. You are the artist! Choose whichever one inspires you." She smiles like she just solved the easiest problem in the world.

Next, Leonard raises his hand. "My parents are renovating our house. Should I make what our house used to look like, or what it's going to look like?" Mrs. Norton's answer is a version of what she told Sheila, "You are the artist, it's your choice, isn't that wonderful?" *Blah blah blah*. Leonard is always showing off about the mansion he lives in. He told me that he and his brothers each have their own bathroom, plus there's a guest suite with a kitchen upstairs, plus a clubhouse in the backyard.

Zahara, my best friend, pokes me. She's missing her two bottom teeth because her adult teeth never grew in after she lost the baby ones. So she has a lisp. "Psst!" she whispers. "Why don't you pick one of your houses and put your whole family together in it?" Zahara looks at me knowingly. She is one of very few people who actually knows how demented my family is. She must have figured out how awful this art project would be for me.

I decide to make my grandparents' house because my first house with Nelson has too many holes punched in the walls that my parents have given up repairing. First I work on my grandmother's garden. I use strips of green furry fabric for the grass and I arrange yellow plastic beads for the flower petals, and then I find toothpicks in another basket for flower stems. The stems are too long so I look around for a pair of scissors to cut them in half.

Sheila walks by. "You're so funny, Harper! You don't even have a flower garden in front of your house!" She turns and calls out, "Mrs. Norton, Is it okay to create a fantasy house or does it have to be real?"

Mrs. Norton puts down the pipe cleaners she's twisting together and walks over. "Well, girls, it is tempting to create our dream house, isn't it? But this is an activity to help us map real patterns of co-habitation." She clears her throat. "Remember when we made igloos out of sugar cubes in third grade? And last year, we used shoeboxes to show how communities migrate from one place to another? This year we are moving from *global* to *local*, by focusing on our own homes." She reminds us that class will be over in fifteen minutes, and to use our remaining time constructively.

I sit there like an idiot, surrounded by magic markers, baskets of glittery stickers and plastic beads, the oversized flower stem toothpicks, and pieces of fabric. Everyone else is bustling around, grabbing materials from baskets and talking loudly. I just want to close my eyes and disappear.

✤   ✤   ✤

I'll start from the beginning, when I was born. I was born Harper Chase Solomon-Shuster which already was a cool beginning because nobody could tell from my name whether I was a boy or a girl. For your information, I'm a girl.

The pictures in our family photo album show that I am usually smiling but if you look closely, you'll see a nervous look in my eyes, even when I was just one and two years old. My older brother, Nelson Lawdry Solomon-Shuster, who was three when I was born, was very mischievous and they had to "keep an eye on him at all times," as Mom likes to say. In early pictures I see that there's a tall gate blocking the entrance to my bedroom. I always assumed it was to keep me from crawling around the house as a baby, but recently it occurred to me that maybe my parents put the gate there to keep Nelson away from me.

I don't remember much about my early years, but I remember a story Mom told me. She said that one afternoon, when I was four and Nelson was seven, she planned to bring us to the zoo but it started to rain. When she told us we needed to change the plan because of the weather, Nelson started raging. When he rages, he screams and punches and throws whatever he can get his hands on. Mom said she was trying to physically restrain him (she says "contain," but it means the same thing as restrain), and out of the corner of her eye, she saw me walk over to the fridge, pour myself a drink, put a piece of pizza on a plate and heat it up in the microwave. "You were too young to be so independent," she told me.

As I got older, I learned to manage Nelson better than my parents could. When we played together, I always made sure he got his way. He would choose first when we picked out matchbox cars to race. I'd let him make the rules for our games. I would agree with any flavor he chose for Jell-O. As long as we did what he wanted, we had fun together.

The problems between us started when I began school. That's when I started getting invited to birthday parties, unlike Nelson. Nelson would get really mad when I would come home after a birthday party. He'd push me down and grab my goody bag and run off with it. After awhile I learned to sneak a Ziploc bag with me to the party, and on the car ride home, I would carefully separate the best stuff into my bag, and leave the junky candy and dumb stickers for Nelson's bag. Then when he stole it from me, I didn't really care.

My parents would make a huge fuss over it, though, not knowing I had taken care of the situation. Dad would get all red and angry, and chase Nelson around the house and pin him down to take the candy bag. By then, it was usually all smushed together and everyone was yelling and crying, and I'd have my hands over my ears. Dad would drag Nelson over to me and insist that he apologize, but at that point Nelson was out of his mind, his eyes shiny and dark, punching anything he could get at. I would make funny faces to calm him down, like crossing my eyes and sticking out my tongue. If I was lucky, he'd start to giggle at the funny faces and then I would start giggling, too, until we were both laughing our heads off. Then Dad would storm off, muttering *Goddamn it!* under his breath.

✤   ✤   ✤

Tonight my whole family is having dinner together at Grandma and Grandpa's. This only happens once a month, so it's kind of a special occasion mixed with dread. I never know what Nelson is going to do. My parents describe him as "Dr. Jekyll and Mr. Hyde," the scientist who alternates between being a gentleman and a tyrant. It's true that with Nelson, you never know which one will be walking through the door. I guess you could say he's predictably unpredictable.

Grandma has made one of Nelson's favorites, spanakopita. It's a Greek pastry filled with feta cheese and spinach and garlic, and it takes her over an hour to prepare because it involves layering thin sheets of pastry dough, one at a time, in the pan. Today we made it together, sort of. Actually all I did was stir the bowl that had the filling in it. Grandma's in charge of the pastry dough. It's so thin that it always falls apart in my hands so she does that part.

Nelson and Mom and Dad knock on the door and I run to let them in. My parents hug me like they haven't seen me in a year, even though I just saw them yesterday. Nelson smiles and pats me on the head. "Hey, Harper," he says. I leap over and give him a bear hug. He's in a good mood!

Grandma walks in from the kitchen, wiping her hands on her apron, and distributes hugs to everyone. Grandma is the same height as me: we're both five feet, two inches tall. She's followed by Grandpa, in his navy sweater with the army pin on his chest. He's not much of a hugger. He's a hand shaker. He walks over to Nelson, looks him in the eye, and shakes his hand. "Good to see you, boy," he says.

I let out a deep breath. The house smells great. Not just from the spanakopita, but also from the cherry pie that Grandma baked. It's my favorite.

The clock in the dining room chimes six o'clock and we sit down at the table. No one picks up their forks until Grandpa sits down. He's the patriarch. "Who wants to say grace?" Grandpa asks, as he lowers himself into his chair at the end of the table. Nelson speaks up right away, "I do."

In our family, saying grace is different every time. Whoever says it has the right to make it their own. Nelson starts to speak and I notice his smile is tight. "I want to thank Grandma and Grandpa for making dinner tonight," he says, and then he turns to Dad and glares at him. "You are *such an asshole!*" he barks.

Mom says "Nelson!" and Dad drops his head so everyone can see his bald spot.

Nelson grabs a bread roll and bites into it, tearing off pieces with his teeth like an animal eating its prey. I can see the muscles in Dad's jaw tense with anger as he stares at his plate. Mom looks like she might start crying. Even her heart-shaped earrings look sad. Grandma's fingers find my hand in the chair where I'm sitting next to her. I want to run upstairs to my bedroom, away from what's bound to be a horrible dinner. Aside from Nelson's noisy chewing, everyone is quiet until Grandpa clears his throat.

"Did you know a man can be hung in Texas for putting graffiti on another man's cow?" This breaks the tension. Grandpa nods his head and goes on to explain that it's also against the law for a man to let his camels run unleashed on a Texas beach. Apparently, these old laws are still on the books, which means that people in Texas can be arrested and tried under them, though that never happens nowadays. This leads to a conversation between Nelson and Grandpa about the weirdest laws in our country, which includes a law in Topeka, Kansas, where waiters are not allowed to serve wine in teacups. Mom looks at me with tired eyes. I wiggle my eyebrows up and down to cheer her up, and she smiles weakly.

Later, when Grandpa is tucking me into bed, I ask him how he knew to change the topic when Nelson started in on Dad. Grandpa sits up straight at the side of my bed and looks at me. "First lesson I learned in the military," he says, "distract, don't engage, the enemy."

He kisses me goodnight and shuts the door. When I close my eyes, I'm not sure how I feel about his strategy.

✤   ✤   ✤

Before my grandparents moved down the street from us, they lived in Montana. That's where Mom grew up. I only visited them one time in Montana before they moved to Maine, where we all live now. It was a trip I took, just me and Mom, when I was in third grade, two years ago. Dad stayed home with Nelson, who was twelve by then, because Nelson can't go to new places without freaking out. And he certainly couldn't have handled the airplane. When the plane took off, there was so much pressure in my ears I thought my head would explode. Mom gave me gum to chew. That helped. No way could Nelson have handled that part, not to mention he would have had to sit with a seatbelt and would have had to be quiet. Maybe if he was all zonked out on his meds it would have worked, but anyway, it was just me and Mom. It's rare when I get her all to myself.

We went to Montana because it was my grandparents' anniversary, and there was going to be a fancy dinner. All of the relatives were coming, but we were the only ones who were arriving by plane. My aunt picked us up at the airport with my cousin Lily, who was just five years old. She sucked her two middle fingers and rarely took them out of her mouth. Only to eat or to ask a question. My aunt gave me a big hug first, and then she hugged my mom for a long time. I heard Mom sniffling and after awhile the hug ended, but they held each other's hands and whispered to each other, which was annoying because I couldn't hear what they were saying.

"Why is your muvver crying?" Lily pulled her fingers out to ask, and quickly followed up with, "Where's your bruvver? And your favver?" Her fingers went back into her mouth.

"Sometimes people cry when they are happy," I explained, repeating what my mother had once told me. Then I skipped over to the baggage area and grabbed my purple rolling luggage off the moving track.

During that visit, there was a lot of mysterious whispering and crying, and by the time we were back on the plane, Mom announced that Grandma and Grandpa would be moving to Maine, to live closer to us. "Yippee!" I said, doing a little wiggly dance in my seat.

I found out later that the reason they moved was for me, to create a safe place for me when Nelson was out of control, which began to happen less frequently because of his medications, but when it did happen, it was scarier because he was getting so big. It took almost a year for my grandparents to sell their house, around the same time that our neighbors decided to sell their house. Mom told me it was "meant to be" for my grandparents to move onto Harrison Road.

❧   ❧   ❧

It's Saturday morning and Grandma says it's fine for me and Zahara to walk into town. It's a fifteen-minute walk to Main Street from their house, and Zahara needs to buy food for her goldfish. Last summer, Zahara won a goldfish in a plastic bag half-filled with water at the Labor Day fair, but no one knew it was pregnant. Now there's a whole school of goldfish in her fish tank. Zahara's not allowed to have any other pets because her mother is allergic, so she spends a lot of time cleaning the tank and caring for her fish.

On the way to *Friendly Pets*, we stop at the ice cream store for root beer floats. "Zahara," I say, while waiting in line to order, "If you could change one thing about your life, what would it be?"

This was a question that Dr. Knowles asked me the last time I saw him. I knew he was expecting me to say something about having a brother like Nelson, since that's all he ever wants to talk about, so I purposely threw him off that trail. "If I could change *anything* about my life," I said slowly, "then school lunch would be only desserts. Like Monday would be chocolate cake day, Tuesday would be ice cream, Wednesday would be pie. That kind of thing."

Dr. Knowles added, "And Thursday would be candy, and Friday would be cookies?"

I couldn't help but smile. I nodded my head. Dr. Knowles picked up a bowl of M&Ms from the corner of his desk and offered it to me. Maybe he wasn't so bad.

Zahara takes her time thinking. She shuts her eyes and opens them quickly. "If I could change anything about my life, I'd have a penguin as a pet!" I laugh out loud. Of course she would. We shuffle ahead in line.

"Where would you keep him? Penguins like cold weather."

Zahara puts her hands on her hips. "I would have an ice room added to our house. The walls would be made of ice and there would be a pool in the middle so he could swim."

I think about this for a minute and then ask, "What if he's lonely?

Zahara responds right away. "Not everybody needs a companion, Harper.

Some animals are happy by themselves."

I mull this over in the pet store, walking behind Zahara in the aquarium aisle, as she eyes the fake water plants and miniature treasure chests. Is it true that some animals prefer to be alone? What about humans? Mr. Fordham in Social Studies says people are social creatures. I stop and watch Zahara as she examines a plastic scuba diver attached to a water pump.

"Sometimes I feel alone," I say to her backside. She turns around and smiles her half-tooth grin. "Lucky for you we're friends," she lisps. She holds up a box of goldfish flake food and we walk toward the cashier.

Outside of the pet store, the sun is shining and we sit on the bench to count how much money we have left. We empty our pockets—a few crumpled dollar bills and coins—and place them on the wooden seat between us. The quarters and pennies catch the sunlight and sparkle like gems. Zahara separates the coins into small piles and adds them up, counting out loud.

"Hi, girls," I hear a familiar voice and look up to see Mom walking briskly toward us, Nelson trailing a few feet behind. Mom has a fake smile and Nelson is grumbling to himself, staring at the ground. "We were just about to do some errands. Getting some fresh air," Mom tells us. Her face looks a little puffy. Maybe she's been crying.

"Go to hell," Nelson blurts, shifting from one foot to the other. He says it again, more forcefully, and his feet start moving quickly. It's his manic dance. Zahara focuses on the money on the bench, as if nothing unusual is happening.

I jump up before anything worse comes. "We're leaving now," I announce. Zahara cups her hands around the money, trying to scoop it up.

I start walking fast in the opposite direction and I hear Zahara call out, "Wait up, Harper!" Behind me I hear Nelson shouting, something about it being too bright outside, and I start to run.

I run until I'm out of breath, at the end of Main Street where the post office meets the highway. Zahara is jogging a few blocks behind. I bend over to catch my breath. If I were with anyone other than Zahara, I'd want to die. It's bad enough that Nelson starts acting crazy on the sidewalk on Main Street, where anyone can see.

If there's one thing I could change about my life, maybe I wouldn't have a brother.

❧   ❧   ❧

The following weekend, Nelson and I are sitting on the porch at Grandma
and Grandpa's house, looking at old photographs together. The sky is bright
blue and Grandpa is nearby, trimming the rhododendron bush.

"Are you scared of me, Harper?" Nelson asks.

I look at him uncertainly. "Why do you ask?"

He looks down. "Well, Mom and Dad said you're scared of me."

"I'm not scared of you!" I try to laugh but it sounds like there are frogs
in my throat.

"Even when I do scary things, like the time I threw a carton of milk at
your bookshelf, and your china dolls fell and broke?"

Nelson looks sadder than I've ever seen.

"Were you trying to break my dolls that day?"

"No. I was mad about something and it took over my brain," Nelson
explains, rubbing the arm of the wicker chair with his thumb.

I think carefully before I speak. "I like to be with you when you're in a
good mood."

Nelson thinks this over. Then I ask, "What happens when your brain gets
taken over?"

Sometimes, Nelson tells me, like when he's pacing or raging, he's not
even aware of what he's doing, and his body is just acting on its own. He's
even surprised when Mom or Dad later describe how he acted. "It's like my
mind and my body aren't connected." Other times, when he gets really mad
or frustrated, he knows how he's acting but it's like he can't see straight. So
throwing a carton of milk makes sense, and seems like the right thing to do.

My stomach is hurting. How will he ever be okay in the world? I gesture
to him to turn the page in the photo album on his lap, and he does. It's a
picture of us at the beach, me in diapers, and Nelson in a Superman bathing
suit. We're holding shovels and laughing, and our ankles are buried in sand.

✢   ✢   ✢

That night at dinner, after Nelson has gone home, I tell my grandparents
that I'm worried about Nelson's future. Grandma nods knowingly.

"Sweetheart, I hope you know that Nelson isn't your responsibility," she
says.

I stop chewing. "That's ridiculous, Grandma. Of course he's my
responsibility. I'm his only sister. And when you and Grandpa and Mom and

Dad are gone, I'm the one who will be left to look after him."

Grandma looks at Grandpa. Grandpa takes a long drink of water and puts his glass down. "Harper, we all hope that Nelson will get better, and will be independent as an adult. But if he needs help when you're grown up, the government has facilities where he can go."

I stare at them, and my jaw drops open. "Are you *serious?*" I ask. "He's not going to be locked up in a facility somewhere. He's not a bad person!"

Grandpa looks at me curiously. He asks if I've heard the expression, "You can choose your friends but you can't choose your family."

I say yes.

Grandpa says, "Just because you were born into the same family doesn't mean he is your responsibility."

I slam my palm onto the table and push my chair back. I can feel the sting of hot tears behind my eyes. "He's my brother!" I yell, and I run from the table, taking the stairs two at a time up to my room.

✤   ✤   ✤

The worst thing has happened. On my way home from school, I see two police cars and an ambulance in front of my first house. Grandpa, who is driving, tells me to stay in the car and wait until we get to his house to find out what's going on. But when he slows almost to a stop to pass the police cars, I jump out. The front door to the house is open and I race inside. In the mudroom, my father is talking quietly to a police officer, answering questions. I run past him to the living room, where my mother is kneeling on the floor next to my brother, who's lying face down on the rug, his wrists handcuffed behind his back. Two other officers are standing by the couch.

"What happened?" I shout, and my mother motions for me to whisper. I lower myself next to her on the floor, and she reaches her arms around me.

"Get Harper out of here!" I hear Nelson grunt into the rug. Nelson's head is turned away from me, so I can't see his expression. My mother walks me into the kitchen with her arm tightly around me.

She sits me down at the kitchen table. I'm crying so hard I can't speak.

"Harper," she says, "Nelson has to go to the hospital. He was hearing voices telling him to do things. You need to go to Grandma and Grandpa's house while we go with him to the emergency room."

"No!" I say, stamping my foot. "I'm going with you!"

My mother presses me to her chest. I can feel her heart beating and her damp hair smells like peach shampoo. When she releases me, she's crying, too. She tells me that a psychiatric emergency room might be scary for me, and they don't know how long they'll be there, and the best place for me is with Grandma and Grandpa. I feel another pair of hands on my head and I look up to see Grandpa. It's the first time I've seen tears in his eyes.

Grandpa and I stand in the hallway as Nelson is strapped onto a stretcher and wheeled outside. By now, a small crowd has gathered outside of the house. Nelson stares straight above him, into the sky. I break away from my grandfather and run alongside Nelson.

"I love you, Nelson!" I tell him, and pat his chest through the heavy grey blanket. Then he's loaded into the ambulance, and he's gone.

The phone rings a few hours later, at my grandparents' house. I hear my grandmother saying things into the phone that I don't understand, and I get worried. She says things about seclusion and sedation. Then I get to talk on the phone with my father, who sounds calm with a quiet voice.

"You don't need to worry about Nelson," he tells me, "He's in a safe place."

I don't believe him. "He's probably really scared!" I blurt out.

"Actually, Harper, he seems relieved to be here. He wants to feel better."

"What happened when he was hearing voices?" I demand of my father.

My father is silent. Then he says, "Nelson wants to tell you himself about it. Can you wait until he's able to talk with you?"

"I am so angry with you!" I surprise myself with these words, and then my grandmother takes the phone from me. I slump to the ground, my head in my arms, tears and snot on my cheeks.

"Don't worry, Martin," she tells my father, "We'll take good care of her."

I have so many questions for my grandparents, but they have few answers. Where will Nelson sleep? Will he have dinner? Does he have clothes to change into? They keep saying that Nelson needs more help than my parents can give him at home, as if that explains anything. I'm not hungry for dinner, but I sit at the table writing a card to Nelson while my grandparents eat broccoli casserole and sweet potatoes.

> *Dear Nelson,*
> *I want you to know that I love you and I will always be*
> *here for you. I hope you aren't too scared, and that you come home*

soon.
Love,
Harper

The next day, my parents pick me up after school to bring me to the psychiatric hospital in Portland to visit Nelson. On the drive to the hospital, my mother asks, "Do you want us to tell you what happened, or do you want to hear it from Nelson?"

I ask them to tell me what happened.

Mom was in the shower when Nelson arrived home from the Holden School, which is a special school for kids with problems. She found Nelson in the kitchen mumbling to himself and lining up the kitchen knives. When she asked what he was doing, he said that his Id, his Ego, and his Superego were having a disagreement, and that his Id was telling him to get the knives ready because there was going to be a fight.

"Are the Id, the Ego and the Superego real?" I ask.

"They're not real in the sense of something you can see or touch," Mom says. "They're based on a theory that a doctor named Sigmund Freud had about how people's personalities develop."

Mom says that Nelson has been taking a class in school where he learned about Dr. Freud and his theories.

"For Nelson, his Id, Ego and Superego came alive and began talking to him. This is how he explained it to me and Dad: his Id was demanding that Nelson get the knives ready for battle, his Ego was insisting that the battle was not imminent, and his Superego was trying to figure out what was right and wrong in the situation."

Mom looks over her shoulder at me and I motion for her to continue. "It was clear that Nelson was not operating in his right mind, so I called Dad who told me to call the police. We were worried that Nelson was going to hurt himself or someone else with the knives. When the police arrived, they felt he was a danger and they handcuffed him. In the emergency room, the doctors told us that Nelson had a psychotic break with reality. That means he couldn't tell the difference between what was real and what was a fantasy."

Listening to her, I am stunned. She's talking in such a matter-of-fact tone, but what she's saying about Nelson is so bizarre. Is that really what goes on in his head? Houses fly past the car in a blur as we drive. Houses and trees and wide, open fields.

Finally I say, "Do you think Nelson is crazy?"

Mom lets out a deep breath. "Sometimes people hear voices. I'm not sure if they are crazy, or just extremely sensitive. The doctors think Nelson might have a chemical imbalance in his brain, which can be managed by the right medications."

I let this sink in. "Why did he want to tell me himself?"

Now Dad speaks. "Nelson worried that you would be frightened hearing this from me and Mom, and he thought he could explain it in a way that wouldn't be so scary for you."

There's another long silence as I digest everything. I look out the window again. The houses have been replaced by stores like Radio Shack and Best Buy, and four-way intersections with traffic lights. Then we're driving down the strip of fast food restaurants on Route 19: MacDonald's, Taco Bell, Wendy's, Kentucky Fried Chicken. Dad used to call this road "Heart Healthy Alley." The last time we were on Route 19, Nelson got to choose where we went for lunch, and I got to choose where we went for dessert: Burger King and Dairy Queen. Now, all these places look gloomy.

Then I think of something that makes me feel hopeful, and I tell my parents: "If Nelson was truly crazy, I don't think he'd care about how I felt. Maybe he's not crazy, because he's aware of how I feel?"

Mom turns again to look at me and then she looks at Dad. "That's a good point, Harper. We should ask the doctors about that."

Dad nods his head, his hands on the steering wheel. "What a kid," he says.

I wonder, but don't ask: is he talking about me or Nelson?

❧　　❧　　❧

It's freakishly quiet at the entrance to the psychiatric unit. There's a series of locked doors, and we have to be buzzed through each set. Before we get to see Nelson, we meet with a social worker who makes sure we don't have any sharp instruments with us. Her name is Suki and she looks young enough to be a babysitter.

She tells us that Nelson will be observed for a few days and then the doctors will develop a treatment plan. My parents nod their heads and thank her. Why are they thanking her? It's like thanking a substitute teacher who knows nothing about the kids in class. What could she possibly know? I feel like sticking my tongue out at her.

There is a steady stream of staff walking around the unit, one or two making notes on clipboards. We walk through an open room where three teenagers are sitting at a table playing cards. They seem happy enough. But huddled in the corner on the floor, there's a teenage girl who's whimpering and pulling at her hair. Beyond her is an obese boy banging on a door. I look away and my mother reaches down to hold my hand. She gives it a tight squeeze.

We meet with Nelson in the family room, which is a cramped room with stained, overstuffed chairs and dirty walls. There are bars on the windows. As soon as he sees me, he walks over and gives me a hug. I start crying and he tickles my armpits, so then I'm laughing and crying at the same time.

"I'm ready to leave. The food here sucks," he tells my parents. He starts pacing around the furniture and repeats, "I'm ready to leave."

My parents look at each other and my stomach starts to clench.

Dad speaks first. "Nelson, like we told you last night, you'll need to stay a few days so the doctors can evaluate you and try some new medications."

"Asshole!" Nelson practically spits the word out.

My father shakes his head, then my mother speaks. "We want you to feel better so you can come home soon."

Nelson challenges her. "Are you telling the truth, Mom? Do you really want me to come home?"

Mom speaks softly. "Yes. Of course."

Mom's reassurance has a slightly calming influence on Nelson. He seems less tense, but I can tell from my parents' body language that this is going to be a short visit. Even I know that when Nelson starts to pace, it's usually followed by an explosion.

It's time to leave. My father opens the door to the hallway, where a staff person has been standing guard the whole time. He's as big as a football player. "Wrapping up the visit?" he asks, and my father nods.

The staff person turns to my brother. "Time to go back to the rec room, buddy."

Nelson's eyes are looking shiny and dark, but he goes along with the big man. We walk single file back to the open room to say goodbye. The teenagers who were playing cards have switched chairs and are now playing Monopoly, but the girl in the corner hasn't moved. The fat boy is nowhere in sight.

Nelson takes a seat at an empty table. Without looking at us, he raises his hand and waves goodbye. The big man holds his badge near the doorknob and we are buzzed out the first set of locked doors. On the other side, I turn to look at Nelson through the thick glass window. He sits staring straight ahead, his hands folded in his lap.

✤ ✤ ✤

That night I get to have a sleepover at Zahara's. Hanging out with Zahara and her family takes my mind off of Nelson and the psychiatric hospital. She has two older sisters and a little brother Elijah, who follows us around asking if we'll play Legos or transformers with him. Her older sisters mostly spend their time talking on the phone, but tonight their boyfriends are over, goofing around in the kitchen. I like the happy sounds in Zahara's house.

Finally it's Elijah's bedtime and Zahara's mother shoos him away. Once he's asleep, Zahara and I make popcorn and bring it up to her room, along with her mom's laptop, so we can watch the Spy Kids movie for the billionth time.

Before we start the movie, we sit on her bed facing each other, trying to toss popcorn into each other's mouths. Soon there's popcorn all over her bed. "Who's your hero?" Zahara asks me, as we pick popcorn off the bedspread. She gets impatient with how long it takes me to respond, so she answers the question herself.

"My hero is either Angelina Jolie, since she's a famous actress and has a daughter with my name"—and here Zahara breaks into a smile with her missing bottom teeth—"or my hero is Jacques Cousteau, because he taught the world so much about animals in the ocean." She shoves popcorn in her mouth. "Who's yours? You get two choices."

The first person who pops into my head is Nelson, weirdly enough. I say Nelson's name, and she laughs. "No really, Harper, this is serious," and she repeats the question.

I look right in her eyes. "Nelson is my hero because his life is so hard and he never gives up."

Zahara bobs her head from side to side, taking this in. "Yeah, but he's crazy, and you can't choose a crazy person for your hero. You have to pick someone normal." She throws a piece of popcorn in the air and catches it in her mouth.

Her words hit me like a punch in the gut. *Pick someone normal.* I slide off the edge of her bed and sit on the floor, my back against her. How could she say that about Nelson, after everything he's gone through? I thought Zahara was my best friend!

"So who are you going to choose?" she asks. I can hear her opening up the Spy Kids DVD case and putting the movie into the computer. I don't say anything because I can feel my heart pounding in my chest, and I'm afraid I'll start crying. I told her things about Nelson that I never told anyone.

The music from the movie comes on and Zahara leans over the side of the bed, and pokes me in the back. "Let's start the movie so we'll have time to watch the whole thing before bed," she says.

I stand up and turn to her. "I want to go home."

Zahara's eyes open wide in surprise. "Why?"

"I want to go home," I repeat, and I walk across the bedroom and open the door. Making my way down the hallway, I hear Zahara calling after me, "Harper! Come back!"

Downstairs, the kitchen is empty. I call my grandparents to ask them to pick me up. Grandma answers the phone, and though I try to sound fine, my voice is cracking. "Is everything okay, Harper? I thought you were sleeping over."

"Yeah," I tell her, "I changed my mind."

Zahara is walking toward me, carrying my overnight bag. "Why do you want to go home?" she asks, as soon as I hang up the phone. "We were just about to watch the movie."

She drops the overnight bag on the floor between us and I shrug my shoulders. "What's wrong? Are you mad at me?" she asks.

I stare at the floor for what feels like forever while Zahara sits cross-legged on the ground next to me, occasionally asking if I feel okay and why I'm leaving. Finally, I hear Grandpa's car pull up in the driveway and I run past Zahara out the front door.

The tears come as soon as I get in the car, and I start to sob. Grandpa doesn't say anything and he just lets me cry as he drives back to our neighborhood. Once we are in the driveway, he turns off the ignition and pats my knee.

I wipe my nose on my shirtsleeve and turn to Grandpa. "Nobody understands," I say. "Not even Zahara. I thought she was my best friend." Grandpa motions for me to sit closer to him, and I unbuckle my seatbelt and scoot over. His arm surrounds me like a warm blanket.

We sit like that in the car for awhile, and then I tell Grandpa that Zahara and I were supposed to watch the Spy Kids movie. Grandpa asks me to tell him about the movie and why I like it so much.

I tell him how Spy Kids is about a family of spies. A mom, dad, sister, and brother. Everyone has super powers, and everyone keeps secrets. At first, the kids aren't aware that the parents are spies and the parents don't realize that the kids are spies. The kids and parents lead totally separate lives until they intersect when they go on all of these wacky missions. Somehow, against the odds, they complete their assignments and in the end they gain a lot of respect for each other.

"A family of super powers and secrets," Grandpa says, stroking his chin. "Sounds familiar."

I look at him, waiting for him to continue, then the front door opens. Grandma stands in the doorway as light from the house pours onto the driveway. She's holding the phone and signals for us to come inside. "Zahara's on the phone," she calls out.

Grandpa takes a long look at me. "The best super power, I think," he says, "is not keeping secrets."

He opens the car door and I feel a whoosh of cool night air.

"You coming?" he turns and asks.

"In a minute," I say.

He nods. I watch as he walks on the stone path from the driveway toward the house. He walks slowly, but with purpose. In the light, Grandma's hair looks more white than grey, and I remember her once telling me that *normal* is a setting on a dishwasher. I take some deep breaths in the car like Dr. Knowles showed me to do, and then it's time to go inside.

SUSAN LANIER

ESCAPE

I was in college five states away
when Mother called   a short conversation
the police   she said   picked up your brother
in a women's bathing suit at the public pool

five states away   they picked up my brother
bouncing at the end of the diving board
arms extended   he always had volume
did they cuff him? I forgot to ask

in a short conversation   my mother said
she watched from the window   my brother
alone in the backyard flip his hands
over and over   five states away

confide in his palms   the backs
of his hands   a short conversation
was he wrapped in a straitjacket? I
fingered my button   forgot to ask

EVENINGS, I DRINK WHITE

against your need
more on nights after
you call   even if you were
lucid   since your word way
is striated with scarred
root bulge and fissure

your disease is a jail
and looking out from it
all you see are jailers or
false accusers

If only that were all
but your mind projects
into the space around you
three dimensional mirrors
turbulent seas

anyone engulfed in the drama
will only find Poseidon shape-
shifting himself from memory
to dream
          still   I brave
the word-slaver and coyote
evasions because one
card in each suit   if I can only
find it   bears the child
I grew up with and his face
looks out at me   longs
for me

to claim him
protect him
from snakes and
poisonous vapors slipping
out
and in
through the bars

OUT OF REACH

You let your cigarettes burn out
in the ashtray as if the swirls of smoke
were family. You keep them
beside your plate.

When you were little
I wouldn't hold your hand, your warts
hard as fat ticks. You carry the mark
of our father like a sullen, hidden tattoo.
I never know when he will
possess you.
        I would hide from him
when I was three, four, a possum as high
in the hemlock as I could climb or jammed
like a rat against the wall under the bed.
His rage shook the house. His arm
was long. His belt slipped through loops.
The metal edge of his instructions.

The yellow jackets were beautiful.
We would squat down beside
the overturned flowerpot
and watch them crawl
from the hole, heavy in the belly,
pause, then off they'd buzz.
        As soon as you
could walk I'd take you out through the long
grass, down to the sluggish, muddy Olentangy.
Swag-roofed, bedraggled shacks on the wash,
soft rot underfoot. We would find things.

Rusty scissors, a fetid can, the neck
of a broken bottle, cap on. We did not
carry them home.

You are happiest when you eat. Mouth
full and chatty, the threads of your thought
fray and fly apart. I cannot follow you.
I live alone.

I COULD NOT LOOK AWAY

from the cowlick on the crown
of my baby brother's head.
His fine white hair swirling
out in perfect order. I would
trace it with my finger,
stare at it as he slept,
until it lifted out,
whorled in.
      Was sorry
he didn't stay a baby
later when he ground
cigarettes out on his wrists
and left his hair a thicket,
dirty and tangled, as if
the expansion of that spiral
had flung out sense
and the only thing left
was the empty
center of the vortex
like the point of a burn.

JANE ST. CLAIR

TALKING BERKELEY DOWN

As usual my brother calls me in the middle of the night with suicidal tendencies.

"I just can't take it anymore," he says. "I'm going to get fired from here. I'm looking at my medicine right this minute. I know which combination will do it. I'm going to do it this time. Friday I'm going to do it for real. Tell Mom I love her."

"How do you know which combination for sure?"

"From the Hemlock Society book."

"They might have it wrong. You might get it wrong. You just sound tired, that's all."

"I am. I'm tired. No one likes me here. I'm just too different from other people, my reactions are too bizarre and I'm tired of trying to fit in. No one likes me, that's all. No one likes me. I can't make it in Wisconsin."

"I like you. You just sound tired. Why don't you take some time off? Call them and tell them you have the flu. Everybody's got the flu these days."

"Then they'll fire me for sure."

"But you just said you're going to get fired anyway."

"You just don't understand."

I do understand, I thought. He and I are about to have another conversation absent logic, absent reason. A geometry made from chaos, a system of theorems no sane person could discern.

"Look," I say to Berkeley. "Have you ever driven up to Green Bay? That's not far. Why don't you take a couple of days off and go up to Green Bay? Mess around."

"I can't. I already owe $22,000 on MasterCard."

"Then what the hell difference can it make? You told me you were going to kill yourself on Friday. Friday, for real, no backsies. You still have five days left before Friday and you may as well screw MasterCard and your job and go up to Green Bay."

"What's in Green Bay?"

"I don't know. The Packers. Maybe a museum about the Packers."

"I'm not into the Packers. Your ideas take energy and I'm tired."

But I am tired too, indeed almost as tired of Berkeley's manic depression as he is. It has been seven long years since his first nervous breakdown during senior year in college. Back then Berkeley made some bad scores on his Graduate Record Exams, his girlfriend told him to walk, and our father was dying slowly of lung cancer. The pressure built up inside Berkeley like a crimped hose, and he exploded quietly, quietly . . . and then just as quietly, he mixed a bottle of our mother's Valium into vodka and tomato juice. The tomato juice was typical of Berkeley's upscale style. A Bloody Mary suicide: nice touch. When he was little, Berkeley asked Santa Claus for a silk paisley smoking jacket.

That night my parents and I sat in the waiting room outside the Emergency Center at Cook County Hospital in Chicago, where Berkeley in an unconscious state had been driven in the back of the highest paid taxi in town.

We three sat in the hospital waiting room, steeped in the antiseptic and Pine-Sol smells of the hospital, and we drank sedimented coffee out of Styrofoam cups and didn't say anything to each other. My parents didn't try to ask me to explain why a team of doctors were using a mechanical pump to rid Berkeley of poisons floating in a Bloody Mary and I wasn't sure I could explain it to them anyway. When Letterman finally signed off, we sat there in silence, not talking about Berkeley or Dad's cancer or the pain we were in or nothing.

A doctor came in late the next morning, and told us we could take Berkeley home now. My mother thanked him but she didn't ask for the name of a psychiatrist. The doctor didn't ask anything either; he just made general remarks like priests do when they preside over funerals of people they've never met, such remarks like "Your son seems like a very nice young man."

We putzed around with hospital accountant-types, and then my parents, my brother and I walked out of the hospital and into our car. In our four-way silence, we looked to Berkeley to say the first words and he did. He always did carry the family.

"I could use some food," he said.

"Me too," said Mother with a kind of giddy enthusiasm and relief that the subject was roses.

"You know, we're in a great neighborhood for delis," Berkeley said. "I know a great deli where they make great pastrami sandwiches. It's right around here."

"Great," said my father.

"Boy, I'd just love a great pastrami sandwich," Mother glowed.

"Me too. Show us where we can get a great pastrami sandwich," my father agreed.

Berkeley was right: the sandwiches were great. They came on rye bread to die for with thinly sliced, thickly flavored pieces of pastrami piled higher than the length of your middle finger. They came with potato salad. We ordered four of them and we ate them in silence, except the air was thick with what was between us and it felt like slime from outer space, gumming up your mind and your stomach and settling everywhere inside you; yet it was something no one could acknowledge because it would have made the unbelievable real. It was left unspoken that day as we chomped on those sandwiches and left what we could not digest to hang between us for years.

Berkeley's very first suicide attempt was on a Friday, and by Monday he was back in his college dorm. He didn't crack up again until rejection letters started to come in from graduate schools. Then he made a complete break from reality.

He often told me that going nuts was better than hallucinogenic drugs, better than anything anyone could ever do with chemicals, even better than quality Ecstasy. The whole world seemed to have meaning—every word anyone said had a significance that stretched from the beginning of time to the end of the world. When he was nuts, he felt lifted up, no longer human, almost an angel.

He said it was complete Enlightenment in the Buddhist sense of the word. He told me the story of a Master who asked his student what is the True Buddha, and the student replied, "Three pounds of flax." That was Enlightenment and flax and it all made perfect sense to Berkeley in a manic high.

Later his heavy-duty intellect interpreted everything in terms of teleological theology—like Teilhard de Chardin's theory that human intelligence could reach the Omega Point of understanding, and that someday the earth will end when everyone reaches the Omega Point all at once. This thought comforted me: I figured if everyone had to become like Berkeley for the world to end, this old world would be around forever.

During his third breakdown, Berkeley walked around Chicago on a February night without clothes, and it is a tribute to the awesome indifference of bus drivers and El train conductors that no one gave a damn that it was two below zero and my brother was naked. Guided by Biblical principles that you give away everything you own, he donated my grandfather's heirloom watch and all his clothes to anyone who would take them.

Berkeley still at the Omega Point rode the Elevated train to the end of the line, where he met an old man who put him in a cardboard box and covered him with a blue blanket. To this day, Berkeley can recite their entire conversation, and to this day, he believes the old man was Jesus Christ, and the blanket was the Holy Shroud. Later Berkeley was picked up by cops and taken to the county mental hospital, where my parents retrieved his body but lost his soul. He went off on this mystical kick, reading the Don Carlos books and doing peyote, and running around with a whacked-out Denny's waitress who chanted ohm for the unity of the universe.

"Frank," he says, jolting me out of my reverie, "are you listening?"

"Yes," I reply. "I still don't see why you can't take some time off and go up to Green Bay. It's only Monday. You always do suicides on Fridays."

"I really am going to do it this time," Berkeley says. "I just can't hack it anymore. You don't understand. I'm too tired to start over again. I'm not making it here. Everyone thinks I'm nuts. My students are dropping my class and complaining to the dean. Their parents are calling up. My department chair is avoiding me. When I try to talk to her, she says she has a meeting to go to and blows me off. She wants to get me fired."

"So you get fired. They won't fire you until the end of the semester. You've got three months yet. That's forever."

Berkeley's latest attempt at employment was a position as a history professor at a small community college in the coldest, most Germanic part of Wisconsin. He moved there in August, and immediately the weather turned bad and become a world-class, record-breaking winter. That was the kind of thing that happened to Berkeley—things like eighty below zero weather.

He had been in and out of graduate schools as well as in and out of mental hospitals and jobs for the past seven years, and yet somehow he had managed to get his PhD in American history. My mother had paid for it because his prognosis was always so poor; she figured a PhD was something no one could take away. And we all recognized that everything had been taken away from Berkeley. Once you lose your mind, it's hard to hold on to people and other things.

Anyway, Berkeley was now teaching an introductory overview of American history and in his perfectionist way, it was killing him. How could you go through the American Revolution in just two weeks? he'd lament. Although the course had been meeting for five months, they were still on the Founding Fathers and even his students knew they'd never get through the Cold War.

"I think they will fire me soon," Berkeley is saying. "It's coming. I feel it coming."

"You're wrong a lot. Just jump ahead to the Civil War. Pick up the pace a little."

I catch myself in my own absurdity: "pick up the pace—" "take a nice vacation before you kill yourself—" oh jeez.

"That would be a total cop-out," Berkeley says. "I'd be selling my soul. These stupid kids haven't even heard of John Locke's theory of revolution and its influence on the American Declaration of Independence. How can they grow up without John Locke, for Christ's sake?"

"Yeah, but if you don't hurry up, they will grow up without the Civil War. They won't know from Scarlet O'Hara."

"All those ugly students stare at me like I'm nuts."

"Look, it's after two a.m."

"You couldn't come down, could you? Frank?"

Don't ask, I think, silently remembering all the times I've tried to take over Berkeley's case. I had assumed, along with all our relatives and long-time friends that his symptoms came from my parents' screwing up his childhood.

Once I moved him away from home and into my apartment on Near North Side in Chicago. My place was a sort of singles' haven where everyone's hitting on everyone—in the bars, the laundromat, the work-out room—wherever. Berkeley immediately sized up the situation and decided what the building needed was Marlon Brando in his "Wild One" persona.

"All the guys here are too nice," he said as he lay on the Oak Street beach checking out the women in bikinis drinking lite beer. "They're all too preppie. These women would go for a guy with a cigarette hanging down one lip, and a black jacket like Brando's."

Berkeley was right. Within days, he had women phoning and banging on the door to meet him. All of these pseudo-feminists with victim complexes wanted to mother the macho guy with the mental disorder.

We lasted less than a month together until nature's little escape valve blew open again for him, and he was lifted out of his hellish reality. I spent three hours on a tin roof one night with him, trying to talk him out of the idea that he was incandescent and could fly down five stories. After that, the women didn't come around anymore and I shipped him back home to my widowed mother.

"Berkeley," I say, "What about Thomas Jefferson? You love Jefferson."

"I showed them slides of Monticello," he replies. "They didn't get it. They didn't even get the significance of his wine cellar and experimental garden—the significance that he could build something like that in the 1780's. They don't appreciate him. I'm so tired of trying. If I lose this job, I'll never work in history again."

"You don't know that for sure," I reply. "If you get fired, you don't put Wisconsin on the resume."

"I'd have it better if I was getting out of prison," Berkeley says. "I can't tell anyone about my depression. They'd all think I'm a nut. Dangerous. If I was getting out of prison, I'd have it better."

"This way you can vote," I say. "Felons can't vote."

"That's real funny, Frank."

"I just get tired of being the sane one," I reply. "I deserve the next nervous breakdown. Or maybe we could go together on the family plan."

"That's real funny."

"Just hang in there."

"It's bad. This time it's bad. Frank. I'm just so tired, so very tired. Frank. I don't have the energy to start over again. To reinvent myself. I've done it so many times. Frank. I've tried so many times."

"Yeah," I say, "but how do you know that suicide wouldn't start some other weird trip out there? I mean, you might have to start over again on some other plane. That might take even more energy. Eternal damnation or some other such goddamn thing. You'd have to get yourself out of that."

"It might just be eternal peace. Sleep. Oblivion."

There was a long pause.

"Frank, do you ever notice all the people who are still smoking? Frank. Not just me, but all the other people?"

He always says my name as if he were calling down a black hole. Frank. Echo, echo. Frank.

"Frank. Do you ever look at all the people who are smoking? They depress me so much. They all have the death wish."

"Maybe they're just addicts," I argue.

"We all cling to something," Berkeley whispers. "You cling to life no matter how bad it gets."

I think about all the little frogs in the Brazilian rain forests that are going extinct because they do everything through their skins. They breathe through their skins, they bring water into themselves through their skins. Mankind is polluting their water and it's killing the frogs who didn't even bother to mate this year. My brother is a man without skin and he lets all the pollution of our times come into himself; he has no crap filter.

"Frank? Are you there?"

"Yes."

"What if it's all just patterns, you know, like six-sided snowflakes and waves hitting a rock and Nietzsche's doctrine of continual reoccurrence?"

"What if what's just patterns?" I asked.

"You know, you and I—just talking together like this over and over. Do you think this is a pattern? Do you think death could break this pattern or do you think is it eternal?"

As usual when I was talking Berkeley down, the hour was growing insanely late, things were making less sense, and old rock songs were going through my head. This time I kept hearing the Beatles song, "She's So Heavy." Everything about Berkeley was heavy: his intellect, his questions, what he was all about. Nothing lite and lively about Berkeley.

"Frank? Frank?"

"Yeah, I'm here."

"I wish you could see things the way I do."

But I'd need a Seeing Eye dog in his world. In his world, I'd be just a blind person with a Seeing Eye dog. If my crazy brother ever does succeed in dying, it would be like Romeo. You could cut him out into little stars and hang him out there and his kind of light would still make us see things we didn't want to see or we weren't ready to see but for some reason, he sees. That all the world would be in love with his light and pay no worship to the garish sun. Whatever.

He's my brother and he's so heavy, man, so heavy.

PETER SCHMITT

THE HANDS

On a ledge above the kitchen door
our mother set the plaster casts
of our hands—like little pies
left there to cool
we'd stuck all our fingers into.

First mine, then three years later
at the same kindergarten—
before he started going
to special schools—my brother's,
for a not quite matched set.

The doctors said he would never read.
But after school, our mother
quietly closed his door
and sat with him and an open book
for hours before she made dinner.

When frustration got the best of him
he'd run from the house,
slamming the kitchen door,
and the little blue plates
of our hands would waver, not wave.

They stayed up there for years,
where a horseshoe might have hung.
But it wasn't by luck
that he now reads.
When we moved, our mother held each hand

in her own, then stacked them in a box.

THE ROPES

The night they tied my brother to a tree,
someone ran to call me from my cabin.
But I got there—as usual—too late;
they'd let him go, and he'd run off to hide,
and cry, not to return until morning.

But I found the tree, around which the kids
In his bunk had danced, and laughed, calling him names
Like *Retard! Dummy!* and I found the ropes,
coiled at the base of the tree like snakes.
That summer, we'd learned about tying knots,

and how a tourniquet stops the flow of blood—
except for my brother, who couldn't, was slow,
who to this day can't tie a knot or make
a bow, yet may know as much about them
as any there that night, or anyone not.

THANKSGIVING: VISITING MY BROTHER
ON THE WARD

Behind the thick, crosshatched glass of the cruiser,
my brother, back for the holiday, breathes
more slowly. A phalanx of uniforms
cloaks the open door, murmuring to him
where he sits. The carving knife is somewhere
out of reach, none of us so much as scratched.
Inside, the bound bird cools on the butcher block.

Later that night I move through many doors, each
locking behind me, each inlaid with the same
heavy glass as the squad car. Through the last
I see my brother's face, fixed as on a graph,
ordinate, abscissa. When he sees mine
he retreats from the common room to his own,
a bare cell he shares with a narrow bed.

He will not speak to me, at first. His fingers
move in perpetual chafe, like a mantis,
his lifelong nervous habit, the edges
of a newspaper shredded on the bed.
This time, his eyes say, we have betrayed him
as never before. This time, he seems to say,
he cannot find a way to forgive us.

At last I persuade him to join the others
finishing the meal, their plastic utensils
working the meat, their low voices broken
by stray whoops of inappropriate laughter.
We sit, though, in a separating silence,
my brother's hand already eroding
his napkin, eyes distant with medication.

If only he were faithful to himself
and took his daily pills . . . But what is the point
of such a constancy when the world itself
has so profoundly turned away? As tonight
I will leave him here, leave all of them here,
the psychotics and depressives, my brother,
to lie on their beds and stare at their ceilings,

and I know that for at least this visit
he will not come home, where our parents now sit
in darkness, their faces streaked and damp. And when
we drive him to the airport, an unmarked
police car following as an escort,
he might be a foreign dignitary
bearing developments back to his country . . .

For now, though, it is just two brothers, beneath
a glaring bulb. The expression on his face
would ask, *Have you gotten what you came for?*
And again I have no answer for him.
But there, at the floor of the bed, all around
the room, are crumbs of paper, as if he were
leaving a trail by which he might be found.

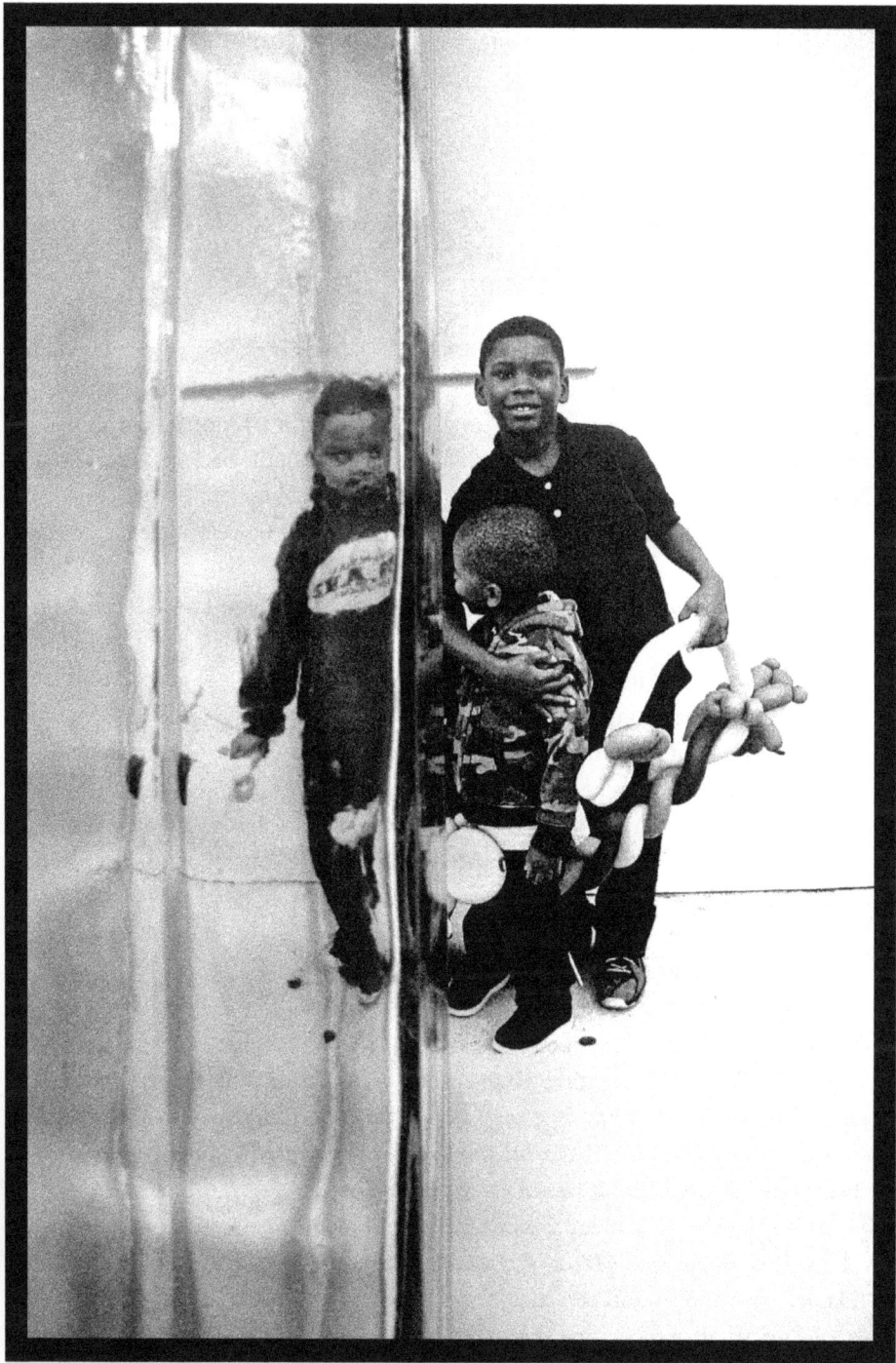

ANDREA ROSENHAFT

I LOVE THAT YOU'RE MY BROTHER

I spent Thanksgiving of 2014 with my brother, Daniel and his girlfriend Sophie at her parents' home in the small city of Hartford, Connecticut. It had snowed there the day before and the children were out in the backyard, building snowmen. Sophie and her mother were cooking in the kitchen.

Daniel and I had a moment alone in the family room. I took his hand and squeezed it.

Hey," I said, trying not to cry. "I just wanted to let you know I'm doing good." I smiled.

That's the best news I could hear," he replied and gave me a smile back.

"I just want to say thanks." I paused. "I couldn't have done it without you." I turned my head towards the football game humming on the television. I couldn't stop the tears of joy.

Daniel was younger than me by eighteen months, but in many ways he took the role of the older sibling. On this Thanksgiving Day, I had turned fifty-three years old in February and he fifty-two in August. It was he I went to for advice when I needed to make a major decision, and his was the first shoulder I cried on when my life began to take a downward tumble.

We fought when we were kids growing up in our three-bedroom apartment in Queens, an outer borough of New York City. My bedroom, although it was a young girl's fantasy with bouquets of pink flowers sprayed across the wallpaper, pink shag carpeting and white furniture with pink trim, was a converted dining room off the kitchen. I resented Daniel because his bedroom was larger and it was closer to my parents' bedroom, which was at the other end of the apartment. Once I got up the nerve to question my parents about this unfair arrangement, they responded that it seemed fitting because Daniel was younger and because he was a boy.

I grew up fearing that a masked man would sneak up the fire escape located by the kitchen window (our apartment was one level above the street) and kidnap me. I believed that my parents would never hear me if I screamed because my bedroom was so far away. To escape my fears I delved into books that pleased our parents, especially our father. My prized possession as a child was a complete thirty-five-volume set of *The Bobbsey Twins* series. I brought my books to the dinner table and propped them up against my plate, an action that Daniel protested mightily.

"Mom, look what Andrea's doing again."

My father, with a scotch by his side would grunt in the direction of my brother. "You should try reading."

Our father drank, mostly scotch, mostly Johnnie Walker Red. He wasn't a violent drunk, but his tongue could be cruel and sarcastic when he was inebriated, lashing out with no concern for the feelings of whomever stood before him. He possessed enough self-control not to binge drink, but he drank a fair amount of alcohol consistently each day into the evening. He came home from his job as a stockbroker at a prestigious brokerage firm on Wall Street, consumed a glass or two of the amber liquid and disappeared into his bedroom, passed out.

"Daddy's tired," Mom would say. "He works hard." Not mentioning the drinks we learned that he had also loaded up on from the bar car on the Long Island Railroad he took home each day.

Our mother protected us as best she could from our father's alcoholism. Making excuses for him. Running interference for him. But she couldn't always shield us from him.

When I was thirteen and Daniel was twelve, our parents called a formal family meeting. We never discussed emotions in our family and we hid behind the veil of day-to-day events, so anything larger that was happening got pushed into the background. The four of us were awkwardly seated on the gold crushed velvet couches in the living room. My parents appeared uncomfortable, Daniel and I were expectant.

My mother spoke first. "Daddy has a problem, but he's going to get help. It's called al-co-ho-li-sm," she told us, drawing out the offensive word as though she wanted it to sink in forever. "He's going to go to something called Alcoholics Anonymous and stop drinking."

Daniel and I looked at each other. His erratic behavior finally had a reason. We weren't at fault. Our father went out every evening and after ninety days showed us his coin. He wanted both of us to attend Alateen, an offshoot of AA for the teenage children of its members. I went to please him and cowered silently in the chaos of the unruly group as the other adolescents shared their horror stories. Daniel wasn't as worried about pleasing our father and outright refused to go.

This was the first time I felt united with Daniel over something that had happened in our family. Until then he and I had taken different roles growing up; I was the quiet one, the sensitive one who read a great deal and spent more time alone. Daniel was more outgoing, more likely to spend time out of the house with his friends, more likely to rebel. He got a lot of flak from our father who put a great deal of value on education and appreciation of the finer things in life such as good art. The walls of our apartment were covered with paintings that he had inherited from his parents who were collectors in Europe before the war.

Following the disclosure of this thing called alcoholism, Daniel and I retreated to his bedroom to play the Atari game Pong that our parents had purchased for us and had hooked up to his television set because his room was larger. I felt the beginnings of a bond with Daniel and I think he felt it as well.

Our mother eventually opened a knitting store in the neighborhood to support our family after Dad lost his job. I hung out there after school and did my homework while Daniel roamed the streets with his friends. Anything to avoid going home where our father had planted himself, now depressed. Our mother told us he had been covering up an underlying depression with the alcohol and now that he wasn't drinking, the depression was evident.

Being home alone with him when our mother wasn't there was terrifying. When he deigned to leave his bedroom, he was demanding.

"Have you done your homework yet? Is your room clean? Time to start dinner."

When I graduated from high school I knew that I had to get as far away from home as possible, but I needed to stay in New York state due to our family's strapped financial situation. I was accepted at the State University of New York at Buffalo, four hundred miles from our home in Queens. The next year Daniel joined me up in the cold, wintry city.

Buffalo, home of chicken wings and blue cheese, was where Daniel and I really become close. He and I transcended the sibling rivalry of our childhood and became friends. Our relationship grew to include not only love, but respect and mutual admiration. He was able to see me away from home, as a social creature with friends, managing classes and two varsity sports. I saw him attending classes, taking care of his responsibilities and finally free from our father's unrealistic expectations.

"Yeah, I'm getting high almost every night in the dorm with the rest of the crowd," I told Daniel. "But I'm still making it to classes and basketball practice."

"I'm fooling around with a couple of drugs too. I miss some of my eight o'clock classes. Never should have signed up for those."

"What do you think Mom and Dad would do if they knew?"

"I dunno. Probably stop sending the money."

Knowing that the other was close by was enough and that feeling of reassurance that we were there for each other, regardless, set the stage for the rest of our lives.

When we were home for winter break in my senior year of college, Daniel's junior year, our parents, in another rare family meeting, announced they were divorcing.

Several days before, my mother had told us she was going shopping with one of her girlfriends. Watching out of the living room window, I saw her get into a strange car. I said to Daniel, "I think Mom's having an affair."

"No! What? Are you kidding?" He laughed at my suspicions.

Now they told us that our mother had a boyfriend and she wanted to be with him. The marriage had been over for some time.

"Andrea knew," Daniel blurted out, "that Mom was having an affair."

I graduated, moved back to Queens and took a job at an advertising agency. Daniel followed a year later, taking a job with the same brokerage firm on Wall Street that my father had worked for. In our early twenties, we were doing what was expected of us, forging a career and hanging out with friends. Daniel was dating, but I was having difficulty meeting men.

Having inherited my father's propensity for depression and addiction, during my twenties and thirties, my life took a precipitous downward trajectory. I dabbled in cocaine and when a psychiatrist prescribed me Dexedrine, speed, for a worsening depression, it suppressed my appetite. I dropped to ninety-two pounds and was diagnosed with anorexia. I became addicted to the highs of seeing my bones jut through my pale skin and caressed my body feeling for the sharp edges poking through my hips and at my collar. I loved getting on the scale in the morning and watching the numbers drop. After two extended hospitalizations I lost the career I had worked so hard for, one that I had climbed my way up to from a secretarial position.

Feeling ashamed and adrift, the depression worsened and in 1990, I attempted suicide by taking an overdose. I was subsequently diagnosed with borderline personality disorder (BPD) and sent to a private psychiatric hospital in a suburb north of New York City that housed a long-term unit specializing in treating this difficult diagnosis. BPD is seen as a more intrusive and pervasive illness, more damaging to my core. When they tried to explain it to me, my first thought was that I was irreparably broken. An image of a dead animal lying contorted by the side of the road came to mind.

I was on that unit for almost a year, discharged to a supervised residence in late 1991. I stayed there for three years, then purchased my own apartment. My mother and Daniel made the trip up from Queens and later down from Connecticut where they had moved—my mother to start a new business with my brother in software development. My father came once or twice for a "recommended" family session, then withdrew into his own world. He was hurt at some of the accusations that my psychiatrist from the hospital had thrown at him about possible transgressions that occurred while he was drinking. Although my mother and Daniel defended him, his fragile ego was close to imploding.

My mother and Daniel stayed right with me. It would have been easy for Daniel to slip out of my life in gradual increments. My mother was supposed to hang in there. She was my mother. Daniel was under no such obligation. There was no rule for brothers and sisters like there was for mothers and daughters stating that they were stuck with each other regardless of the circumstances.

By the beginning of my forties, in 2000, my life had improved measurably. I had recovered enough to return to graduate school and earn my master's degree in social work. I wanted to counsel others who were in pain, and give them what had been given to me by my therapists and psychiatrists.

In December of 2001, my mother and Daniel asked me to come up to Connecticut. We sat in the family room and the reluctance that filled the air reminded me of the family meetings that punctuated my childhood. Solemnly, my mother told me that she had been diagnosed with pancreatic cancer and was expected to have only six months to live. Daniel already knew. He had accompanied her to all the doctor visits.

Mom lasted three months. The last month of her life she was bedridden with a gangrenous foot. She was able to hire a private nurse to attend to her needs during the day, but I made my way up to her house after work and slept besides her in her king-size bed. I wanted to take care of her, I wanted to be there for her when she needed me although I felt it wouldn't even come close to what she had done for me.

She and Daniel were busy putting her affairs—both for the business and for her personal life—in order. He was remarkable in how collected he was able to remain, knowing that soon our mother would die. One evening we were at her home and eating dinner on trays with her in her room. My mother asked me about the flag that was waving on the wall across from the bed. There was no flag. I looked at my brother, alarmed. I turned to soothe her as she became agitated. She took a swing at me. Crying, I motioned to the phone. Daniel called 911.

My mother was lying silently in the hospital bed. I sat beside her, prepared to stay all night. Daniel had left, saying he would be return in an hour. I didn't know where he disappeared to. The doctor came in and put the stethoscope to Mom's chest. He looked at me and shook his head. "I'm sorry," he said. "She's gone."

Daniel came walking into her room. Looking at him my mouth opened, but I couldn't speak.

"I know," he said quickly. "I met the doctor in the hall."

He held his hand out for me to get up and helped me on with my coat. His arm around my shoulders, he guided me gently out the door. I thought about looking back, but I couldn't. I was afraid I would never leave. It was very early the next morning as we walked down the empty hospital corridor. As our shoes echoed on the tile floor, Daniel tightened his grip on my shoulders.

We sat Shiva at my mother's house. It was the only place big enough to welcome all the people who wanted to pay their respects.

My mom and I had been best friends. We spent many weekends together shopping, getting manicures and just hanging out because we enjoyed each other's company. Suddenly there was a huge hole in my life. Daniel understood and he checked in with me frequently.

"Just calling to see how you're doing." I'd hear his deep voice on my phone.

"I miss her."

"Yeah, me too." We'd be silent for a moment, both of us lost in our separate memories of our mother. "Call me anytime you need to," he'd remind me. "You're going to make it through this. We both will."

"Yeah I know. Thanks."

It was Daniel and I now and barely a buzz from our father who was still living in the apartment where we were raised in Queens. We each spoke to him every week or two just to make sure he was still breathing, but Daniel had taken over our mother's computer software development company and I was ensconced in my first clinical position as a social worker in Westchester County, outside of New York City.

In late 2005 I experienced another depressive episode and needed to be hospitalized. And then a similar one in early 2006. My clinical responsibilities were severely curtailed at work and I resigned, humiliated. Perhaps it was a long-delayed reaction to the death of my mother. Part of the internal world of BPD includes an ongoing feeling of chaos and emptiness which I liken to being locked in a small windowless room and being hurled violently from wall to wall, coming to rest bloody and bruised on a cold cement floor. Perhaps it was just time for me to fall apart.

This breakdown required four additional inpatient hospitalizations and several courses of electroconvulsive therapy. I went back on the rolls of Social Security Disability. I viewed this disengagement from society as a complete failure.

Daniel never wavered. He showed up. He knew when to make me laugh and when to stay silent and comfort me with his physicality. We were both aware of our mother's absence. He had a wife now, Cindy, whom he had married in 2003 on a sunny day on Fire Island in view of the Atlantic Ocean.

He was consistent for the entire three years it took for me to slowly, so slowly regain my emotional and physical health, for the last hospitalization of this series was for anorexia. He was there for the journey, for the little slips and slides that were inevitable. For the days I'd call him howling like a wounded animal from the floor of my living room.

"I can't do this anymore. It hurts too much."

He listened to the screeches over the phone.

"Go find Zoe or Lucy (I had adopted two cats after my mother died) and hold them close."

He waited until I hunted down one or both of my girls.

"Got her? Good. Give her a good hug and kiss. Feel better? Call me later. Let me know how you're doing. Love you more."

By the summer of 2008 I had been working with a new psychiatrist, who was also a therapist, for several years. She didn't take insurance and that was one more way that Daniel was helping me out. He was giving me the money to see her. She was encouraging me to return to work, starting slowly on a part-time basis. I found a position two days a week at a mental health clinic in

Queens, not far from where my father still lived. It was a long commute from Westchester, but they had been willing to take a chance on me.

Two days turned into four days, then after nine months in 2009, my part-time job became full time. I was myself again, on medications that were working well for me. I had made friends at work, had developed an active social life that was filling the gap left by my mother's death. I had also discovered a passion for writing through classes I had taken before I started working. I loved the feeling of creating something from nothing, the feeling of choosing exactly the right word and of crafting a sentence, then a paragraph and finally a finished piece. Gradually I had been able to develop an identity for myself as a published writer and as a social worker, far away from that of an ill person, the lens from which I had viewed myself for the prior three years.

I told Daniel, "I don't feel like a sick person any more. I mean I still have a mental illness, but I don't feel like it defines me like it did a year ago."

"That's terrific," he answered.

I tried to pound home how important this was. "I can say I'm a social worker now, again, and a writer. I don't have to say I'm on Social Security anymore and not working. No one has to know." I let that sink in.

"That's great A." As we had gotten older he had gotten into the habit of calling me by my first initial for short, but I still called him by his full name. "Keep on movin' forward. Don't let anything stop you now."

In the spring of 2010 Daniel called me at work. "Dad says he needs some groceries and he doesn't feel well enough to get down to the store. Can you swing by after work and pick up a couple of things for him?"

Surprised I said sure. "I'll call him and see what he needs."

When I walked into his apartment I was overwhelmed by the filth and the stench. The once pristine white tile floors of the foyer where I had played on my hands and knees were black with grime and littered with dead roaches. The apartment reeked of stale body odor and garbage not taken out to the chute. My father appeared, thin, clad in boxer shorts with an unkempt grey beard. He put his face up to mine and puckered his lips as if to kiss me. Disgusted, I recoiled.

Shopping done I returned to the apartment to put away the food. Opening the fridge, I saw rotted food and shelves coated with mold. Flies flew out. The odor was revolting.

Alarmed I called Daniel and described what I had seen. "What are we going to do?" The shopping trips became a weekly ritual, sometimes twice a week. I might forget something or purchase an incorrect item and the cruel, snide remarks from my childhood found their way into my father's lexicon. "Why did you get me this shit cake?"

The defenseless little girl emerged and said nothing, swallowing her hurt. I just left for the hour-long drive in the dark back to Westchester.

Migraines started to plague me regularly. I had hints of them since my thirties but now they made a regular, painful appearance.

I got a case opened for our father with Adult Protective Services. They came in haz-mat suits and cleaned out the apartment. He got angry because we threw out a roach infested antique settee with a torn rattan backing.

One afternoon Daniel called me. "I haven't been able to get in touch with him for three days. He's not answering his phone. Can you go over and check on him?"

I found him lying naked on the once again filthy foyer floor, barely conscious. "Water," he whispered. I called 911 and he was admitted to the hospital.

In 2011 Daniel got our father to agree to move up closer to him in Connecticut and rented a studio apartment. We cleaned out the apartment in Queens and packed up all the paintings, china from my parents' wedding, and ceramic and metal sculptures. We wore gloves and threw away our clothes after we were done.

I took the risk of reading to my father a piece of my writing once, an essay I had written about how much I loved the artwork I had inherited from him and my mother. I was in his apartment, waiting while I was doing his laundry. I made myself vulnerable to the fire that was known to explode from his tongue. I made the mistake of trusting that I could try to connect with him through the pastime that had become my passion. I thought that would be enough. Looking up I met his eyes, questioningly and received a dull stare from glazed-over pupils and a slacked jaw in return. "Ehh," was the only comment he had. He didn't even care enough to make the effort to be sarcastic.

Daniel and I met for coffee and talked about how we hoped he wouldn't last much longer.

"What's keeping him going?" we asked each other. "Why doesn't he just die and leave us alone?"

In the spring of 2013 he collapsed several times in the bathroom of his apartment and called Daniel to come pick him up. I left work early one day to take him to the emergency room and he never left. He had sepsis and his liver was failing. He was transferred to a palliative care facility and died ten days later. We had him cremated and tossed his ashes in The Long Island Sound. There was no memorial service, no sitting Shiva, like we did for my mother.

I thought I would feel a sense of relief after my father died. I thought I would feel at peace and would feel free. But I found that I was trapped by my own feelings of anger and resentment from which I was unable to extricate myself.

"Daddy what did you do to me?" I asked in the dark as I cried myself to sleep night after night. These ugly feelings first manifested themselves in a persistent migraine that began in June, two months after his death and lasted until late September, when my neurologist threw up his hands and sent me to The Cleveland Clinic's headache program, one of the best in the country. I went for their three-week outpatient program, nine hours a day and returned significantly improved, though not cured.

The elation lasted several months until my father's ghost made himself known by ripping a chasm through my soul, otherwise known as depression. The depression returned gradually; at first my psychiatrist and I thought my long-time medication had ceased working, but none of the others we tried seemed to help.

I reluctantly told Daniel what was going on, apologizing for what I perceived as a deficit in my character.

"I'm sorry this is happening again. I'm trying so hard not to let it."

"I know, A. Hang in there. We'll get through it."

The thoughts started around 2:00 a.m. Saturday morning on a cold day in early March of 2014. I woke up from a disturbed sleep. *"I want to die. I should kill myself. I deserve to die. I would be better off. Everyone in my life would be better off without me. I wouldn't be a burden any longer. Die. Die. Die."* The last thought felt like a spike in my brain, much like the migraine had months ago. I tried to fight the thoughts for hours. With my reasonable side. With my logical side. To no avail.

By 5:00 a.m. I gave up trying. I padded into the kitchen and swallowed thirty capsules of Cymbalta because that's all I had. I wasn't sure if it was enough to kill me, but I was hoping it was.

"Is there anything else I can do for you?" The doctor's voice cut through my reverie. I had not died. I had gotten sick, taken a cab to the emergency room and wound up on the cardiac floor of a medical hospital attached to a heart monitor.

I hesitated. The tears started again. Through them I asked the doctor if he would call my brother. Fifteen minutes later he returned with a phone in his hand. "Your brother wants to speak to you."

I sobbed into the phone. "Danny, I'm so sorry. Please don't be mad at me. I'm okay," I lied. "I'm so sorry. Please don't be angry. I love you."

He listened to me cry for a long time, just listened to me sob and breathe, breathe and sob. "It'll be okay. I'll come down tomorrow afternoon."

I gave the phone back to the doctor, he looked at me and gently nodded. I turned over and tried for I don't how many times that day not to cry but I couldn't hold back.

Sometime the next afternoon, Daniel walked in but seemed to fly into the room, appearing from nowhere. I tried to get up from the bed and he reached down and pulled me up and I stood close to him. He wrapped his arms around me and I reached up to him and wrapped my arms around his thick chest and we hugged tight. For a long time.

"Danny I'm so sorry. Please I'm sorry. I didn't mean to hurt you. Everything just hurt so much. I just didn't know what to do. Nothing was working anymore. Please don't let me go. Please just hold me." The last sentence came out as a whimper.

"Shhh," he whispered and held me tightly. He just held me and didn't let go. I didn't want him to let go. He was my brother; our mother was dead, our father was dead, he was a father, but he was all I had.

I don't know how much longer we stood there, I on my tiptoes, he holding me tight pressed to his chest, my arms clasped around him, but finally he eased me back down to my bed and folded the covers back over me.

Sitting down in a chair the nurse brought in, he sat down and our eyes met. "Hey," he said softly. "I'm here for you always. You never ever have to be afraid to tell me anything."

"I was so afraid," I sobbed. "I didn't want to be a bother. You have your own life and your own stuff going on."

He reached out, took my hand and squeezed it and put it back. "Wanna see a picture of your niece? She's sitting at the bar by the pool in Puerto Rico.

I smiled. "Yeah, let me see my niece downing one." He pulled out his phone and showed me a photo of a six-year-old girl with pink sunglasses sitting at the bar in front of a pool with turquoise water behind her. Emma was sipping a pink concoction with an umbrella in it through a straw and grinning wildly for the camera.

We chatted calmly. I was trying hard, very hard not to cry. He asked me what was going to happen now and I told him I was going to be transferred over to New York Presbyterian, a psychiatric hospital, probably tomorrow morning. "Danny, it's starting all over again. I had a good run but now I don't know."

"We'll make it. I love you, all right?" He stood up, stretching, all six feet of him. "I gotta go. Let me know what's going on every step of the way." As swiftly as he had entered the room, he was gone.

IV
DISCOVERY

ANN PODRACKY

GOSSIP AND LOVE

Even the maintenance men were talking. During a time and in a neighborhood where things like this were not supposed to happen, my brother Bernard had gotten Libby Goldstein pregnant. Libby was in her last year of high school and Bernard, admired for winning the school science fair for three years in a row, had just entered college in upstate New York on a scholarship. For the first time in all our years of living in Arverne in the Rockaways, my family had become the main topic of project gossip.

The neighbor gossips, whose heads seemed eternally wrapped in fat pink sponge curlers, said my father was suicidal because Bernard was his first-born son. They said Libby's parents didn't care because they thought their daughter was a whore anyway. If there was a wedding, Libby's parents had already told the Maniscalos in 2A that they would not pay for the liquor.

One day, three of the gossip offspring, hanging upside down on the monkey bars in the project playground, shouted to me, "Is it true your brother stuck his thing in that girl and got her pregnant?"

"They love each other," I shouted back. I was ten years old and crazy for teenage romance books.

Still hanging upside down, the three of them broke into a chant, "Your brother's penis loves her hole. Your brother's penis loves her hole." I ran from them into my building's unlit stairwell. Sitting on one of the dark green metal steps, I closed my eyes and imagined the taunters' feet and hands losing their grip on the monkey bars. I pictured their bodies falling slowly headfirst onto the concrete ground. Death by monkey bars. Besides reading romance books, I had also grown fond of wishing death to people I considered mean.

The following day when my father announced to my younger brother Frank and me, "Your big brother's getting married," I was relieved. A brief meeting between Libby's parents and mine, over cheesecake and instant coffee, had already taken place. It was agreed that Bernard and Libby would be married in the basement of a rabbi in another neighborhood. "I'm not giving up handball practice for that," Frank told my father and my father did not get as angry as I'd expected.

The rabbi's basement had orange floor tiles. Libby and I were the only ones smiling at the ceremony. The only girl in my family, I looked forward to having a sister-in-law.

For their honeymoon, my parents drove Bernard and Libby to a motel on Cross Bay Boulevard. I sat in the front of the car, wearing a thick plaid winter coat, squashed between the worried looks on my parents' faces. As the streetlights flashed into the car I turned my head back to look at the newlyweds. I wanted to see what young love looked like.

Bernard and Libby were sitting apart from one another.

"I'm going to read my books tonight," Bernard announced.

"No, you're not," Libby said. She winked at me as she moved closer to my brother and took his hand. I forgot the look on my parents' faces. It was winter but suddenly I could smell the ocean.

SHARON LEDER

IN SISTERHOOD

The last time I saw my sister Rachel, in a flowered moo-moo, love beads and blonde braids, she was behind the wheel of the Red Squirrel, waving good-by to me from Gate 40, the Port Authority. She was eighteen.

A year later, 1974, I knew Rachel was still in trouble, when she called me from the Church of Perfect Planetary Peace in Portland, Oregon. She was quitting the church. She was disillusioned with Mark, the church's spiritual leader, and would no longer be driving the Red Squirrel, their cross-country bus.

I was twenty-six, living in a commune with five other women in a dilapidated but stately brownstone on East Fourth, around the corner from the Men's Shelter and the Hell's Angels. I was getting a divorce from a marriage gone bad, working days as a waitress on 14th Street, nights as a graduate assistant teaching English Composition at City College. Reading *Sisterhood Is Powerful* and *The Dialectics of Sex,* I began questioning religion too, but in a different way than my sister. If women weren't to be kept down, maybe traditional religions needed a complete overhaul.

Over the phone, Rachel told me she had been sleeping with Mark and hoped to become Mrs. Mark, the mother, so-to-speak, of the church community. "Before I discovered the church was a front for drug-trafficking," she said, "I learned that Mark was promiscuous. I wasn't jealous, Sara. I just couldn't accept his not making me Wife Number One; you know, to lead the church with him. There's nothing for me in Portland anymore."

How had Rachel become so screwed up? How could Mark, a Jesus look-alike who shook my hand feebly at Port Authority, have bewitched my intelligent, resourceful sister? She was born into the same cultural Judaism as me. Why in hell's name did she mix herself up with a fake guru, a drug-pushing womanizer? Why didn't she follow Kabbalah, if she wanted a more spiritual connection? Utterly torn, I felt a knee-jerk response to save Rachel from ruin, an angry need to challenge her low self-esteem and male dependency, and a self-protective urge not to complicate my already hanging-on-a-limb life.

At City College, my PhD dissertation advisor expected to see my Chapter One in a month. A bald spot had already appeared from stress on my brown-haired head. How would I meet my deadline with a loose kid sister on my hands? Minding Rachel and sticking to my writing would be difficult, I thought, yet she could benefit from the order my commune afforded, the routines.

"We have room," I finally said, "but we also have rules. We rotate cleaning and shopping, we have weekly house meetings, and we're all in psychotherapy. The system would be good for you."

"I don't need a shrink," she blurted. "Waive the dumb therapy requirement."

"Can't," I said. "Take it or leave it. Plus we chip in for rent and groceries."

"No problem there," Rachel chirped. "I have a waitressing job lined up a few blocks from your commune."

"Huh," I managed. "How did that happen?"

"Mark's connections. He considers me one of his wives and set me up with the owner of the Dolly Deli."

In no time, Rachel attached herself romantically to Bernie, the deli owner, a greasy man approaching middle age, trying to make the Dolly Deli compete with the famous Second Avenue Deli, two blocks away. Rachel became a favorite with the regulars, the one she talked about the most being Major Bill, a former military man in his sixties whose diabetes was wearing his body down. She earned great tips and soon moved out of the commune into her own apartment. I could hardly believe how swiftly she was putting the broken pieces of her life together. Maybe, I thought, I can focus on my writing again.

But one night, before Rachel moved out, she sat me down in the kitchen, after the others had gone to bed. Outside, I heard homeless men shuffling towards the shelter.

"Sara, give me one reason to continue living," she said.

I sat there dumbfounded, frightened. Rachel had been making so much progress, I had no idea she was depressed.

"See, you can't," she said. "That's why I'm leaving the commune."

I looked at Rachel's pale face, her sandy hair and full lips. I had that sinking sense of failure and guilt I used to have when I babysat for her and couldn't stop her crying.

Now I said to her, "I can only give you the reason I have for living. I can't give you your reason. That has to come from you."

"Intellectual bullshit," she said.

"But Rachel, you're creating your own reasons—you drove cross country, lived out west among strangers, formed an intimate relationship. It didn't work out. Fine! You picked yourself up, returned home, found a job, an apartment of your own."

"That's surviving," she said. "Not living. I can survive, but the question is why should I want to?"

I hoped her sad question didn't mean she had already given up. I hoped she was still searching.

"I thought I found my place with Mark, but I was wrong."

So, was it only a man who could save Rachel? "Why Mark?" I asked her. "Why a church? And now, why Bernie?"

"I thought Mark's church would be a love community. I thought he would lead me to God." She looked at me with heavy-lidded eyes. "But Mark let me down. And *your* commune doesn't run on love, either. Bernie may not love me yet, but he says his customers love me, and the deli needs me. Maybe with Bernie, God won't let me down . . . again."

❧   ❧   ❧

"What good is God?" Rachel had wanted to know ten years ago when our father died, from a long illness.

It was a large question, but our mother, who was now forced to work for the first time since she was a teenager, and who was distraught and overwhelmed by our loss, answered Rachel mechanically: "Daddy's *with* God now, where he should be." We were a family of untutored Jews, almost totally assimilated. Our mother naively believed the folklore of *bashert*, that events, good and bad, were meant to be.

I remember Rachel crying out, "Then, I want the God Daddy's with to tell *me* what to do. Why doesn't God talk to me?"

❧   ❧   ❧

When our mother remarried, Rachel latched onto Stanley like a needy kitten. Stanley, a refugee who fled anti-Semitism in Romania, told Rachel if she worked hard, she'd have a good life. When he recounted the oppression and poverty his family experienced in the old country, and he blessed America for religious freedom, Rachel hung onto every word.

But our mother and Stanley divorced. Rachel watched our mother struggle joylessly to support our family on her own, working two jobs, night and day. Rachel wanted to know why the *bashert* world God created was filled with disappointment and suffering. It was then Rachel, at fifteen, attempted to take her life, thankfully without success.

Rachel overate, expanded like a yeast roll, and played hooky from high school before following Mark and driving the Red Squirrel cross-country. She must have concluded that life wasn't worth living without a man. And she must have believed that the God of love Mark purported to embody was different from the God who accepted people's pain as meant to be, like our mother had said.

My mother's life led me in a different direction. She was a high school dropout during the Great Depression and was raised to find a husband, unprepared for life on her own.

Determined never to be dependent on anyone, I went to college and joined a consciousness-raising cell of Redstockings, a nationwide movement of diverse women who sought to change society to improve women's lives. Traditional religion seemed to be part of the problem, not the solution, and goddesses, rather than God, offered succor to some. So, when my early marriage needed dissolution, I left it, thinking marriage was the problem, not a hard-hearted God. Being single is no tragedy, I thought, and women could change the world if they had greater autonomy. They needed to find, and follow, their *own* drummers.

✤   ✤   ✤

I felt guilty that I couldn't keep close tabs on Rachel at the deli because I was working two jobs and trying to meet my writing deadline. When I did drop in, Rachel served me coffee but had no time to chat. She'd zoom past Major Bill at a corner table and lift latkes off his plate. She'd smile at me and say: "Just snacking."

Her uniform was getting snug around her chest.

✤   ✤   ✤

After a year, Rachel looked completely different. From collar to calf she wore a long apron. Her cheeks filled out like two oversized plums, and her hair was pushed into a kerchief, like a Russian *babushka*. She danced around the deli, serving tables, carving roasts, greeting customers, telling jokes. Did I know this Rachel? On the phone, she was upbeat, spoke about fixing up her new place, learning the ropes at the deli, and "becoming tight," as she put it, with Bernie.

Her dramatic changes made me suspicious. Though I was Rachel's senior, she suddenly looked older than me—full-bosomed with sandy hair, appearing ashen. I was a pencil compared to her. How could she have turned from the quintessential lovechild into a seasoned hostess and savvy shop manager? I asked my landlord, Arnold, about her boss, Bernie. Arnold knew everyone in the neighborhood. He told me the Dolly Deli was failing and the Mafia was supporting it.

"Rachel, you don't know what you're doing," I told her over the phone. "Bernie's involved with Mafia. He's too old for you, in his forties. You're just a baby. You were just allowed to vote. You know the kind of women he sees. What's wrong with you?"

"I have more of life's encyclopedia in my little pinky than you have in both hands," she snapped. "What business in New York *hasn't* rubbed elbows with Mafia? I know Bernie's imperfect, no man of God. He's afraid of the big commitment, sees floozies for sex. But he says he needs me in the deli." She smirked. "It needs to dawn on him we have a damned good relationship. We're *bashert.*"

"Are you sleeping with him?"

"Not yet," she laughed. She began scheming about how to convince Bernie to pop the question. If that didn't work, she'd propose to him herself. I was terrified she was caught in a web of money, sex, and intrigue she wouldn't be able to escape. I could only think of platitudes: "Think before you swim," I told her; "there are other fish in the sea."

"You sound just like Mom!"

"Okay, then," I said. "Come with me to consciousness-raising."

"No thanks! I don't want your cockamamie, alternate lifestyles. I found my kind of love."

"Damn it, Rachel," I said. "Grow up on your own." At the same time, my heart broke not knowing how to steer her out of the rut she was digging for herself.

✤   ✤   ✤

A few months later, Rachel called saying it was urgent that I come to her apartment. "I'm quitting the deli," she announced. "I'm moving in with Major Bill."

"But Rachel, you're a magnificent waitress. You're making a living."

Tears streamed down her face. "I proposed to Bernie last night. The jerk refused me. I've slaved for him in the restaurant, turned the place around. For what? I can't wait tables there anymore. Too humiliating. I'm moving to Coney Island with Major Bill."

"You can't mean that old guy in the World War II uniform."

"That's him. He'll let me live rent-free in exchange for my being his home care aide. He'll pay me extra for assisting him in his accounting business."

"I can't see you with Bill. This is nonsense. You've got to stop this, Rachel!" I felt like shaking her, but I took her hand.

"Let go of me!" she cried, wiggling away. She rose off the couch and floated toward the third story window overlooking Second Avenue, crowded with wheeler-dealers, hookers, bums, bikers, students, and hipsters. Seeing her lift the sash, I thought she was about to fling herself onto the street. I lunged forward to stop her, when she swiveled around and said brightly, "You're dead wrong about Bill. No one else in the God-damned world has given me the reason for living."

"What's the reason?"

She lifted two books off a snack table. "Bill turned me on to Machiavelli and Ayn Rand," she said, waving copies of *The Prince* and *Atlas Shrugged* in my face. "We're on this earth to prove they're wrong!"

I agreed with her completely, but I needed to know what she was getting at. "What do you mean?"

"They say the world is like countries at war, and peace is just our superficial stand-still from the real action of life."

"So, the reason for living?" I repeated.

"Discipline," Rachel said. "God wants us to master the violence that fills the world. We fight tooth and nail for our own little piece of pie, clobbering everyone in our way. We need to figure out how to meet our needs without running all over the other guy, so that the world doesn't turn out to be one huge hell hole." She beamed at me, like she'd finally found the God she'd been searching for.

Her language was rough, but I had to admit, her insight was good. She wanted a better, fairer world, like the activists I was reading. But was it that kind of discipline my sister needed? She wasn't clobbering anybody. "Since when have *you* been hurting people?" I asked. "If you move in with Bill, you'll be his servant. You'll be giving up your freedom. Isn't freedom as important as discipline? Didn't God free the slaves from Egypt?"

"Your version of freedom is just egotistic self-interest," she shouted. "I've been reading Baba Ram Das *Be Here Now* and Meher Baba."

Words flew out of my mouth. "You want someone to show you the way? I'll show you a much better way than Bill's, or Bernie's, or Mark's."

"Really?" Her voice rose several octaves. "What's the way?"

"Move back into the commune, enroll in City College where I teach Composition. I'll help you write your assignments. No one has to know. You can write about the new play at the Lafayette, *For Colored Girls Who've Considered Suicide When the Rainbow Is Enuf.* Tranzania Beverly has this fabulous insight at the end of the play: 'I found God in myself and she is beautiful.'"

The hopeful light in Rachel's eyes snuffed out. "You don't know me at all. I'm in trouble, but your plan isn't for me. You have your academic schemes— be a teacher, write a book. I'm the blue-collar member of the family. With Bill, I'll learn home care, accounting, discipline, and put my life in order. Bill says I'm a victim of permissiveness. No thanks, Sis. I have to do this my way."

✤　✤　✤

Meanwhile, my dissertation advisor wrote a searing comment in red on my draft of Chapter One of The Fiction of New England Writer Elizabeth Drew Stoddard: "You're not supposed to be writing a feminist manifesto."

Why the heck not? I thought, my face boiling. Why is he unsympathetic to my approach?

A strange impulse overcame me. Rachel hadn't called me since she moved in with Major Bill. I had mailed her my chapter because I wanted her to know how I was spending my time. Given her penchant for reading, I thought she could offer a thoughtful response. I decided to call her. Seven a.m. "I know it's early," I said. "But I figured with Bill's discipline, you might be up."

"We're up. We're heading to Vegas."

"Vegas?"

"Major Bill's seeing big clients, Eddie Murphy, Phyllis Diller."

Sure, I thought, disbelieving. What grandiosity in this Bill!

"Everything okay?" she asked

"My advisor sent my chapter back. It took me months to write it. Now he wants revision."

"Why?"

"He wants biography, not feminist analysis. He wants me to write about Stoddard's family, her education, her attitude towards children."

"Maybe your advisor wants help seeing Elizabeth more fully," she said. "If he knew what her parents were like, who her teachers were, whether she was loved, maybe he'd see her more the way you do. Don't you sympathize better if you know where the person is coming from?"

I was floored. There was sense in what she said, more sense than I, in my anger, could come upon. Was my advisor finding ways to support me through the system? I felt so compelled to prove a woman writer's *work* needed more attention than her *life*, I hadn't trusted my advisor to be on my side. "Maybe you're right about my advisor," I said reluctantly.

"You've delved into your subject," she said. "Anyone who reads your chapter can tell. You just have to say what you know differently."

Was this my sister speaking? I considered her words. Maybe there *was* a way to show Stoddard's fiction flowing from her experience and becoming transformed into art. I had to laugh at myself. Here I had been trying to mold my sister in *my* image.

"You know, if you're in trouble, Sara," she said, "I'll change my plans. I'll be in the Village in no time."

Rachel stunned me into silence. I felt deeply tied to her. Finally, I asked, "What about Bill? Doesn't he expect you to be in Vegas with him?"

"Family emergency trumps everything," she said. "You helped me, remember?"

I remembered. "What were you doing again in Vegas?" I asked.

She told me about the stars she and Bill would be doing accounting for, their acts she'd be seeing on stage. She sounded happy. "Enjoy Vegas!" I said. "I wish you both a wonderful trip."

I hung up the phone, still concerned about my sister, but at least with the knowledge she was creating her own path, however strange it seemed to me. I brewed a cup of coffee and wondered: Has Rachel heard from God? In no time, I began rewriting Chapter One.

ELAINE P. MORGAN

THERE'S ALWAYS ANOTHER WAY

After both of our parents died, my fifty-three-year-old sister came to live with me. She was an intellectually challenged adult who had been kept at home and protected from the outside world for all of her life. She arrived telling me, "I can't" because our mother always told her she couldn't because she was "retarded." I was a fifty-five year old who was accustomed to thinking I could.

My sister's "laundry list" of what she couldn't do included learning how to draw her own bath water, learning to tie her own shoelaces, learning to operate a microwave, learning to wash her hair and learning to identify colors. The solutions to these problems were simple. I told her to put her head under the faucet, scrub with shampoo and then rinse. I tagged the buttons on the microwave and told her to press her finger on the "tagged only" buttons. Also, to wear loafer shoes without shoelaces and how to run water in the bathtub and to test the water before diving in. I also told her I would help her to learn colors and arrange for art lessons to shore up what I would be attempting to teach her. I wasn't sure if she could learn colors but I told her we would give it our best shot. I also imparted my philosophy for living to her, "If you can't do something one way, there's always another way which will work for you. Let's see if Mom was wrong. Okay?" I, of course, was not sure my philosophy would apply to her but I loved her enough to give it a try. I wasn't trained in any area of education for people such as herself but I figured I would simply "play it by ear."

Our color lessons began at breakfast that winter. I would hold fruit in my hand and repeat, "This is a banana. It is yellow. This is an apple. It is red. This is an orange. It is the color orange. That dog is black. That dog is white. My hair is gray." When spring and summer arrived, the lessons encompassed my pointing and repeating, "The sky is blue. The grass is green. This flower is pink. That flower is purple." One morning, tears flooded my eyes when I asked my sister what was the color of the outfit she was wearing and she answered, "Banana yellow." I shouted, "That's right! You can do it, Sis!"

The problem of "I can't read" was more perplexing for me. Also very distressing for my sister as she was aware of her inability and often said, "I can't read like you," until the day I found photos in a magazine of aboriginal cave wall paintings dating back a few thousand years. I was then able to show my sister with credibility that people didn't always have the alphabet to write with so they instead drew pictures for people to "read" in order to communicate with each other. I then proceeded to teach my sister how to read labels on cans and boxes, picture signs on highways, restaurants, public restrooms and supermarket logos. She also learned how to separate the dog food from the cat food by observing the pictures of the animals on the cans, as well as identifying cans of vegetables, fruits and brand names of boxes of tea and cereals, among many other food and beverage products. In addition, photos accompanying newspapers and magazine articles, as well as the covers on paperback and hardcover novels.

I also taught my sister to read the expressions on the faces of people and animals on books and magazines. I would then ask her "Who is happy? Who is sad? Who is tired? Who is angry?" She became very proficient at reading these expressions as well.

I reminded my sister that she was not blind and that anything she saw, could interpret and then tell me or anyone else what it meant was called "reading." I said, "This is the way people used to read before the alphabet was invented." The following year my sister told me there was an automobile accident on Main Street. I asked her how she knew it. She replied, "I read it in the newspaper." I felt a lump in my throat and tears flooded my eyes as I realized my intellectually challenged sister had mastered the "art of reading" with the capacity she had. She then began referring to herself as someone who could read. As a result, she became more and more positive about exploring the other hidden abilities she did possess.

When my sister arrived to live with me, I initially thought our relationship would be a "one-way street." I eventually learned I was mistaken. My intellectually challenged sister was my teacher and, sitting at her feet, I learned there truly is always another way and that anyone's poor self-image and self-esteem could be transformed through love, patience and the art of mirroring their positive yet hidden abilities.

Today, I don't have to think "I could" anymore. I know I can because of her.

DEBORAH BURCH-LAVIS

AM I MY SISTER'S DAUGHTER?

I stood looking out over the desolate graveyard after my sister's funeral. Only a few family members lingered, including my two nieces, Tammy—or Sissy as I always called her—and Cynthia, and the oldest of my three nephews, Bill. The graveyard appeared neglected. Dirt dominated more than grass, and the graves bore few markers and very few flowers. The empty graveyard seemed to go on endlessly and resembled a desert more than the coastal prairie in which it was placed. Only a couple of misshapen, solitary scrub oak trees in the distance broke the monotony. Would my sister Tamah be dismayed to know she would be resting in such a place?

Interrupting my musing, Sissy moved closer to me and said, "You know, Cynthia always thought you might be our sister instead of our aunt."

"What? What made her think that?" I asked, stunned that my nieces would have discussed this possibility and curious at the timing. Why now at her mother's funeral would my niece raise this question? Memories and regrets surfaced for me around Tamah's death. An aching sadness had moved into my consciousness next to the loneliness and melancholy that still colored most of my waking hours since my mother's death only six months back. I assumed Tamah's children must be experiencing similar emotions. What did the possibility of my being their sister instead of their aunt have to do with anything they were feeling?

Sissy continued, "You know, you are so close to us in age, with only eighteen months between you and Bill. And out of all the photos of Grandma and my mother, we thought it strange that we never saw one of Grandma pregnant or with you as a newborn."

"Strange, maybe, but then there aren't many of my mother overall. Also, I can't believe your mother could've kept this kind of secret or that she would've let your Grandma and Grandpa provide for me in ways she claimed they never provided for her. She was too jealous, don't you think?"

"True, she was very jealous of you, but have you ever wondered?"

"My birth certificate shows your Grandma and Grandpa as my parents, and I found the registration of my birth in the official government records for Harris County."

"Don't you think since Grandpa was a lawyer, he could've altered those records?"

"Perhaps, but I doubt it."

I was caught off guard by my nieces discussing the notion of my being their sister. I didn't know the tale my mother told me years ago had surfaced among my sister's children. According to my mother, the gossips in Liberty, Texas, a small East Texas town halfway between Beaumont and Houston, had circulated the rumor I was Tamah's illegitimate child.

My mother in one of her tirades against Liberty said, "Those people can be vicious. You know, they spread that spiteful story you were Tamah's child."

"No, I didn't know. Why would they say something like that?" I asked.

"Who knows? People envied Tamah. She was pretty and popular. You wouldn't believe the boyfriends she had. When your grandfather heard it, he told your father to do something about it."

"What did Daddy do?"

"He moved us to Houston, away from the gossips. It was mean and typical of those people, but let's not talk about it anymore." I was shocked to hear this story, but I was not surprised that people would have questions. Tamah was sixteen years older than I, and my mother was forty when I was born. I am sure the move to Houston added to the rumors more than quieted them. I had questions, but I had learned never to cross my mother, so I kept quiet, thinking I might ask them later. However, I never did.

Knowing about this rumor helped bring some clarity to a few of the mysteries in my life. I understood for the first time why my mother dragged out my birth certificate to show my new friends after we moved back to Liberty when I was ten. It embarrassed me, and I had no idea why she did it. I guessed it was another of her attempts to create status for us, although I did not see how a birth certificate contributed. This ritual somehow seemed connected to her animosity toward Liberty, but again, I did not understand. All I knew was that she hated the town and was obsessed with maintaining the *right* position in Liberty society.

Liberty was my father's hometown. His father owned one of the largest construction companies in town and several rent houses. They were a well-known family, with my grandfather running for county commissioner and my father for county attorney. My father loved Liberty, proud that when he walked down Main Street and to the courthouse, everyone called him by name. He felt at home, but my mother did not.

My mother was born in Newton, a small East Texas town close to the Louisiana border, where her father served as County Judge and owned a saw mill and acres of timber land. My mother was obsessed with being *somebody*, the people in this world who mattered she said. To her that meant they had money, political status, or were from a prominent family. She married my father because she thought he was one of those *somebodies*. As a lawyer from a well-respected family in the community, he was on his way to greatness in her eyes.

From the time I was ten until I married and left Liberty at eighteen, I watched my mother try to position us as important people in the town. She had us join the right church and the country club and pushed me into being a Rainbow Girl, an exclusive and secretive group of girls formed as a branch of the Masonic Lodge. She beamed when I came home having not been black balled. Each member voted on new members, and if only one were against someone, the girl received a black ball. On the other hand, my mother herself never socialized with anyone in the town, never attended the church, and never went to the country club.

She told my father often, "Liberty is hell on earth." She transferred much of her disdain for the town to me. I felt out of place with versions of city mouse and country mouse playing out for me in many of my interactions with my country peers. I often did not understand their colloquialisms or they mine. I ended up with a rock barely missing my head when a boy on the playground told me he was going to *chunk* a rock at me, and I will never forget the laughter when I called a sofa a *divan*. For me though it was the loss of anonymity the city provided that I missed. In Houston our movement and words were not of interest to anyone, but in Liberty, they were scrutinized and discussed. What the townspeople did not know, they made up. By the time the story had passed from one to another, to another and another, it had little truth left in it, the way the childhood game of Telephone works.

Bringing me out of my thoughts, Bill walked up and asked if we were ready to head home. I started to ask him if he had similar thoughts to his sisters but decided the idea was too fanciful for my sensible nephew to entertain. He and Sissy were the only of my sister's children to whom I had been close. We played together like brothers and sisters. I wondered could I indeed be one of my sister's children. Is Bill my brother and Sissy my sister? Thinking that way made calling her *Sissy* take on new meaning.

I imagined all of my nieces and nephews, two red heads and three blonds, and me as one family. While Sissy looks like her mother and a little like me, I do not resemble the rest of them. However, I do not look too much like my father either; only our olive skin tone was similar. He had black hair, brown eyes, a straight pointed nose, and a strong jaw with a broad smile. I have hazel eyes, reddish brown hair, a pug nose, and a weak pointed chin. My chin resembles my mother's more than my sister's, and my nose, my sister's more than my mother's. My mother had a prominent hooked nose ending in a point, blue eyes the color of the sky, red hair, and very pale skin. Like my father I could spend hours in the sun and tan, but my mother would burn in minutes. My sister had my mother's blue eyes, but her jaw was closer to Daddy's very square one. If I ran our faces through the FBI's face recognition software used on television, how many points of similarities would we have, I wondered.

I had not entertained these thoughts before, with any questions around my birth well below the surface of my consciousness until now. Sissy's inquiry launched me on a quest to determine if any possibility existed for the Liberty gossips to be spreading the truth for once. With my mother and sister gone, I felt compelled to explore who I am. I had postponed going through the family photos, letters, and files my mother had left behind since I was still recovering from losing her, but perhaps I would find some answers there.

On the four-hour drive back to Houston from Corpus Christi, I had plenty of time to think about my nieces' suspicions and talked to my second husband Jim about my own doubts.

"Do you think it's possible?" he asked me.

"I don't think so. You didn't know my sister, but we weren't close and haven't talked in years. Her selfishness when Daddy died and her destroying his will a few years before caused me to shut her out of my life."

"What do you mean by her *selfishness*?"

"She barged into my mother's house after Daddy died, loud, obnoxious, and drunk as usual. I tried to get her and her son, David, to go to a hotel nearby because I felt my mother wasn't up to company, but my sister refused. At the funeral, she created a scene when she was asked to ride in the second car in the procession. I think she was drunk then, too. When we got to the gravesite, she again ranted about how she was being treated as second fiddle, and she should be first with my family second. I was embarrassed and sad that my mother had to deal with my sister when she was so distraught over Daddy's death."

"She sounds like a troubled soul."

"True. I'm sure she was. I told you we believe she destroyed Daddy's will. That broke my heart. The will was handwritten as Daddy knew it had to be to be legal without witnesses in Texas."

I thought back to my mother's call when she found the will. She said, "Please come over now!" She was breathless, almost hysterical. She recognized my father would not be able to write another one. His macular degeneration had caused him to lose most of his vision, and the strokes he suffered resulted in his being confined to his bed, barely able to eat, and not able to read and write anymore. When I came into their house, my mother handed me the will, her hands shaking and her face scarlet. Written on lined notebook paper, it was distinctly my Daddy's writing; the penmanship careful and the words almost poetic, despite the legalese. Someone had torn off the back two pages and crossed out the dates and the names. Tears came to my eyes as I looked at it.

My mother said, "Who'd do such a thing?"

"I don't know. Who's been here?"

"No one, except your sister and that weasel Royce. Remember, they visited a few weekends ago. You don't think Tamah did this do you?"

"I certainly would hope not, but who else?"

Neither of us wanted to believe my sister had done such a thing, but despite my mother's low opinion of Tamah's second husband Royce, I suspected my sister more than him as the culprit. No one else had been in the house or would have had access or motive. I surmised from my mother's comments that Daddy had left more to my children and me should my mother no longer be living when he died than to Tamah. Tamah, who was known for flying into rages, particularly when drinking, must have been furious that our father had favored me in any way over her. Had her anger been so great she destroyed the will? She had placed it back in its hiding place among my Daddy's legal papers, probably hoping he would not find it, which would leave him to die intestate. Then, she and Royce would inherit the *boatload of money* they claimed my parents had.

Their frequent discussions about the money they would inherit were insulting and painful. I preferred my parents alive and well over any amount of money. I tried to correct their misconceptions about how much money my parents had. I told them my mother and father only had the house they lived in, what was left of the Liberty property, which was not much, and whatever savings they had accumulated. My mother, however, bragged about her inheritance from her father. I knew little about how much she inherited, but I suspected my mother exaggerated as she often did about her family and her money.

All of my life, my mother had supported our family on the small salary she made working as an operator at Southwestern Bell Telephone Company. Daddy, practicing law even after retirement, made very little money. My mother said he was too honest to be a rich lawyer. He frequently provided his legal expertise to people who could not afford to pay him. He simply wanted to help them.

Until we moved back to Liberty, I witnessed his drinking keeping him at the local bar more than at work. Once back in his hometown, where he joined his college roommate's law practice, Daddy stopped drinking, but his income was half of what my mother's was. His primary income once he retired was Social Security and the money he and his brother collected from the few remaining rent houses. Watching Tamah and Royce covet a huge inheritance coming their way caused me to resent my sister. I had trouble understanding such selfishness.

While I looked over Daddy's will, my mother's flushed face hovered over me. I was sure this episode had caused her already elevated blood pressure to rise dangerously high. "Please find a lawyer for us right away," my mother pleaded. "Your Daddy wants a new will, and I need to do one, too."

Once my mother and father had created new wills, they were much more at ease, but every time they saw me for the next few months, they would bring up my sister's actions, clearly still distressed. My father and my sister argued every time she would visit before the defacing of the will; I imagined if his health had allowed, he would have confronted her if he saw her. However, he never had a chance. Shortly after the new wills were created, he was hospitalized. We tried to get my sister to come see him. She refused, saying her health was too bad, which was a common excuse she used anytime they needed anything. Now, I wonder if she was afraid to face him and perhaps felt some guilt over what she had done; however, I suspected she carried no guilt. She either was not well enough or did not want to inconvenience herself. She showed up only after he was gone, to attend his funeral and I suspected to check to see that the defaced will was still in its hiding place.

A few weeks after my father's funeral, my mother called me. "Your sister called today wanting to know when your Daddy's will is to be probated."

"That's a strange question, don't you think. What did you tell her?"

"That it doesn't need to be probated. She said she was going to the courthouse to find out for herself."

"Don't worry, Mama. She will learn everything went to you, as Daddy wanted and as it should."

"You know, I wish she'd just leave well enough alone."

If my sister went to the courthouse, we never found out, and she never said any more about it. Within a year of my father's death, my mother moved in with me, and I took care of her until she died almost ten years after my father. During that time, my sister never visited, but she called my mother every week. They would talk like a couple of close friends, discussing the plots of the soap operas they both watched, but my mother never asked her about the will as far as I know and never brought it up with me again either.

I could not let it go though and after Sissy's questions, I imagined a plot right at home in my mother's and sister's soap opera world to explain my sister's actions. Perhaps her destruction of the will was connected to her giving me up when I was born. I imagined agreements between my sister and our parents. What if I were her child and she had struck a deal with them to give me up if she would someday be their sole heir. She bought her freedom and secured her future by giving me to them. Maybe that explained her extreme anger over the will and her motivation to destroy it. Although an interesting story, I suspect jealousy, perhaps sibling rivalry, motivated my sister more than any kind of deeply hidden family secret.

Whatever motivated her, the will episode and all of the other examples of selfishness I witnessed caused me to avoid my sister. I never visited her and exchanged only a few words when she called to talk to my mother. Since she is gone, I regret not talking to her before it was too late.

Now, I only have family photographs. Looking at them, I see me as a baby in my sister's arms. Tamah looks so young and attractive. She would have been only sixteen years old. The photos must have been taken shortly before she ran away from home to marry her first husband Garry, who joined the Army soon after they eloped. The two of them rarely returned to see me, my mother, or my father.

My sister told me when I was older that she married so young because she had to babysit me all the time. She decided if she were going to have to take care of a baby, it might as well be her own. And that was how it was. She gave birth to Bill eighteen months after I was born and then in another eighteen months, came Sissy, then three more children in succession about every two years following. When she got to five children, she stopped. The contact I had with her and her children consisted mostly of our summer vacations to visit them on whatever Army post they were living, places such as Leavenworth, Kansas, Fort Leonard Wood, Missouri, Omaha, Nebraska, and Bloomington, Minnesota. We would pack up the car and drive until we got to the trailer park or other base housing. We would spend a week with my sister's family and then drive back home. They came to visit us, but not often. My memories of those times when I was six or seven are of sitting for hours in my tiny blue rocking chair stationed at the front door so that I could see the minute their car pulled into the driveway.

In the family photos, I found none with my mother holding me and only a few of her sitting with me while I played in the yard. I also found no photos of my mother pregnant, but none of my sister either. In those years, women probably would not have wanted their photos taken when pregnant. The romance of the baby bumps so popular in today's social media had not yet emerged.

In the spirit of the *Who's your Daddy?* billboards that had sprouted up around Houston, my niece sent me two photos of men she did not know that she found in her mother's house after the funeral. She believed them to be my sister's boyfriends when she lived in Liberty. Both men had dark, curly hair and dark eyes, and they were wearing T-shirts and jeans. They looked very much like James Dean. One was standing next to a motorcycle and one next to a car. I wondered, is it possible one of these men might be my father? The photos did not give me the answers I sought.

So, I started digging through the files my mother and father left behind. In them, I found my original birth certificate. I also found a request for a maternity leave of absence my mother submitted to the telephone company for six months around the time of my birth date. Would she have requested or gotten such a leave if not pregnant? I doubt it.

My niece collected some of her mother's hair and I had some of my mother's. I considered having the DNA analyzed but decided against it. I did send in my saliva to a Web site, which determines DNA and maps it to country origin and closest relatives. With it, I found out that I am related to my mother's side of the family with a very high DNA connection to my first cousin, her brother's son. While the DNA relationships are not as clear on my father's side, I have found nothing yet to suggest he is not my father.

Where does that leave me? Am I my sister's daughter? I think not. Why can't I answer with a definitive, "No, I am not"? Why the doubt? I wonder if it would even matter. What change would it make in who I am? I would have had a different life as a child. Instead of being reared as an only child, I would have been the oldest of six children. Instead of the feeling I always had of loneliness, the emptiness and absence of any family connections when growing up, and the sense of being out of time with parents old enough to be my grandparents, I would have been surrounded by others and moved often from Army post to Army post. So, yes, it would matter in that the surface of my life would have been different, but would I be?

Although not of the magnitude of the life changing family secrets from one of Faulkner's novels, my birthright does matter to me, not as some overwhelming question on which my entire being hinges, but more as a nagging feeling of uneasiness. The blood and DNA that make up the biological me would be roughly the same if my sister is my mother. However, if Tamah is my mother, who is my father? The father I knew was the one who took care of me most of my life. I love him so much and was much closer to him than to my mother. I do not want to give him up as my father, blood or not.

I also can't help but marvel at how my sister and mother played the roles they did all my life. My mother often created stories around the events in her life, many exaggerated and more myth than reality, but this one would have been huge to have achieved. I doubt my sister or mother could have kept such a secret and deceived me and others for so many years.

My exploration into who I am leaves me believing what I want to believe. I am not sure that I am not my sister's daughter, but I am sure my mother and father are the ones I remember as my parents. My sister I choose to continue to see as only my sister. With all of them gone, I cannot ask them, but I wonder if I could, would they tell me the truth now? I doubt it. The truth we lived was the truth they created and the only reality I know.

LORETTA DIANE WALKER

BREAKING THE ICE

We cannot speak of him—the weather remains a safe topic,
fills empty beats of silence so we don't have to reveal ourselves.

Winter's early morning light drips
from the bare branches
of a chinaberry tree.

Streamers of toilet paper are interlopers
in my neighbor's yard,
waving where leaves normally shake
under the wind's nervous hands.

Some child thought this prank funny.
Maybe fate smiled at us, too?
The way she brought us together.

The church where we gather has a gloomy face.
Neither light nor trees can change its disposition.
Perhaps the black hearse parked outside
highjacked its joy.

Linked by blood and shock,
we meet for the first time.
Grief clogs the air while we look for him
in each other's faces.
Our names are listed like royalty in the obituary,
written as though we grew together.

Outside bewilderment dancing around us,
choreographed by betrayal.
My friend leads me by the arm like a wounded puppy
and gives a voice to the mystery.
She says my name, introduces you as my sister.
We exchange greetings
with the finesse of polite strangers.

Silence keeps a steady beat on our tongues
while we hold each other with our eyes.
This is the only comfort we have to offer
one another while our father lays in his coffin.
The answers to our unasked questions are sealed
in his cold mouth.

MAUREEN TOLMAN FLANNERY

FISHING FOR FATHER

1. First Indications from the Unknown Half-Sister

. . . and then she says from somewhere out of left field
I think your father was my father too while I am thinking I don't even know
you and who the hell are you to be claiming my dad who had only two
daughters and you're not one of them but then she goes on with her story
of fractured childhood on the cliff-rim of existence always inches from the
plunge into the canyon of hunger and her beautiful mother beaten but not
beaten down abandoned young by a brutal drunk of a husband who had
dragged them among the west's transients from bunk house to mining camp
sheep wagon to rental shack lacking every convenience barely protected from
predators of the wild by my father the clandestine benefactor of their marginal
lives until I wonder how to convey my sorrow over the girlhood she does not
regret with its disastrous lessons blessings miracles since I'm flooded with
guilt about the unearned ease of my life having felt always entitled as the child
of the landed because the rancher was my father so that I could anticipate
everything easy just because I had been born to the woman he married and
not the one he must have loved and by what specious privilege did I expect to
be ranch-housed and helped with homework comforted always with paternal
attention even a horse or a prairie dog if I so much as mentioned it

2. *Comparing Memories with the Half-Sister*

Find breach in his being, a fissure between the secrets
and a man unlikely to have them.

Two sisters and their half-sister, formerly unknown,
might miter the misfit edges,

join the gapped corners of a life already over,
pull fallibility into the frame of his goodness.

Their discordant recollections could, even now,
piece together

the light-hearted life of everyone's party
with the sullen spouse who'd walk out on his wife's tirades

the dutiful husband
with the passionate lover of some other life

the dance-with-me dad
with the unacknowledged giver of mysterious gifts

the respected family man
with the clandestine caretaker of someone else's family

the charmer
with the man disarmed by what might come to pass

the fisherman
with a one unable to clean his own catch

the rancher
with the man who brought provisions to the hired man's shed

the admired community leader
with the meeter of strangers in dark places

the church elder
with the self-blaming, self-proclaimed sinner.

Invite them all to the table,
the altar where we are all related.

3. Test Results
Eighty-five percent probability of sibling kinship

85% accurate accusation that my father
was loving another woman when I was one year old

a cold hard DNA explanation
for my mother's possessive hold on her own girls
why she became ever more demanding
and less content as he met each new demand

15% chance her reactions were irrational

low odds his heart was ever hers after that
high likelihood she always felt unloved
had reasons for not trusting
for thrusting herself into the arms of her church

genetic explanation for her chronic displeasure
with a seemingly easy life
why she didn't encourage me to be a ranch girl
never wanted him to go fishing

85 degrees of silent rage that seethed inside my mother's psyche
and made her seem the crazy one

high odds that the lives of all involved were complicated
by the possibility of this probability

85 creases in the portrait he wanted saved
innumerable reasons for holding his secrets
one answer to the question he took to the grave

0% probability my childhood can actually have been
what I believed it to be

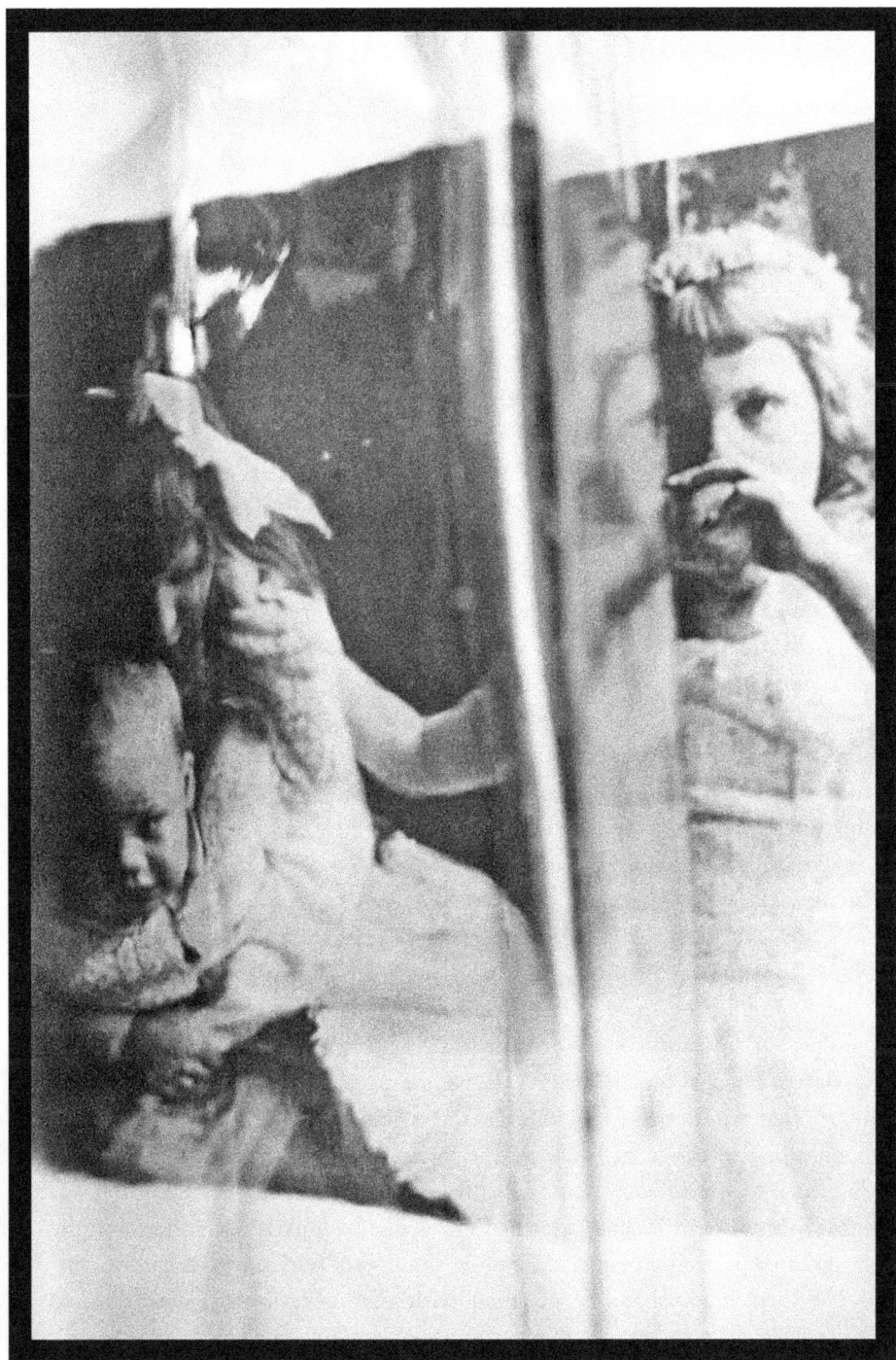

HEATHER MACDONALD STOREY

THE SISTER WHO WASN'T THERE

I don't remember how I knew about her, I just did. I knew she had been named Jacqueline so of course that meant she was a girl. No one talked about her or when she was born and of course there was no visual proof she existed. As children, no one paid much attention to the adults' conversations and if they noticed our interest, the topic was quickly turned to other matters. My grandmother had a saying *little pitchers have big ears*. I never knew what it meant back then but as I got older I understood.

In my teens, all I knew was I had a sister that my mother had placed for adoption at birth. I thought she was born after my sister who was three years younger than I and she gently resided in a part of my mind that only surfaced every few years. When I married and had children of my own, I thought of her more often. Perhaps it was the maternal part of me that was more active because I was now a mother. I also found in my thirties, forties and fifties she had become Jacqueline. The use of her name made her a real person and not a figment of my imagination.

As I reached middle age, as society calls it, and my family had married and moved around the country, I found myself fantasizing about how Jacqueline and I would meet. I never thought of when, just how it would happen and I always felt a meeting was inevitable. Our paths were meant to cross and the reality of my growing older never seemed to matter. She would come.

That was another of my fantasies, I was not going to find her; one day there would be a knock at my door and it would be Jacqueline. Living in another province with a different name never deterred my plans for this reunion. I was now in my late fifties and it seemed Jacqueline had taken up residence in my mind on a permanent basis, still I never thought of initiating a search for her.

Then, my husband and I, along with another couple, were traveling to Winnipeg for a military reunion, stopping for a few days in Ontario to visit family. The other couple stayed at their daughter's and we went on to my sister who lived a couple of hours away. The first evening, as we sat talking, Donna asked me if she could talk about something personal. Thinking she had found a new male friend and wanted me to meet him while we were there, I told her to go ahead. I was very surprised when she broached the subject of finding our sister Jacqueline. She had been to the Children's Aid Society and had filled out papers for herself; she also had papers for our youngest sister and for me. Donna then informed me our younger sister was not in favor and wanted nothing to do with it as she thought this would destroy our mother's reputation. Also since mother was now deceased, why bother.

I spent the next day trying to make Berta understand how important this was to all of us, at least to Donna and me. The day before we left to continue our trip, against Berta's wishes we filled out the papers and Donna mailed them the following day. I was not very optimistic about what the letter would produce and I didn't have much faith in Jacqueline being found this way; it was not the scenario my mind had planned.

Two weeks after we returned home I received a phone call from Donna. She excitedly told me she had a letter from our sister. She also informed me her name was not Jacqueline, it was Sandra. I found this disturbing. I had never considered that her adoptive parents might have changed her name. To me she had been Jacqueline for over fifty years, now I had to get used to her being Sandra. The letters flew back and forth between Donna and our lost sister for several weeks before Sandra decided she was ready for a face-to-face meeting with us.

As my husband and I journeyed to Ontario for our first meeting, I was excited but nervous. What would she be like? Would she accept us as her family? What if she was wealthy and thought we just wanted to meet her for whatever monetary gain she might offer? We already knew she was a widow and had two married daughters, one with three children. What if her daughters didn't want anything to do with us and influenced her decisions? My thoughts were like a hamster on a wheel going round and round but not getting anywhere. I had rented out the prime real estate in my mind to negative thoughts and they were not very good tenants.

The day I had dreamed of for so long was finally at hand and all I felt was fear of the unknown I couldn't control. I was not thinking about how this woman was being affected by this life altering change. Sandra had never dreamed when she wrote the first letter seeking her birth mother that it would set in motion a chain of events that would lead her to discovering she had three sisters. She had only Donna's letters telling her what we were like and I worried that she might have said the wrong thing or might have sounded negative. I was loathe to admit it but some of my thoughts stemmed from good old-fashion jealousy. This was not going the way I had visualized it all these years. My Jacqueline, now Sandra, had not initiated the contact with me. I couldn't put myself in her place or feel what she must be feeling. I also knew I didn't like myself much right then.

We had made plans to meet at the mall and go for coffee for our first contact. My husband was supportive but thought it should only be the four of us at this initial meeting to not overwhelm her with too many people. Donna and I went together; Berta was at work and would be meeting us there. There was not a lot of talk as we traveled into the city, I think it had finally hit us just how big a step we were taking and how these steps would influence four lives forever after. We were all women in the later stages of our quite normal lives; one divorced twice, two of us still with our life partners, and Sandra a widow. How could we bring all these dynamics together and hurt no one in the process? When we got out of the car and started toward the mall entrance we just looked at each other and smiled, no words were exchanged. What was there to say?

Three sisters met and stood waiting for the fourth to appear. She had said she would wear a rose and we all furtively scanned the faces of the women passing us. Then she was there and I literally thought my legs would buckle. It was like our mother had appeared; none of us resemble our mother but here was her image. I have no recollection of what we talked about or how long we stayed in the coffee shop; I think it was about an hour. We set up a family lunch for the next day.

There was not much conversation on the way back to Donna's home. Donna did not invite any of her grown children to come and mine were too far away to include them. Berta does not have children and I know they would not have been included if she had. A fine line was being drawn in the sand and I learned later that evening that while Berta was willing to come to the lunch date the next day, she did not want to be included in future meetings. She had not approved of the search in the beginning and felt no keener about developing a relationship with Sandra now that the first meeting was over.

Later that evening, I asked Donna how she felt about building a relationship with Sandra and received only a shrug. I realized then that as Berta and Donna were so close, both living in the same village and their limited social life revolving around each other, the choices Berta made would ultimately be Donna's as well.

I lay in bed that night talking with my husband about our meeting and his meeting her the next day. My first impressions were that now that they had made contact, heard her story and seen her, Donna and Berta were losing interest. I told my husband I didn't think that was fair. I also worried how this would affect Sandra and if she would take it as another rejection from a family who didn't want or need her around. My feelings of jealousy had come full circle and now became righteous anger towards my two sisters. Boyd pointed out that I had no control over other people's lives and whatever the two of them decided to do, they would have to live with it. I have a very wise husband at times.

The next day when we all met again, I introduced my husband to my new sister. He gave her a big hug and said welcome Sis. I followed suit with a hug for her and her daughters, my other sisters did not. I happened to be seated across the table from Sandra and I told her the first thing we would change if she were agreeable: to me she would be Sandy and not Sandra. She smiled saying no one had ever called her Sandy and she was fine with it from me. I watched in fascination as the meal progressed, she sat like my mother and used her fork like her; it was like sitting across the table from my mother. It seemed so sad later, when the three of us were talking; they could not see any similarities between Sandy and our mother at all.

When Boyd and I left for New Brunswick the following day, I knew in my heart Donna and Berta would probably not further any relationship with our new sister. A few days after I arrived home I called Sandy and told her I would give her any information she would like to have including pictures of her birth mother and grandparents and that, although there were many miles between us, I hoped we could build a strong foundation for a new relationship. I am happy to say this has developed far better than I could have expected. The most amazing thing I have learned about my new sister is that she holds no animosity toward our mother.

In our long conversations she has often remarked, "We don't know how we would have acted back then. It was wartime and she already had you, and my birth father paid for her confinement in the birthing home. I also had good parents. I was the apple of my father's eye even after he had two children of his own."

I once had a sister who wasn't there—no pictures or trace of that young life, no squabbles over toys or girlish laughter over boys; those are the things we missed. The life experiences of two women who have raised their children and seen both loss and happiness in their lives; that is what we have now. Today we have fifteen years of shared memories, we talk on the phone at least once a week and we visit each other's home as often as we can. My life is richer and I think hers is too. My fantasy that Jacqueline, the sister who wasn't there, would one day find me has given way to a deeper and richer reality. Her name is Sandy and we have found each other.

CHARLOTTE JONES

WHEN THINGS COME TO LIGHT

I have a twenty-three carat kunzite gemstone that I never wear and try to forget I have. I accidentally inherited it when my sister died.

Most women would be thrilled to have something like this; its sparkling pale pink brilliance draws you in. The stone, most likely from Afghanistan, is reputed to enhance a person's capacity for devotion. It is supposed to be the ideal precious stone for lovers. Perhaps that's what bothers me about it. So I keep it hidden in the shadows of my closet, tucked away where I won't run across it and succumb to the temptation to wear it.

It was a gift to my sister on her fifty-fourth birthday from her Arizona boyfriend, a jeweler she had been involved with for over two years. Only problem was, she was married and lived with her husband in Colorado. One week after receiving this exquisite gift, she had a massive stroke. I boarded the first flight to Colorado I could get and arrived in time to say goodbye. I will never know if, in her coma, she sensed my presence, but I like to believe she did. I held her hand—I can still remember how quickly it grew cold when she died.

I ran across the unset stone in her purse while I retrieved her driver's license so the coroner could verify her age. I knew her husband, a struggling entrepreneur, hadn't given her the stone, so I slipped it into my pocket. At a time like this, I didn't want him discovering her affair, one I had known about from the beginning. Her husband had been by her bedside for twenty-four hours straight, was exhausted and distraught. I would keep her secret safe.

She was born in 1943, but had managed to change the date on her license to 1948. She believed in lying about her age, even telling me when I was eight to claim I was only seven. She was twelve years older and I idolized her. Even with the age difference, we were very close and talked at least once a week after I moved away. We had no secrets, or so I thought. In the photo on her driver's license, she had black hair, but she had recently dyed it red, which better suited her personality.

She loved a practical joke. Before hosting a Christmas dinner at her house, she got stacks of books about Buddha from the library, just to upset our fundamentalist Christian parents. She could play anything on the piano, even Mozart's *Turkish March*, after hearing it only once. I called her "the perfect bitch with perfect pitch." Her hundreds of piano students adored her. She kept a Chinese porcelain box on the piano and, if students showed up with long nails, she cut them and put the trimmings in the box. On recital day, the box was always empty. When the students asked what happened to the nail clippings, she held out a plate of cookies and said, "I like my chocolate chip cookies crunchy. Won't you have one?" Her wicked throaty guffaw then rang out.

The next few days after her death, I forced myself to stay strong so I could console my parents, negotiate between them and her husband on whether she would be cremated or not, write the eulogy, figure out what clothes she would be buried in, help pick out the casket. There was no time for grieving over losing my only sibling. That would have to wait until later.

The worst task of all was calling her boyfriend to tell him she was gone. I'll admit I was enraged that my sister had put me in such an awkward situation. He was heartbroken, even more so when I told him he couldn't come to the funeral. It just wouldn't be right. I asked him about the stone, did he want me to mail it back to him? "No," he said. "I want you to have it." Then he told me about other things I needed to smuggle out of her house so her husband wouldn't find them: pictures of the two of them stashed in her nightstand, other jewelry he had given her. Those, I did send back. I learned he thought she was only thirty-nine. "I've seen her naked," he said. "No way was she fifty-four."

I never talked to her boyfriend again, though I wrote him once and he wrote back with weird stories about how my sister and he were once druids and had been married in a former life. I never wrote back, but I wonder if he doesn't regret his decision to give me this beautiful gemstone.

Several months later, I took the stone to a jeweler, got it set and planned to wear it. Then I told my husband the whole story. He looked at the stone, admired it, but then said, "I don't know. It's a symbol of betrayal, don't you think?"

It's true. As her executor, I learned more about my sister than I really wanted to know. How she'd lied, not just about the affair and about her age, but about many, many more things, making me wonder if I ever really knew her. She had told me she was accepted to a PhD program in music in Arizona, but I found no application form or acceptance letter in her filing cabinet, just a certificate for a weekend course in Past Life Regression, something she had never mentioned an interest in. I called the school and they had no record of such a student. Even at the funeral, her friends asked if I'd enjoyed having my sister stay with me for the summer in Arizona. When I explained I lived in Texas, confusion washed over their faces. Had she told any of us the truth?

As I started to settle her estate, I discovered she had not filed an income tax return for several years. Her calendar showed an upcoming IRS audit. She also had constructed an elaborate, but fake, legal scheme to embezzle money from her own husband. Nearly $100,000 was missing from an investment account and I suspect it had been moved to an offshore account in the Cayman Islands. When I decoded her address book and tracked down someone who might know where the money was, this person suggested we meet in a cave in the mountains so our conversation wouldn't be overheard. He worried his phone was tapped. My sister must have been planning to go underground or at least to run away with her lover. I quickly resigned as her executor. There are some things you just don't want to know. I don't believe my brother-in-law ever found the money.

As painful as it is, I now wonder if my sister was a pathological liar. If I had only known how troubled she was, perhaps I could have helped her.

Even before the funeral, her husband went into a frenzy to get rid of her things. As we sorted the items into "things to donate," "things to give to friends," "things to throw away," he revealed that he did know about the affair. She had told him one night in a fit of anger. To my shock, she'd had affairs throughout their thirty years of marriage. I asked him how he had put up with all this. He simply said, "I loved her." Should I have told him about the stone then? Maybe some secrets are better kept.

Eighteen years have passed since her death and this is the first time I haven't cried on the anniversary date. My confusion and anger have been replaced with mostly happy memories of our childhood—hiking in the mountains, dancing "The Twist." I can hear my sister laughing now as we plotted our rendition of *Chopsticks* specifically designed to drive our folks crazy. I played the bass part. She played the melody as we sat side-by-side on the piano bench. We played the first verse straight. The second, she played totally off-key while I played the bass as intended. The third, we reversed roles; and the fourth and final verse, we both played wildly out of tune until someone yelled from the kitchen, "Stop that this instant!" I miss her a lot.

Her husband was extremely generous and gave me all her Indian turquoise jewelry. He and I have become good friends now. I almost always wear something that belonged to her. Her jewelry keeps her close to my heart.

Still, I don't wear that luminous pink stone. The interesting thing about kunzite is that it fades when exposed to sunlight. That's another good reason to keep it hidden in a dark closet.

PAULA MACKAY

MY SISTER'S SHOES

My closet is filled with shoes, most of them a half size too big.

Black leather Mary Janes, barely worn but for a few minor scuffs across their rounded toes.

Brown, mid-calf dress boots—soft to the touch but tough on the arches. They made their debut at a meeting in cowboy country last week. I may never wear them again.

And next to those, mud-splattered garden rubbers, red as a Brandywine tomato. When she first offered to let me have them, I thought they were too bright for my personality. Now I practically live in them come spring.

There are two empty shoeboxes in the closet as well. During a mid-winter cleaning frenzy, I packed the tan oxfords and another pair I can't even remember into a bag for Goodwill. I knew replacements would soon be on the way.

Circumstantial evidence aside, I'm no shoe fanatic. I rarely buy them, and when I do, they're usually from REI. Hiking boots, sport sandals, cross trainers—these are more my typical style. Most of my fancier footwear once belonged to my twin sister, Pam. Every time I visit her in Berkeley, it seems, I inherit a pair of Eccos or some other quality brand sold at Nordstrom.

"Do you like these?" Pam asks. There's a bit of hesitation in her voice, like she's sorry to see them go. Then comes the resolve, followed by her ultimate selling point. "They're practically new!"

Recently, Pam's tastes have gone from laced shoes and pull-ons to slightly bulkier models secured with Velcro. They're easier to slide over her swollen feet and to fasten with jerky hands. If a pair of shoes becomes uncomfortable—or Pam tires of looking at them, poised and motionless on the platform of her wheelchair—they're destined to become mine.

✤   ✤   ✤

Pam and I started out as two eggs. She was sunny-side up; I was soft-boiled. In virtually every photograph from our childhood, Pam beams at the camera while I stand solemnly by her side, looking like someone just stole my Raggedy Ann.

Had we been identical twins, we would have shared one hundred percent of our genetic makeup—carbon copies, so to speak. But Pam and I are no more genetically similar than we are to our siblings. Which makes sense, given that she's the spitting image of one of our older sisters and I could reasonably be mistaken for the other.

All we knew was that we shared the same crib, the same stroller, the same haircut, the same blue eyes, the same birthday, the same birthday cake. Every morning, we awoke and took a bath together before my mother dressed us in the matching clothes she'd crafted on her Singer. We spent our days laughing and crying in sync, and went to bed listening to the same fairytales and the sound of each other's breathing as we drifted off to sleep. Identical or not, we were The Twins—a two-for-one deal. And that, we were told, made us special.

Was it nature or nurture that molded us into such distinct personalities? I was a restless infant, known for keeping my parents company while they watched *The Tonight Show* into the wee hours. Pam was more relaxed and outgoing, having earned her nickname, "Pam the Ham," almost as soon as she could talk. She was a pint-sized flirt with our oldest sister's boyfriend, asking him to marry her every time she sat playfully in his lap, and at six or seven, she pulled down her pants for one of the Flaherty boys next door in exchange for a bag of penny candy. I can just see her now, savoring a Tootsie Roll in our driveway, bragging that *she* had gotten the better end of *that* bargain! I gladly conceded the spotlight, observing the people around me from behind my shyness like it was a one-way window. We were perfect complements.

Our dualism was even more pronounced at school, where my efforts to disappear were paralleled by Pam's to flaunt her colors. In her fifth-grade performance as the Hunchback's court jester, she cartwheeled across the stage in her flamboyant, polka-dotted pajamas while belting out, "Who is the monster and who is the man?" to the enchanted audience. That same year, I pushed my limits as Abigail Adams, feeling more like Quasimodo than the First Lady of the United States when I had to kiss John—aka the studly Bruce Hardy—in front of my parents and peers.

Pam and I partitioned our intellectual resources to further minimize competition. I excelled at science and math, she struggled with algebra and had to endure excruciating tutoring sessions with my father, who hung a blackboard in our kitchen and lectured her on the Pythagorean Theorem as if triangles really mattered. Meanwhile, in Social and Cultural History—the last class we ever took together—Pam blazed through blue notebooks during exams while I sat paralyzed at my desk, unable to focus on anything but the sound of her pen scrambling across the page.

Before we had finished high school, Pam's enthusiasm for politics and a good argument had already positioned her for a future in law. My more eclectic background included forays into social work and environmental activism before I settled on wildlife conservation. Although our paths differed, I ultimately trailed her all over the country—from Vermont to D.C. to Colorado, and finally, to the West Coast, where we're currently separated by eight hundred miles of shoreline. Through the years, we've diverged and come together again like a braided river, with Pam consistently carving channels ahead of me like she did at our birth.

✤   ✤   ✤

When I was a teenager, my friend Rachel's mother had multiple sclerosis. Mrs. Lieberman was an elegant woman, her disease barely made visible by her nodding head and a lack of balance when she rose from her chair. My mother was ill, too, with cancer, so Rachel and I were kindred spirits of sorts. The only thing all the *other* kids had to worry about was who was making out with whom and what kind of jeans they had on at the time.

Not that I didn't think about boys. In Boston, David Flaherty had wooed me from kindergarten straight through to the fourth grade—the year we moved to the suburbs. I recall the hot summer day my mother told me I had to start wearing a shirt when playing outside with David, those tiny pink nipples apparently no longer appropriate for public viewing. By the time I'd reached junior high and was ready for a training bra, my budding desires were well hidden beneath my family woes.

After school and on weekends, Rachel and I would perch on her bed commiserating like cellmates, taking life way too seriously given our innocence and youth. In addition to being lonely, we both had regular run-ins with our mothers, who had the strong wills necessary to manage their hectic households and failing bodies. But I always felt mine was the lousier hand. At least Mrs. Lieberman had two breasts and didn't have to wear a wig to the grocery store.

I worshipped my mother behind closed doors but cringed when she put on pastel petticoats to go square dancing, or drove Pam and me to school in her yellow Chevy Nova—her tangerine White Stag jacket zipped up over a flannel nightgown. Rachel's mother seemed so much more hip, with her thrift shops and bulk foods and artwork from faraway countries. And then there were our fathers.

Papa Lieberman, as I referred to him then, was a tall, doting professor who prepared exotic meals and insisted I join in. "You're not going to turn down Papa Lieberman's famous vegetarian casserole, are you?" he'd ask, taking mock offense if I said I had to get home. In contrast, my dad—a descendent of the warring MacKay clan and a number cruncher for the defense industry— often sent me running from our own meat-and-potatoes dinner in tears. His temper piled our plates high with tension, my older brother and me receiving the largest portions. Although I knew the Liebermans had their conflicts, too, I begrudged Rachel her close-knit family and found myself wishing the tables were turned.

✤   ✤   ✤

Nearly two decades later, I stopped by to see Mr. and Mrs. Lieberman during a visit to Massachusetts. My mother was long gone, my father, remarried and estranged from my siblings and me. Parentless, I was eager to see the Liebermans again and to introduce them to Robert, the man who would soon become my second husband.

Mr. Lieberman answered the door. Warm and gracious as usual, he looked very tired—not the type of tired that comes from taking a long hike in the mountains, but that relentless, emotional exhaustion that knows no respite. We exchanged hugs and hellos, and he went to get his wife.

Some things hadn't changed. Books and magazines were scattered about, and I recognized Rachel and her siblings in the framed photos on the shelves. But the furniture was sparse, and Mrs. Lieberman's comfy chair—the one I used to see her reading in so often—was no longer there. Peeking around the corner, I saw medical equipment in the next room, its sterility penetrating me like a sharp needle. Once, this place had felt like home to me: the aroma of a hearty soup, Rachel's brothers racing up and down the stairs, the family's black Lab barking in anticipation. Now the house was quiet, and there was nothing cooking on the stove.

Mrs. Lieberman emerged in a power wheelchair, much like the one Pam relies on today. Her dark eyes bore their familiar spark. But her body belonged to the disease.

The four of us gathered in the living room, Robert and I talking about how we'd met in graduate school and recently moved to Vermont. Mr. and Mrs. Lieberman, their faces shining, caught me up on Rachel and their grandchildren. We touched upon the past, too, although this seemed like sacred ground.

Then one of them asked, "How's Pam?" There was an awkward silence. I'd intended to tell them, perhaps even come in part to solicit their empathy. Now I felt guilty. Mrs. Lieberman embodied my deepest fears about the future, and I'm sure it showed on my face. I often wondered what it was like for my mother to see her illness through our frightened eyes, and how she reconciled this perspective with her fervor to protect her two baby girls. Many mornings, I'd find her propped up with pillows in her home hospital bed, staring at her hairless head in the mirror across the room. I wanted to move that damn mirror, replace it with a pretty painting.

"Actually, she was diagnosed with MS about a year ago," I said, unable to lie to my old friend's parents. My voice wavered as I started to convey the details.

Mr. Lieberman got up and left the room. Maybe it was more than he could bear, hearing about a woman Rachel's age just beginning her journey with a disease he knew all too well. Or maybe he just wanted to give us a private moment with Mrs. Lieberman, who spoke slowly and with sheer determination.

"Please don't worry that Pam will end up like me," she said. "Not everyone ends up like me."

✤ ✤ ✤

Summer, 1997. Robert and I had traveled to Quebec to go canoeing at La Mauricie National Park. On the rainy afternoon of our arrival, we checked into a spa for a pre-camping splurge. I decided to call Pam from a payphone after my massage, just to touch base before we paddled off into the wilderness.

"Hi, Paula," answered a voice as familiar to me as my own. Her heavy tone made me anxious, despite the scent of lavender oil wafting from my skin.

"What's wrong, Pam?"

"I got some bad news today. The doctors think I have multiple sclerosis."

Although Pam sounded shaky, she didn't break down. I held myself together, too, as I didn't want to be the one to set us off. Ever since we were kids, neither of us could stand to see the other get into trouble; if one of us got slapped, we both began to cry. Our emotional dynamic became even more complex when we were teens. I started dating before Pam, and I often stayed out late with my boyfriend to avoid coming home. There was hell to pay if I missed my curfew, which happened more frequently than I care to remember. After being confronted by my father in the stairwell, I'd find Pam sniffling in the bed next to mine. "Why do you have to piss him off like that?" she'd whisper into the darkness, misdirecting her anger toward me. Over time, we'd learned to beef up the membrane between us so that we could endure one another's heartaches—the loss of our mother, my short-lived first marriage, Pam's imminent divorce from her college sweetheart, Sam. But it didn't take much to open up old wounds, or to create new ones from raw material.

Bracing myself against the wall, the phone's cord stretched taut, I listened to Pam describe how they'd ruled out lupus and Lyme disease—two of the usual suspects. She was being treated for carpal tunnel syndrome, but that didn't explain her fuzzy vision. With more tests, they'd finally found the culprit. Her MRI showed lesions in her brain, linked to the neurological attacks she'd been experiencing for years.

Did she say *years*?

Gradually, the memories fell into place. Pam's clumsiness during our day hikes in the Rockies, where she'd tire out quickly and complain that her legs were on fire. "You should drink more," I'd say, urging her to go farther. And that backpacking trip into the Maroon Bells, where Sam and I hopped effortlessly across a stream, only to see Pam stumble like a drunk into the water behind us. And then there was the ski hut expedition near Aspen, which concluded with Sam sporting two loaded packs—one on his back, the other dangling from his chest—so Pam could snowplow down the trail unencumbered. She was deathly afraid of falling.

Still, I couldn't fully absorb the impact of what I was hearing. I'd spent most of my life terrified of cancer, dreading it would someday come back for Pam or me. Cancer had consumed our childhood, beginning with our mother's left breast and not satiated until it had picked away at her bones. But MS? How could that be? We were only thirty-three years old.

✤   ✤   ✤

Sometimes a fine line separates our friends from our foes. Take gray squirrels, for instance. When they cache nuts in the soil, they provide an important ecological service by helping to regenerate the trees that dropped them. But if they decide to move indoors, squirrels can chew through the plastic coating surrounding your electrical wires, potentially causing a short in the system. Worst-case scenario: your entire house burns down.

The same principle applies to your immune cells. They defend your body from foreign invaders, but become downright dangerous if they turn their forces against the cells insulating your central nervous system. When they attack this insulation, called the myelin sheath, the nerve fibers that send signals to and from the brain, spinal cord, and optic nerve don't function properly. The damaged myelin forms scar tissue (sclerosis) in multiple places. Multiple sclerosis.

Although MS is typically a progressive disease, its course varies widely from person to person. Many people experience remissions between attacks, while others decline more steadily. Women are diagnosed with MS two to three times more often than men, most between the ages of twenty and fifty. Symptoms run the gamut as well, from blurred vision and poor coordination to blindness and paralysis. Some have cognitive issues, some don't. Some can walk, some can't. An estimated two million people live with MS worldwide. None of them, including Pam, knows the story of how their disease began or where it will lead them as it unfolds.

✤   ✤   ✤

I love to walk. In the forest. In meadows. Along rivers. Even in the city. Each passing step brings calmness, relief. I move forward. I breathe. Walking feels like survival. Walking allows me to leaves my demons behind.

Sitting does the opposite. My back hurts, my butt goes numb, and finally, so does my mind. Thoughts no longer flow. I'm like a clogged artery, a heart attack waiting to happen. I need to get up. Get out. Get going.

"When you have worn out your shoes," writes Emerson, "the strength of the sole leather has passed into the fibre of your body." I burn through a pair of hiking boots in a single summer, maybe two. But what about Pam's shoes, with their intact soles and unmarred leather? Does it count if I wear them out for her? Or will their strength remain locked inside forever, a lasting testament to her immobility?

For the most part, Pam takes it all in her stride. On weekdays, she braves San Francisco's public transportation system to get into work, her office located so many floors up in a skyscraper I become lightheaded just thinking about it. Weekends bring downtime with her husband, Norris, and September kicks off the sacred football season—which means don't even bother trying to reach her on Sundays. Norris grew up in Seattle, making Pam a diehard Seahawks fan. I have a statue of the Buddha in my garden. Pam's is graced with green and blue Seahawks gnomes.

But living with MS has changed Pam—how could it not? Her contagious laughter is harder to come by these days, and she's often preoccupied with getting from Point A to Point B. There are the barriers most of us don't ever have to worry about—the bathroom without a grab bar, a broken elevator to the train—and the myriad inconveniences we all have to face. Yet the last thing she wants is for people to feel sorry for her, as though she's any less a person because her immune cells don't know how to behave themselves. I've seen the way some strangers look at her—or don't—and it makes me want to scream, "Hey, that's my twin sister, and she'll kick your ass at Scrabble!"

The truth is I'm the one who can't embrace Pam's disease. Not an hour goes by when I don't yearn to rewrite the script, or at least hit rewind. If I could, I'd strap her leg to mine and enter a three-legged race like we used to do at camp. If I could, I'd help her scramble up those peaks again and wait for her at stream crossings. If I could, I'd carry her to the other side.

✤   ✤   ✤

Singer k.d. lang's voice filters through the hospital speakers, her liquid melody pierced by the industrial noises of the MRI scanner. With my head immobilized in a padded vice and my body enveloped in metal, the unsettling sounds help distract me from the claustrophobia I acquired from my mother. Pam has described this strange, pseudo-musical experience to me in the past, how she can hear familiar tunes in the thrums, pings, and pounding jackhammers permeating her skull. Maybe it's the anti-anxiety drug at work, but I can see what she means. Within minutes, lang is accompanied by the rhythm of "I want my, I want my, I want my MTV."

The trouble started with a persistent twitch in my right eyelid. I found it annoying at first but became more concerned when muscles in my back, arms, and legs began to twitch, too. I also had some inflammation in my feet, and my balance seemed way out of whack. Although I suspected these symptoms were somehow tied to hormonal changes—isn't everything for a middle-aged woman?—I decided to pay a visit to my physician.

"With today's medications, people do really, really well with MS." The doctor was perusing my medical chart, focused heavily on my family history. After we reviewed my symptoms further, he suggested I see a neurologist to make sure Pam and I hadn't inherited the same fate. "Even if you do have MS," he said, "I'm sure you'll be just fine. I know women who keep running marathons." *Yeah*, I thought. *And I know a woman who would pass up front-row tickets to the Super Bowl to be able to walk from her bedroom to the toilet.*

✤　✤　✤

According to the National Multiple Sclerosis Society, the average person in the United States has a 1 in 750 chance of developing MS. The risk increases to 1 in 40 when a close relative, including a fraternal twin, has the disease, and to 1 in 4 if that relative is an identical twin. In other words, if Pam and I had started as one egg, I would have a twenty-five percent chance of having MS. Because this figure isn't one hundred percent, genetics alone can't explain who gets MS and who doesn't. Some researchers suspect that an infectious agent—the Epstein-Barr virus, for example—might trigger the disease process in genetically pre-disposed people. A lack of sunlight and the Vitamin D it produces could be another factor; MS is less common closer to the equator. Theories abound, but there are still more questions than answers.

By remarkable coincidence, I was referred to the same MS specialist Pam saw in San Francisco when she was first diagnosed. Dr. K now works in Seattle, a leader in her field. The day before Thanksgiving, she listened carefully to my complaints and performed a basic neurological exam. She didn't find anything particularly alarming but wanted me to have an MRI so we could rule out MS. Within a couple of hours, I was being slid into the tube with the k.d. lang/Dire Straits duo.

Dr. K texted me to say my MRI looked good before I even left the hospital. Relieved, I decided to put the whole thing to rest for a while—until I received a copy of the MRI report in the mail a week or so later. Some of the details surprised me.

T2/FLAIR SIGNAL ABNORMALITY IS PRESENT ADJACENT TO THE OCCIPITAL REGION OF THE RIGHT LATERAL VENTRICLE MEASURING APPROXIMATELY 11 X 6 MM.

MINIMAL WHITE MATTER SIGNAL ABNORMALITY IS INDETERMINANT. IN THE PROPER CLINICAL SETTING THIS MAY REPRESENT DEMYELINATING DISEASE, HOWEVER APPEARANCE WOULD NOT BE CLASSIC.

Although I was no medical expert, I understood the terms *abnormality* and *demyelinating disease* and didn't want to see either of them associated with my MRI. I emailed Dr. K and we connected by phone on a snowy day in mid-December. I ducked into the doorway of a local bank when I received her call, my cell phone pressed hard against my ear.

"Can we talk about my results now that I've seen the report?" I asked, clenching my jaw so she wouldn't hear my teeth chatter. She pulled up my records and read the findings aloud. I probed her on the meaning of abnormality and how it applied to my right lateral ventricle.

"You might want to come back for another MRI in a year. Just to be safe."

❧   ❧   ❧

Pam and I were eight years old, still living in Boston. It would be another year before our parents relocated to the suburbs to evade forced busing, the court's controversial attempt to desegregate the public schools. Another year before my mother found a tumor in her breast, causing my intrinsic worry to metastasize into full-blown anxiety. Another year before I had to wear those ugly green glasses, before I walked into Bridge Elementary knowing nobody and wary of everybody. For the moment, there was only Kilroy to contend with. And that was bad enough.

When I try to imagine Kilroy today, I can't distinguish him from the quintessential neighborhood bully. Scrappy. Mean smirk. Dirty blonde bangs draped over his eyes. The first time Kilroy cornered Pam and me, we were hanging out with David Flaherty—who ran home to get his older brother. Now it was just the two of us on our little red bikes, rainbow streamers hanging from our handlebars, spokes decorated with neon plastic covers that went click-click-click as we rode.

Pam was ahead of me when Kilroy stepped in front of her, causing her to backpedal hard on her coaster brake. I came to an abrupt stop, too, like I'd hit an invisible wall. *We should have taken a different street!* I thought, wishing we were closer to David's house. Kilroy straddled Pam's front tire, spewed some tough words in her face. But it wasn't until he gave her shoulder a shove that I broke myself free.

"You leave my sister alone," I yelled, jumping off my bicycle and running full speed toward Kilroy's chest. The next thing I knew, I was somersaulting backwards along the sidewalk, pavement scraping the skin off my elbows. Lying there dazed and looking up at the sky, I heard the comforting sound of a neighbor's voice. She emerged from her doorway waving her arms, hollering at Kilroy that he should be ashamed of himself for picking on girls. *Is Pam okay?* The memory goes black.

❧   ❧   ❧

Sclerosis has another definition: an inability or reluctance to adapt or compromise; excessive resistance to change.

On the eve of our fiftieth birthday, Pam and I had a huge fight. I'd felt it brewing over the phone for months—probably much longer—but it didn't surface until we were strolling along the shore of Puget Sound. She and Norris had just arrived in Seattle for our traditional birthday rendezvous. We were discussing plans for the celebration when Pam suddenly proposed we each go our own way the next day and meet up for dinner late in the afternoon. I stopped walking, unable to speak. We'd been talking about this birthday since before we'd turned forty-nine.

"I don't identify with being a twin like you do," she said in her lawyerly voice, like she was describing one of her cases about software mergers. "We're basically just siblings born at the same time."

Robert and Norris glanced at each other nervously.

"What can you possibly mean by that?" I asked, peering down at her through my sunglasses. I hoped she couldn't see the water in my eyes.

"All I'm saying is that spending our actual birthday together isn't a big deal to me. I could just as happily watch the Seahawks game with Norris and celebrate with you later."

The Seahawks? Are you fucking kidding me? I felt myself start to panic. Not only had I gone to a lot of effort exploring options for our fiftieth—which had now been usurped by football—but Pam was dismissing our twinhood as a fluke of nature and nothing more. In her mind, we weren't special after all. We were run-of-the-mill sisters.

The conversation quickly escalated. Selfish. Ungrateful. Pam and I pummeled each other with words while Robert threw a Hail Mary, trying in vain to remind us of how much we loved each other. I finally muttered something that got under her skin and she zipped away, sobbing, in her electric wheelchair. As I watched her go, I thought about how profoundly unalike we were—our temperaments and interests; her passion for sports, mine for the outdoors. In many ways she was right—we really *were* just sisters. If we weren't, would we even be friends?

I knew Pam could be stubborn—she got that from my father. I suppose I did, too. But was she really willing to sacrifice our birthday plans just to bring home her point? What I didn't know was that she'd been wrestling for weeks with how to tell me she wanted more than anything to see the Seahawks play on her birthday. I didn't know that the following year, I'd go bear-watching with Robert on our fifty-first, having decided that Pam *was* right about one thing: we both had to do what made us happiest, even if that meant letting go. Most of all—and this had taken me half a century to understand—I didn't know what it was like to be Pam.

It's easy for me to box Pam into being a victim—a grown woman rendered powerless by disease. In my low moments, I can see myself that way, too: first, a mother with cancer, then a twin with MS, and now even a small chance that I have it as well. Instinctively, I try to take control; Pam pushes back, then vice versa. Each of us wanting more—and at the same time, less—from the other. Both of us trying to be whole in a life that has always been divided by two.

✤   ✤   ✤

Pam and I are at "The Walk Shop" in Berkeley. We come here every Christmas to check out the latest shoe styles. Pam eyes a funky new boot sitting high on the rack. I'm dubious—it looks narrow for her foot—but I get it for her anyway. "This is so cute," she says, coveting the boot with her hands. "What do you think?" I glance down at my feet, unsure how to answer.

V.
LOSS

TIM J. MYERS

TO MY SIBLING, MISCARRIED 1957

Catching a fragrance of nectarines
from the basket on the table,
I feel how strange it is
that you're not here,
find myself wondering who you might have been.

At my grade school, well-meaning nuns
gave us their strange perfunctory tale
of unborn babies drifting in Limbo.
But I was born, and have come to fruit,
my sons on the floor here
giggling and bucking like horses,
as if five short years ago
neither was compounded of infinite nothingness.

Now that the mystery of Me is a bit clearer
in the mystery of Them,
I think of you who never came from our mother,

you who are less now than
a fragrance of nectarines

in a breeze from the window so slight
only my new-shaven face can feel it.

THE NIGHT WE TALKED

It was bound to happen, heavy as water's
sullen anger against the dam,
bees in swarm-wrath pressing from the hive—

He'd called me to say his second daughter
my sister had died, and what I am
still twists around that sentence, alive

as she is not: *Tim. Mary's dead.*
She'd raked herself through burning years
of anorexia-bulimia, how many times

had I told her, *You have to tell Dad
how you feel!* But mostly our fears
for her went numb, anaesthetized

by the family story, Dad's doctor life,
pillar of community, eleven children
in Catholic schools—and of course

he couldn't listen, not even to his wife
my mother. The thing stayed hidden,
successful professional cannot endorse

by recognition so human an obscenity.
And after she died he kept that omerta oath
like a Mafioso—which he was not.

No killer. Just a man. The mystery
of his beloved girl's anguished truth,
the love between them, poisonous knot,

were not to be discussed. We knew
but could not say. And then that night
years after, when some family altercation

burst into something else: the spew
of rank secrets breaking toward light.
Words led to words; bestial emotion

unleashed became a glowering storm over
the circle of us, sitting on deck
chairs on the porch at midnight. And he said

to me in whispers that seemed to sever
him, *When I was little . . .*—and then some ancient wreck
of his Nebraska childhood, pain that fed

his fear, emerged: a letter he'd once found,
in his father's hand my grandfather,
citing domestic anguish, *I just might leave*

and never come back. Broken by this, bound
to it and fueled, he never was delivered
of that primal fear, could not believe

in more. Out it came, stinking Lazarus.
Then at last—we'd all been drinking—
he hung his drunken head and wept,

suffered like a fool. Each of us,
quiet at last with truth finally speaking,
sat stone-content, now purely desolate.

And yet, and yet, as Issa says,
and yet we sensed some new thing there
not there before, an unseen path

opening in front of us. Does
suffering always turn to prayer,
rise like smoke from offered wrath?

GREGGORY MOORE

HOW THEY SAY IT

Dostoyevsky said or one of his characters (it's interesting to consider how much one presumes the other): There's this rock see, and it's, like, a million tons suspended a hundred feet above your head. It'll be going plenty fast by the time it squishes you dead like a bug, mister. You'll die instantaneously, right? says the one. Sure, says the other. No pain? asks the one guy. I rather doubt it, says the two. But would you be afraid there *would* be pain? I would—that's what he says, that's what I say too: I'd fear it, I do. Dostoyevsky conveys this to me and I explain it to you out there or you see it here for the second time or recognize it in yourself, not the words but something.

I was walking through my old neighborhood. (Isn't that how they say it: THE OLD NEIGHBORHOOD?) But it was truly old now. Newly built when we had moved there thirty years before, there was something unchanged, frozen since then. The house-fronts wore the same faces, retained their phrenological features, just a tumor here or there, just a tumor, nothing but a little ol' tumor. The colors though were not the same, shuffled, redistributed I'm guessing, I could not remember exactly the original shades, only that these were brighter stronger gaudier more artificial-seeming. The topography seemed right, the trees and foliage more abundant, older, more mature but of about the same population as then. Shortly after the funeral I moved to live on campus. I hated it, hated the apartments that followed one after the other as I worked my way through the cluster of complexes built with students in mind, I shouldn't have come back. I shouldn't have come back, and two years later my father had left with the Rams for St. Louis and I had moved to Seattle for grad school, leaving my mother alone in the house where our pixie left us.

The old neighborhood appears deserted, the wind is blowing, the air is so clear, the light is beautiful and I'm out for a walk in the perfectly comfortable sharp brisk clear. I'm walking in the direction of the clouds, for some reason all wind-shuttled to a northern distance, clustered far away for my viewing pleasure. The moon is full and big and bright early this evening, luminescent white and pale daytime grayblue occupying the same celestial plane. The old neighborhood has been left to me. The roots of an old tree break through the ground, skim the surface through the grass. The poem carved into the trunk by a teenage me while my sister watched can still be read, surviving juvenilia:

> Another time, another place
> Shoot a death ray into space
> Another place, another time
> Give a little, change your mind
> Another day, another life
> Live it different, how you might
> Another fate, another line
> Move a little, what do you find?

It seems every house has wind chimes and every tree is rustling, there's no traffic anywhere, every car an idle metal shell today, for all I know never-driven props. It's like a diorama approximating the old neighborhood thirty years later, a good job all in all, impressive, a virtual resurrection. I am wondering why but not sure at what, *Why does it exist*, I think that's it, *Why does it exist*, not the cause-and-effect why, the bigger one: *Why?* Why am I shown what I am shown, why do I see what I see, and what is it? At least that something, a feeling, not these words, "why am I at least that not these," not why but something out there. Eventually people filter back in, are let in, a man and his dog, he shortens the lead, bringing it around his wedding-ring hand in loops, a responsible courteous dog-owner in a Raiders cap. The dog is cute, puffy white fur well kempt, of pleasant demeanor, too small to pose a threat. The man smiles, says "How're you doin'?" genuinely, sincerely, seemingly not a miserable man. "I'm fine, thanks" I say since I believe it really was a question, "How are you?" I want to know, especially as there's little doubt he's well, it's almost too far for him to answer over a shoulder, "Good" he says, "Good" I say. A jogger wearing headphones waddles along the street; we acknowledge each other with smiles.

Five, she's five back in that old neighborhood, where we've moved because of CHOC, our dad having gotten a job with the Rams. She's five, and one of the sidewalks has an acute turn just below the crest of a steep suburban hill. I'm pulling into the neighborhood, left, in and down, about to make a sharp right, and a little to the left I see her taking the turn too fast, her Big Wheel sliding off the curb, staying upright but drifting towards the asphalt declivity, her mortal terror, her little feet pushing at the ground without finding a foothold, her little body spasming. I jerked the car out of its turn and accelerated to across the mouth of the downhill flow. By the time I stepped onto the pavement she had made some progress slowing the black-wheeled vehicle by sheer futile friction, but she was on the way down, the grade too much for her and her panic. I grabbed the back of the little blue seat. At this angle she was heavier than I had anticipated, and I could only slow her and slide down with her, stepping and shuffling. I knew she would be all right now and even that she would have lived had she tumbled from the top, probably just bumped and bruised but no worse for wear and tear in the long haul, not even psychologically, just left with a little tale: "Remember when I fell down the hill and scraped my arm and got that big bump on my forehead with the ugly scab? It was three weeks before it was completely gone." But at the time she didn't know, she was panicked and afraid not of death, not the words, the concept still a bit obscure but something, a present suffering, an overwhelming anxiety, the terror on her face, her little moans. "It's okay" I said to my tiny little sister, my baby baby baby, "it's okay." "Per-ry" she sobbed and screamed. "It's okay," my footfalls already leveling out, the ground flattening. We stopped, clearly out of danger, even had it been the gravest sort, but she screamed and wailed, I grabbed her from behind, came around her, took her pixie frame in my arms, I said her name, "it's okay," I said her name, her name. She screamed, still in a panic. She knew I was there, knew she was okay, but the fear she couldn't name had not subsided, she screamed, not yet, I said her name, not yet, not yet.

    I wonder if at six she remembered, if at seven she could have recalled this on her last day, "Do you remember the time . . . ?" I envision her answering, but in here she talks like she's my age: "Oh my God! I was so scared, Perry. It was the strangest thing. There was just this terror! Remember how I screamed, the panic? I couldn't shake it even after we'd stopped. So strange to recall it now. It wasn't me." She wasn't eight, so even if she remembered, but I never asked so I don't know, just that it would be different. "Oh yeah" she might have said, "I was so scared I was gonna fall." "Aw, little scaredy" I would say and tickle her. She would have been tired, I think, but they told me it was a good day for her, a good morning, she was just tired. She knew then, the concept no longer obscure, *Tell Perry I love him.* She was swaddled in one of the terry cloth robes I had given her as presents (yellow for her last birthday, completing a rainbow, "I can wear any color I like!" she had said, paying no mind to having outgrown most of the others), and I would have tickled her and made her giggle, tired but she loved me and she felt I loved her, "felt" because she couldn't know, *No one ever knows or loves another.* I remember the first time I heard that line, "Yes" I said with the wonder of recognition, the *conocer,* "that's right." But she would have felt she knew, and it would have so happened she was right. Did she know anyway that I loved her as she did her best to make me know by proxy that she loved me? There's enough doubt in this overrated world to choke a fucking moose. I'd said "It won't be for long, a semester." "What does that mean" she asked. "You know, like from the start of school to Christmas vacation, except I'm going in July." "After fireworks" she burst out, hopeful animation. "Yes, I wouldn't miss that with you. That's our Ooh-Aah Day. We have to do it every year." She beamed, my parents standing behind me, loving the enthusiasm I could always get from her no matter what kind of day she was having. "You'll be back in time for Christmas, though, and my birthday. Is Amsterdam good? Do they have caribou?" "Is caribou like a duck?" "No!" she laughed, "it's a moooooooose!" "Where did you learn that?" I tickled. "In school" she squawked. "I think it's cold enough for mooses. Mooses? Meese? Meeses?" "Is it cold like where I was born?" That was Boston in January, where/ when she came two months early on a New Year's trip back East after the Giants ended the 49ers' quest to repeat. "Something like that" I answered. "It's warm here" she said. "You're right: Southern California is pretty warm." "Southern C-A. I like it, but I wish there would be snow. I want it to be all white one day." "Never happen" I said. "I know" she agreed. From her perspective she had more actual cause to know that I loved her than to predict the weather, not being some child climatology prodigy after all—and she happened to be right, so. "You'll miss Halloween, and Thanksgiving too." "I know" I said, "I know." "How I wish you would stay" she said. "You're going to make me cry, Pix." It may be an inconsistency to allow this nick of name (the stupid things we say), but there, a nice thought, a little snapshot pix, that word, term, endearment, nice thought outside the context, that context, gone yet surveyed regretfully from here/now. "Why" she asked, little big eyes taking me in. "Because I'll miss you. I'm going to Amsterdam because it's a great thing for me to get to do, but I love you, and even though it's great, it doesn't make up for the things I have to give up to do it, like miss Halloween and Thanksgiving or even just seeing you every day, because I love you, little pixie, my little baby baby sister," poking at her sides with my hands like little beaks, she laughed, you, like that, "I want to be with you all the days. Well, except when you bug me." I tickled her, she laughed, "I'm not a baby and I don't bug you!" "Oh yes you are and yes you do. I should call you babybug!" "I don't, but if you don't watch out I will, just you wait and watch!" And maybe when she said *Tell Perry I love him* she felt she knew, being right after all, please, at least that.

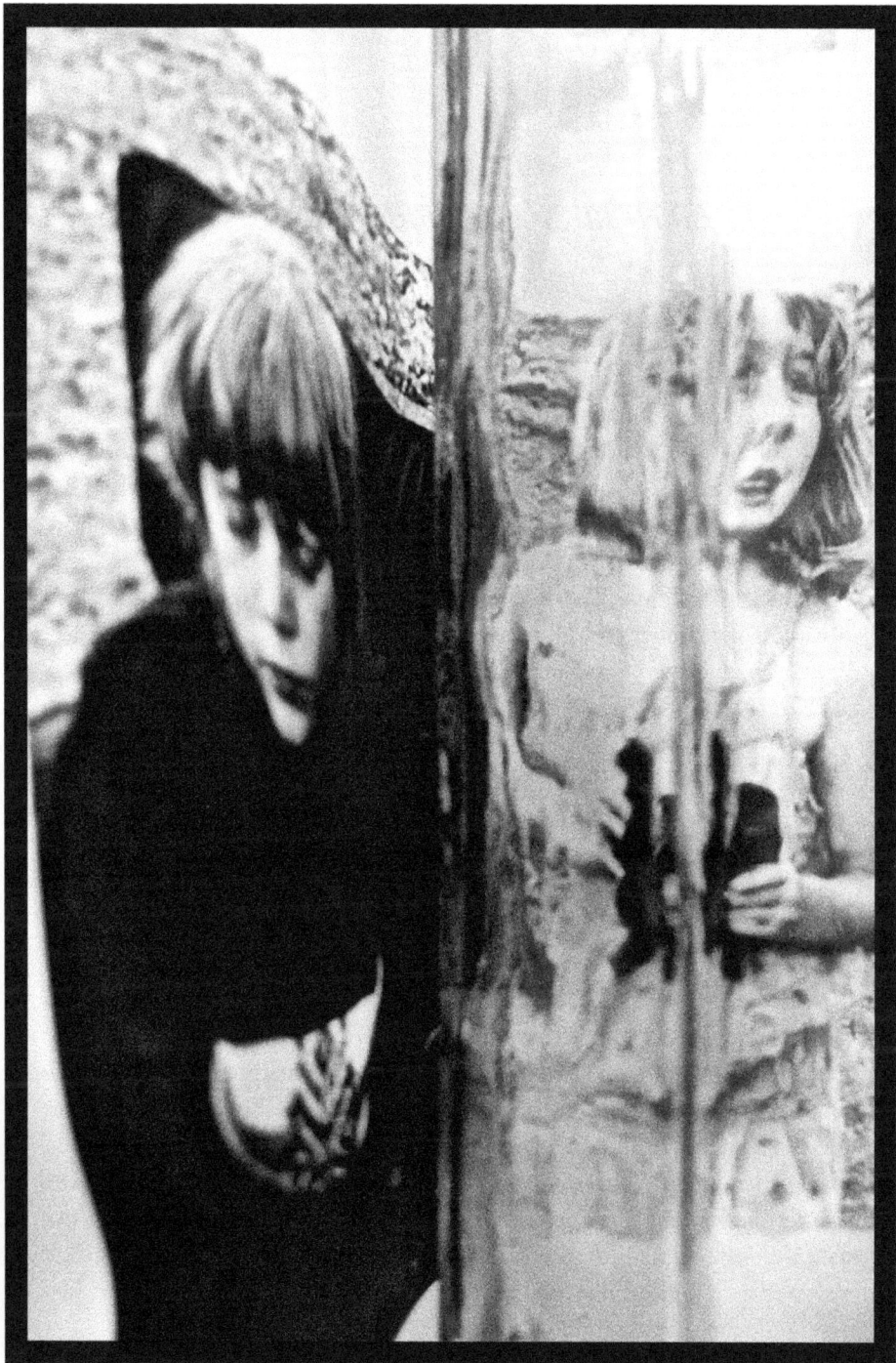

ROSEANN LLOYD

NEITHER HERE NOR THERE: WHAT THEY SAID

It's been two weeks since my brother Lloyd said he'd be back, I said to my friend. We breathed the moist air of linden tree, silver maples. Still June, the humidity hadn't hit us yet. *He promised me. He said he'd help me out after my foot surgery.* She quoted a poem, *He's not lost, the trees in the forest know where he is.* That day a deputy had found his van on a back road in the Boundary Waters, far from where he said he was going. His friends rushed to help Search and Rescue, to walk the cold trail, to watch the orange rubber boats drop into the clear water, to witness his clothes spread along the untended trail to Whisky Jack Lake. *He was wired for the wilderness. A woman in Ely said he was a legend up here—I wouldn't go where he would.*

❧   ❧   ❧

By July, the hope of rescue had gone. *I'm sorry we couldn't bring Lloyd home,* his friend Laura said at the memorial service. July 1st. I still saw his body lying in the woods, slowly sinking into the boggy June earth. Maybe he wouldn't have minded his bones resting there. Grade school friends teased us for our last name: *Hey, Skelton . . . The toe bone's connected to the heel bone, the heel bone's connected to the foot bone . . . .* He died in a place he loved. How many people can say that? Woods by the water. Trillium, Lady's Slipper, Dutchman's Britches. *His* Boundary Waters, *his* land and water, *his* edge of heaven. His disappearance was a personal offense to all those who love that endless maze and claim it for their own. A friend told me later, *When I heard about your brother, I took my dog and went up north to camp, to paint more water and stars.* Other people asked, *How could this happen?* As if the Boundary Waters is paradise—surely they haven't ever paddled a big lake like Saganaga in a storm, waves tipping the canoe, rain erasing the four directions like watercolors.

✦ ✦ ✦

Sinking into stormy memory, I took on another consolation: Lloyd's hatred of embalming. He'd recoiled when we saw our younger brother's body laid out, his swollen neck unable to be doctored by the undertaker. Oh, Philip. *No embalming, no embalming*, Lloyd said when our father died some thirty years later. But that story is neither here nor there. This is the story of the way I made it through that first summer, learning to walk again, wiped out by sorrow. *He died in a place he loved. When will a hiker stumble on his body?*

✦ ✦ ✦

Sometime along summer's beautiful turning, the sheriff told us there wouldn't be another search. *By this length of time after a death,* he said, slowly, gently— awkwardly, even—*we won't be able to find a body. By now the animals will have taken him.* Silence followed the sheriff's sentence. When I reported it to friends, they said, *What? The animals?* My daughter said, *I thought bears ate blueberries.* Our mother said, *What kind of animal could haul off a grown man?* My husband said, *Everybody is protein for somebody.* My nightmares conjured up mountain lions, bobcats, cougars. The sheriff added, *The most we can hope for—someday a hiker will come across his skull.* His skull? The skull would tell us nothing about his suffering. It wouldn't tell us if his feet gave out, or his lungs, or his heart. It wouldn't even tell us the location of his death.

✦ ✦ ✦

The skull only leads us back to mysteries, to childhood, to playing in the dark, to singing . . . *the head bone's connected to the neck bone.* The skull leads us to harvest and Halloween, dressing our kids up in scary costumes, that one twilight when my brother and I draped vines and stalks from the compost heap on our heads and ran towards the kids singing out, *We're the ghosts of the compost.* The skull has a candle in it; it leads us back in time to Shakespeare; forward to latter day saints of mystery, Abby, the TV forensic scientist with her skull T-shirt, *Hey, Bones, what's shakin'?*

CHRISTINE SIKORSKI

THE TRUTH ABOUT MY BROTHER
(Michael, 1957-1995)

My brother wore a tin hat and needed oil. He could spin his arms
    like propellers.
I would cling to his back and we would fly over Milwaukee to the Lake.

My brother had a team of horses he drove daily to deliver milk
    house-to-house in big metal cans.
He was kind to the horses, who pulled wagons 30 feet long.

My brother could turn his hiking boots into roller skates.
He gave squealing neighbor children rides in his arms.

My brother was a basket of fish. My brother was a warm hat.
My brother was harmonica music and crisp watermelon.

My brother was the set of lungs I used for 35 years.
He was a hand grenade. He was the truth told slant.

My brother was green camouflage. He was Campbell's soup.
He was a firecracker taped to a Hot Wheels car and a footrace
    around the block.

My brother was a shout across a long field, a slide down a snowy hill,
a Christmas card, a croquet set, a finger painting, a German chocolate cake.

My brother was a pink, sardonic rabbit, a peal of thunder, a joke
    told before bed.
He was a diagram in ball point, high top tennies, a jeans jacket
    lined with red.

He was a sack of marbles, a well-fingered guitar, a chemistry set,
     tambourine, and kazoo.
He was licorice and electricity, a garter snake and a wooden raft,
     a plastic army man and a tiny flag.

He was my fort, my protection, my army base.
My brother was a general. He won the war.

ARRANGING PHOTOS BEFORE THE FUNERAL

Boy on a bicycle. Boy on a train. Boy in the cockpit of an airplane, waving. Boy of four, boy of seven, boy with a prayer book, boy with his front teeth missing. Boy with an Easter egg in each hand, one in his mouth, one on his head. Boy with cheeks blown into a pumpkin face. Boy with no guile. Boy on a couch sleeping, cat on his chest. Boy in a pyramid, second from top. Boy on a bench, girl beside him. Boy on a bicycle broken in half. Sweet boy demolished by the bulk of a car. Body flying through gray sky, through rain. Broken boy and his broken mother. Missing boy and his lost mother. Boy in heaven and here on earth, the sound of his sister keening.

FOR THE BROTHERS

For Cindy's, struck by lightning
For Janet's, leapt from a bridge
For mine, hit by a car
For my mother's, blown up in the war

For Carol's, of leukemia
For Cheryl's, by a train
For Rachel's, drowned at nine
For Carol's, burst artery in the brain

For Kay's, who drank till he was poisoned
For Caroline's, when the plane went down
For Amanda's, though she will not say how
For Julie's, of his own gun

For yours, if he's already gone
I have made a little song:

too young too young
you left us too young

ELIZABETH BRULE' FARRELL

FINDING A SISTER

My sister, who was nine years older, seemed mysterious and alluring to me as a young girl. When I was nine and she was eighteen, everything she did seemed intriguing. Her world in the 1960s involved slicking her skin with baby oil and lounging beneath the sun, then soaking in a tub with luminous bubbles that made a romance of getting clean. She would turn on her transistor radio and loudly sing along while indulging in rituals to smooth, powder, and curl, emerging from the bathroom ready for her evening date.

Being the mischievous younger sister, I would rush to the front door so I could greet her date to entertain him with my array of adolescent jokes, never able to figure out the magic my sister cast upon those who waited patiently in our living room. She always kissed my cheek before she left, the room still smelling of her Jean Nate perfume as I returned to our shared bedroom trying to stay awake until she came home.

One night my glamorous sister was brought home hours early. Her date told our mother that she was drunk and had embarrassed him at the restaurant. It was then that our mother tried to educate him about what having diabetes meant, and that my sister was experiencing a diabetic reaction that made her slur her words and lose her balance, and needed to eat immediately. He appeared understanding for the moment but she never saw him again. Having acquired type 1 diabetes in childhood, she took three shots of insulin a day. Once she allowed me to pretend to be her nurse, and as I pinched the skin of her arm so she could inject herself, I became afraid and let it go before she slid in the needle. I had hurt her and could not forgive myself. My tears soaked the Peter Pan collar of her shirt.

Through the next few years she dated often but never could find a partner who was willing to go forward into an unknown future living with her disease. Public knowledge and the support groups we now have nearly fifty years later were not readily available. My sister died in her early twenties in a diabetic coma. She gave up hope that anyone might love her enough to create a life with her, raise a family, or of pursuing a career she could enjoy. She became afraid of the stories she heard about losing limbs and becoming blind, limitations that seemed dire to a woman so young who felt quite alone. Unfortunately our mother, who had been a photographer's model in the 1950s and valued outward appearances, had no ability to comfort or encourage a daughter who she felt not whole. This was the failing of a mother who did not know any better, but my sister took the failing to be her own.

So one evening she decided, with a sky full of stars and a moon half full, to stop taking her insulin. She once told me she felt like a junkie with tracks on her arms and legs from each injection site. My young arms held her as she cried. On this night she was alone and hastened the effects of not taking her insulin by swallowing a bottle of pills. Taking her own life ended her suffering. Mine was just beginning.

At the funeral our mother pushed into my palm Valium and handed me a glass of scotch to drink them down. She told me not to shed a tear or talk to anyone about what had happened. I was thirteen and my sister twenty-two when she closed her eyes forever. Obeying our insistent mother, I did not know this would be the start of years of numbing memories, of pushing away reality. A different time than our current one in which AA, grieving groups, therapy, and many other opportunities exist for helping each other in whatever situations we find ourselves.

I flourished despite keeping my secrets, and was functional enough to graduate college, work in advertising, begin a marriage and raise two sons. I became sober and tried to live the words uttered by Martin Luther King Jr. that we all are wounded, asking us how we use our wounds.

I would use mine to write poems and tell the truth, unafraid to rip open the universe to discover what is positive, turning shame and regret into strength and determination while trying to help others do the same.

For years when I would go grocery shopping and see a woman about the same age that my sister might be had she lived, I would stare at her from across the aisle while pretending to touch the skin of a peach. I would wonder if my sister might wear her hair in that style now, or wear those pants, or choose the items in the cart for her own dinner. I would always smile if I caught her eye, for after all, that woman in some sense of the word is my very sister today.

I will always mourn and miss her, but have been surprised through the following decades of my life to find loving sisters in women of all ages, from a variety of backgrounds and cultures, blessing me with their insights and sharing with each other as only sisters know how to do.

MICHELE WOLF

THE GRIEVING ROOM
For Cathy Wolf, 1958–1982

I.
Your eyes are open, blank, fixed.
They are not like the eyes of the sleeping,
Lids a hairbreadth lifted, eyes calm,
Or, in the trance of a dream, fluttering.
Nor like the eyes stilled in a photograph,
Flat but familiar,
Reliable glimpses into a soul.
Nor even like two glossy stones
At the foot of a pond,
One moment clear and then,
When the wind
Rumples the surface, far away.
They are eyes of the dead.
Pressed to the bed rail, we stand
Over you, a mother flanked
By two daughters only, arm in arm,
Watching as you heave
With each blast of the ventilator.
Your heart repeats
Its jagged scrawl across the screen.
You are already there,
At your destination,
Already worlds beyond our sky.
What do you see, my sweet Cathy,
What do you see?

II.
I cannot bring myself
To touch your cheek, to kiss you,
Take your hand,
This body
That was once my sister.
Later you would show me
Where you had journeyed,
Through shadows to a circle
Of loved ones, floating in a grotto
With soft walls of burgundy-gray cloud.
Each face shone with replenished youth.
Our grandmother Rose, not as she died
But dark haired, in her bloom at forty,
Rocked you against her,
As did the others in turn, overcome
By that silent crying
In which the chest swells
But the eyes no longer tear.
In spite of your weariness
You had reached toward those first
Welcoming arms, the arms
Of our father, who also arrived
Here young, before you began to speak.
And yet how you recognized him,
How you did know him.

III.
In line at the hospital cafeteria
I chose chicken soup for our mother,
Turkey and mashed potatoes for me.
It was the longest wait,
Once your brain had died,
For your sturdy heart to follow.
The room was draped in tinsel and snowflakes.
The speakers were caroling "Deck the Halls."

"Have some cake, dear," offered the serving
Woman. "As much cake as you'd like.
Merry Christmas!"
"Thank you," my voice answered dully,
A reflex. "Merry Christmas to you."
How much I resembled
That life-size mechanical Santa
At the entrance, his slow-motion waving—
The way I chewed, then attempted
To swallow, turkey,
Each bite lodged in my throat,
The way I roused myself this morning
To dress for a funeral.
That was how we spent December 25,
The day on which our present
Was not given, but taken away.
A present we were permitted to borrow,
But too exquisite to keep,
Wrapped in roses,
Scattered with earth.
And one last time,
Before you are lowered,
I touch your polished wooden box.

IV.

For our mother

I sleep to the side in her oversize bed.
When she cries in the night,
I offer my hand,
But even I am unable to reach her.
"Her life was so sad," she blurted out
This morning, eyes filling again,
Reminded of surgeries, tantrums,
Breakdowns—how you never quite fit in.
And in the grocery store or a restaurant
Every voice she hears, the back

Of each young woman's head,
Seems to be yours.
Your kitchen chair
Since you sat on a phone book
To reach the table
Remains cavernous, empty.
She keeps expecting you to return,
Singing one of those sugary
Hit songs as you set out the plates,
Brimming over with news of your students—
How Jasmine no longer reverses her R's
And Adam can write his first name.
Dozens of visitors stop by the house,
Yet no one can comfort her.
She sits on a stiff chair
Tucked in a chamber inside her heart
Where no one can enter.
The curtains are drawn.
It is stuffy with a heavy
Shifting darkness, a room
Full of shadows. She is
Wailing, beseeching,
Quavering, her arms
Uplifted, fingers splayed,
Reaching
At shadows.

KAVANAUGH

SING

I smiled when I found a brown-edged picture among my sister Jean's old photos yesterday. She looked regal—at nine she was a little Liz Taylor look-a-like.

There's Mom, eyes squinting, her hand resting on Jean's shoulder. There's me, I'm a real knock-out leaning into the other side of Mom, wearing high-topped shoes below a pinafore with standout ruffles—my knees too big for my skinny legs, my arm wrapped around Mom's thigh, my thumb inside my face. The floppy curls in my eyes would be red if the photograph were in color. The date on the snapshot's scalloped edge tells me I was four years old at the time it was taken. 1947. I don't remember this time in my life at all. This picture's happy.

❧   ❧   ❧

One mysterious day a year later, life changed for Jean and me. I've pushed that dark day so deep it stinks of mold. Now here it comes, a sourness in my throat.

My five-year-old mind didn't know our dad was leaving Mom. It didn't know Dad arranged for Jean and me to live in a private foster home, fifty cornstalk miles away from our mom who only rode streetcars.

My chest tightens as I summon up that pivotal winter day. Why were we alone in that big backseat? Why was that ominous suitcase in the car? Why was our father standing in the snow waving good-bye? Who were the strangers who drove us to that scary house? Why did they LEAVE US BEHIND and DRIVE AWAY?

There were no answers to quiet my cries. Not then. Not now. I'm sure Jean was traumatized as well, but she saw the event through more worldly eyes.

After all, she was ten.

❧ ❧ ❧

Jean was my protector, my only family as we bumped through three more foster homes, private homes where strangers lived, homes arranged by my father, driven there courtesy of him and his Cadillac. I was afraid of my father and his temper.

I don't know if Jean was afraid. Maybe she had a favorite-daughter relationship with Dad, or maybe at ten she knew how to be brave. She gave me kisses and whispers to soothe my fears. She never showed me hers. Mothers don't.

After the foster homes, Mom married again and we lived with her. Not for long, shorter than a school year. Mom's new husband abused Jean. But I didn't know that was the reason Jean ran away.

The night she split she got real close to my face so I could see her in that midnight moment. She looked into my eyes, put her finger to her lips, stroked my cheek, and kissed me. Then she slipped into the dark.

My memory is murky. I imagine thirteen-year-old Jean transferring from one CTA bus to another across the Southside of Chicago on a March night, maybe carrying a heavy brown shopping bag by its twine handles, finding her way to Dad, and I bet she had a scrap of paper all folded up tiny in her coat pocket with Dad's address on it.

Back in my bed, I skidded into my default position, bug small, eyes tight. I wasn't safe anymore without Jean.

There's no timeframe in my mind, no clock and no calendar to mark Dad and Jean coming to take me, screaming, away from Mom again.

Dad bought a second-hand bicycle for me—with a broken kickstand. I thought it was a gift. After I learned to ride it I discovered the real reason for it. I peddled that bike to the grocery store every week. With the list and the ten-dollar bill he left on the table. Buying the groceries was one of my jobs. I was nine. That kickstand clanged every time the pedal hit it, clack-clack, clack-clack. The store was ten blocks away. I can still hear that kickstand.

Jean had jobs, too. She did the laundry in the ringer washer. She did the cooking, and after the dishes were done, she did her homework. I helped with the laundry and the dishes. Jean was the keeper of the house then, and sometimes she riled me with her bossiness. "Wipe your feet. Stop tracking mud through the kitchen."

Jean went away to college and came back a singer, steeped in coffeehouse music. She had a smoky singing voice, and even though my voice made our parakeet squawk, she insisted I sing along with her. Maybe she thought that would give me confidence. Growing up, I was uncomfortable with people. Jean hoped to see a flower bloom—she would wrench my dreams out of me and then she'd champion every one of them.

As an adult, Jean was brilliantly outspoken. By the end of the Fifties she was a feminist—ahead of the times—and a force others would be wary of. I loved her in a way that can only be described as primal. She had been my lifeline since I was five. I would go feral if anybody criticized her.

Jean needed a heart operation when she was twenty-three. The surgeons discovered she had an infantile aorta, which was the result of rheumatic fever when she was a baby.

They operated and I waited in the hall. After fourteen hours in surgery, she was wheeled out of the operating room.

The pallor of her face put a rock in my throat. Heart surgery in the Fifties left survivors a Chicago gray. She looked dead.

It was the first time death had stood close to me. I trailed behind her blanketed body, sobbing. I can see the rear wheel on the gurney. I can hear it squeak and see it spin, making it difficult for the orderly to push. Nurses were waiting to move her—to a bed in the ICU. Only then did I realize she was still alive.

She needed another aorta fix ten years later. I was there. The tracheotomy damaged her vocal cords and left her with a scratchy voice—annoying and hard to listen to.

That voice.

No more singing.

I know—it wasn't pleasant for her, either, but I really didn't get that then.

Jean went into the hospital one last time when she was in her fifties. It was her heart again. I went to Ann Arbor to be with her.

I never knew what I'd find when I walked into her room. One day, there was nothing but the gauges and cables hanging out of the wall. When I grasped the emptiness, my own heart stopped.

A nurse came running in behind me, breathless. "She's alive–she took a turn and now she's on a respirator. We moved her to ICU."

I found her there, unconscious, damp ringlets stuck to her forehead.

I spent all day and all night, and all the next day with her . . . and into the night, once more. I stared at the respirator tube in her mouth and watched her closed eyes. I listened to the antiseptic room breathe and sigh.

I watched the lines pulse on the machines. I counted floor tiles. I ate Cheetos and chocolate. I tried to read.

Going on midnight, she woke, and I came to life. I knew she'd recover; she always did.

She looked at me, took my hand and pulled it toward her, turned my palm up and touched it with her other forefinger. Then she wrote.

I watched her finger.

I said no.

She wrote the word again. I said no again. Her eyes shone. She nodded her head at me and poked her finger a few times into my palm. "Sing."

I winced.

She stroked my fingers gently.

Midnight in the ICU. I can't carry a tune. I can't remember lyrics. Jean did her happy eye thing.

Yeah.

So I raised my voice and belted out the only song I knew by heart: Janis Joplin's "Oh Lord, Won't You Buy Me a Mercedes Benz." Out at the desk, the nurses clapped.

Jean died six months later. At her memorial, I told the Midnight-in-the-ICU story. There at the podium I channeled my inner Janis Joplin, and one last time, I sang for my sister.

Loud and bad, in front of God and everybody.

SHARON LASK MUNSON

FOREWARNED

You are about to forget the red rose bush
that blooms each May on your birthday,
ingredients for the tart lemon pie
you serve on fine blue china,
the touch of our mother's cool firm hand.

You reach for slippery names,
forgotten titles, mislaid books.
You tape reminders of daily appointments
on bare white walls,
stare bewildered in front of grocery shelves,
torn between stewed tomatoes
or canned peaches swimming in sweet, thick syrup.

Slivers of a puzzle you try to recall
lie scattered, strewn between
cracks in the sidewalk
we jumped over as children.

Roads you used to travel easily
are now slightly beyond reach.
I see you at the crossroads, adrift,
off course in an uncharted realm.
I am forewarned.

SARAH W. BARTLETT

FULL CIRCLE
February 2014, for my sister

Last night you lay curled
before sleep, your fragile frame
barely denting your soft bed. I massaged
your back, arms, hands, legs and feet
the way, in my early years your hand was the last
I felt before sleep soothing me into quiet,
filling holes left by an uneasy mother; holes
you, too, carried and soon enough filled
with resentment at being consigned to care.

But last night, you sighed under my hands
oiling skin thinned with the depletions of time,
smoothing scar and keratosis, the fissured hump
of heel hard and immovable at the end
of withered calf, soaking in tenderness, time
hovering uncertainly overhead as I held you,
crooned our cradle song
"only don't forget to sail
 back again to me."

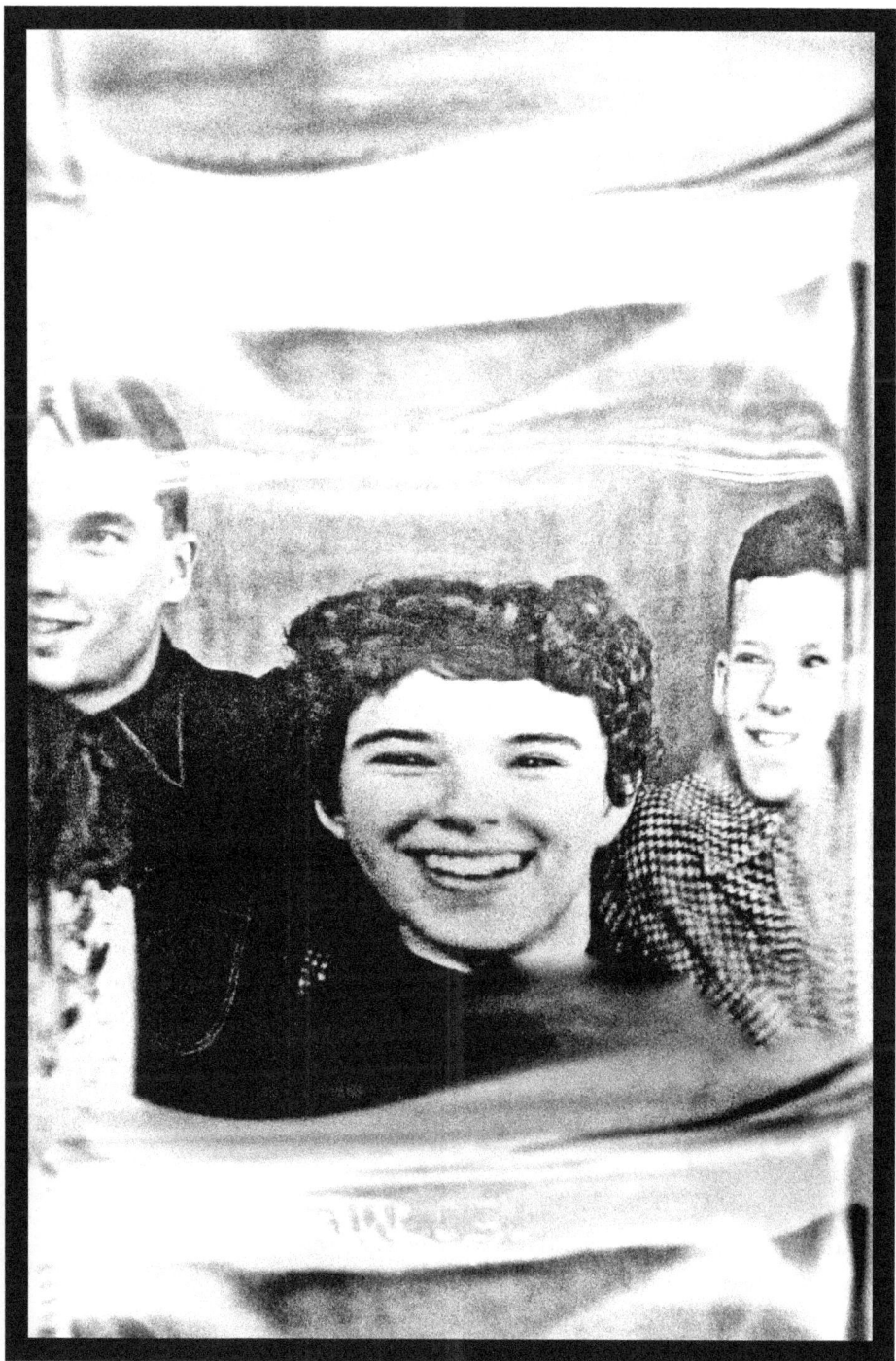

FRANCES RUHLEN McCONNEL

MY BROTHER WITH UNDERPANTS ON HIS HEAD
for Russell Grice Ruhlen, 1942-2011

When I heard they found you naked
with your underpants on your head,
brain discombobulated from the toxins
your liver could no longer wash from your blood

(Hepatitis C), I thought of the three of us kids
the few times we were left alone in that household
of three watchful adults, including Nana, how sometimes
we'd strip, put our undies on our heads and romp
through the house in unholy and ludicrous riot.

Our older brother, the sly instigator,
Lord of Misrule, egging us on and snickering;
myself high on self-horror and fear of getting caught;
and you, our little brother, you were the gleeful imp,
prancing and spinning and cavorting,
leaping from chair to sofa to chair
like an uncaged monkey; pushing me aside in line
to slide our bottoms down our father's regal
red leather armchair, letting out a whoop of delight.

Though I shielded my eyes from the mirrors
that in those days hung on every wall, opening
spaces in the dim rooms, multiplying the light,
multiplying ourselves; you did the hootchy-cootchy,
a skinny-legged kid in time's looking glass.

You with your reckless independence, always,
you laughed and said I could write this poem
after I saw you myself one morning in your last December,
trying to cram your underpants on your head.

Neither you nor I could say what it meant to you
to don those plaid boxers; perhaps you thought
their legs sleeves, or perhaps they were divinely
inspired—a jester's cap with which you could mock
the powers of darkness awaiting you and us all.

A TOUCH OF MORPHINE

A touch of morphine and he is in the brush
somewhere alone with his wounds,
holed up where no one can touch him.
We crawled under the Bridal Wreath bush
when we were small and had our feelings hurt.
The others snapped off branches
and tried to poke us out of there.
Now, no one wants to poke him out.
Besides, after the nurse's scolding, we've put on
the green vinyl gloves and can touch him
only in metaphor. Or sneakily brush
our lips against his forehead.

He said, in the hospital the first time—
is it months ago?—when I smacked him
on the lips hello, he said he couldn't remember
the last time someone else had kissed him.
Today his lips are black, blood in the corners.
It would take a love more powerful
than a sister's to kiss him now.

Our older brother and I woo him
with his childhood names, evoking a lost world,
orphaned together these decades.
Rusty is the name our kids still
know him by—*Uncle Rusty.*

While he was still only a lump and a ridge
Dad watched wobble across Mom's belly,
they started calling him *Snorky.*

When I asked if he remembered
he said, *yes*, but *yes* is his default mode now.
Funny for such a stubborn character.
Another family name was *Muley*.

In high school, he was called *George* as in
the catch-phrase *let George do it*.
Born at the chalkboard in a bone-head
math class when the teacher resorted on him
in despair over his other lackadaisical students.
He shouldn't have been there, but back then
he was shy about showing his smarts, or maybe
not quite believing in them, being last in line
in the family hierarchy. They say people
with many nicknames are much beloved;
but he laments never having been in love back.
Under the thin flannel hospital blanket,
his belly is distended with ascitis;
but he is too fragile to have it drained.
He grew to clamor for that procedure—
Paracentesis: the long needle, the cramps—
mocking the pregnant swelling
under his old man's suspenders.
"Snorky," we whisper at his pillow,
trying to draw him back, "Rusty-dusty,"
giving up his secret names.

Only two of us left to remember this.
And then there'll be one. And then
an extinct culture.

ALEXANDRINA SERGIO

I TELL HER

about the houses she's lived in,
her wedding,
the funny things,
the old political people
we once gleefully skewered with the
sarcasm learned from our Irish mother.
She smiles at the tales—
they're not like how most talk at her,
always quizzing,
saying *You must remember.*
She doesn't, but she still knows how to feel stupid
so she says *Oh yes, I remember.*
I tell her about the snazzy royal blue suit
with nail-head arrows across the front,
better looking than it sounds,
tell about the beach days,
the red two-piece that turned the guys' heads,
and she listens, sometimes looks surprised,
says *I love your memory.*

She's being wisped away as if on indrawn breath,
more there than here.
I scramble to gather up the pieces she's dropped,
give them back to her,
but when she turns
she takes only stories.

ASPERGILLUM

They sprayed holy water on the bikes and the bikers
with their aspergillums, the metal (shakers) that are dipped
into vessels of holy water.
         News Item, *The Hartford Courant*

The priests and deacons
whirl aspergillums,
bless the bikes,
shower each gleaming machine,
each studded rider
with prosperities of
Clear Sky,
Smooth Road,
Safe Journey.

Sister, were I allowed an aspergillum
I would leap, dance it about you,
command its baptism to inundate you
with remembrance of
teen boys who whistled when you walked by,
your fold-out honeymoon apartment,
a first-paycheck red coat,
what you had for lunch,
who visited today,
my name.

This denied,
I would bend, fold my hands,
beg the waters at least to touch you
with gentle fortunes of
Clear Sky,
Smooth Road,
Safe Journey.

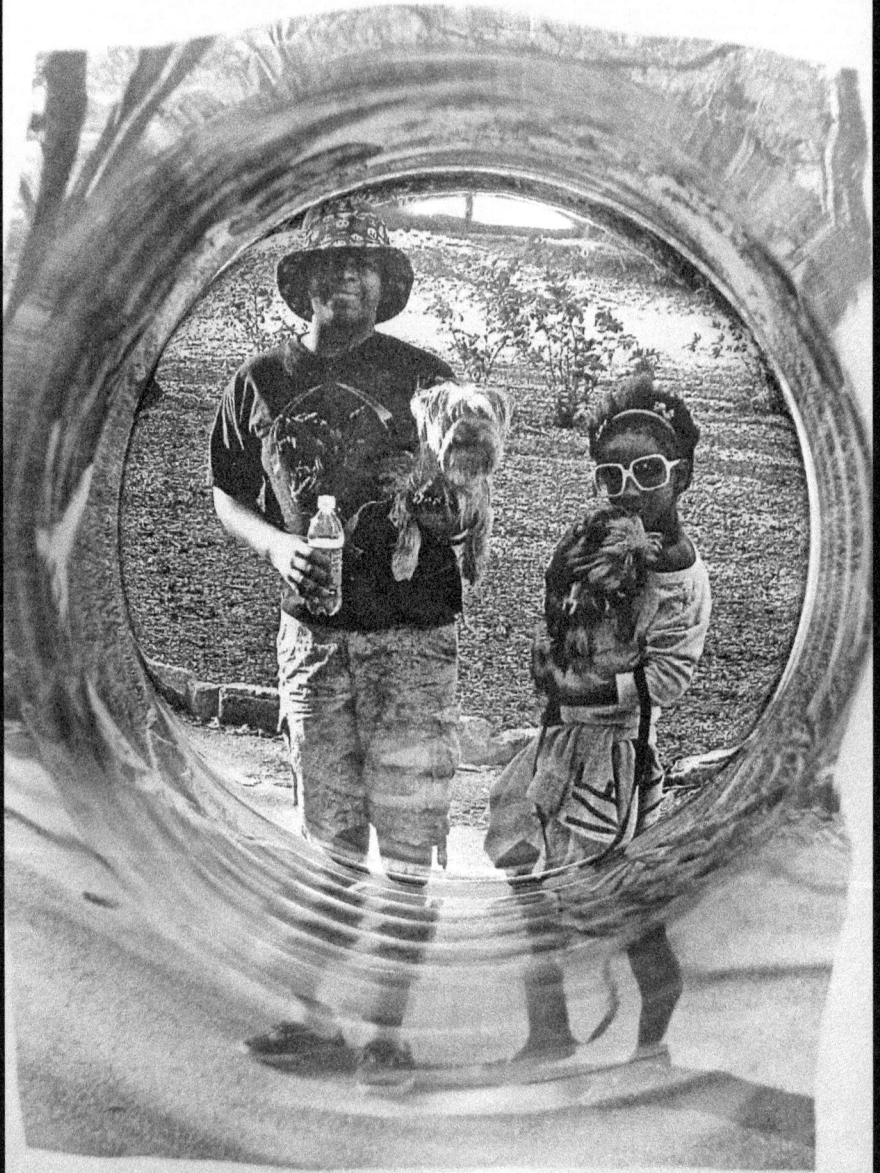

ACKNOWLEDGEMENTS

Laura Apol's "Twin Sister, Stillborn" was previously published in *Crossing the Ladder of Sun* (Michigan State University Press, 2004).

Rachel Squires Bloom previously published "Rutabaga" in *California Quarterly (2010).*

Maureen Tolman Flannery's "Comparing Memories" and "Test Results," now sections of "Fishing for Father," were first published in *Roll: A Collection of Personal Narratives*, edited by CoCo Harris (Telling Our Stories Press, 2012).

Grey Held previously published "The Bested and the Best" in *Pudding Magazine* (2003).

Roseann Lloyd previously published "Neither Here Nor There: What They Said" in *The Boy Who Slept Under the Stars: A Memoir in Poetry* (Holy Cow! Press, 2012).

Katharyn Howd Machan's "Christmas Eve, and I See" first appeared in *When She's Asked to Think of Colors* (Palettes & Quills), "My Brother" in *Negative Capability* and "Virgin Poem" in *Cedar Rock.*

Susan Mahan's "Goddess of the Moon" was first published in *Words Apart Magazine* (2015).

Greggory Moore's "How They Say It," originally appeared as Section 73 of his novel, *The Use of Regret* (2012).

Tania Moore's "The Messenger" originally appeared in *Kestrel.*

Sharon Lask Munson's "Forewarned" first appeared in *Punkin House Digest.*

Timothy J. Myers previously published "To My Sibling, Miscarried 1957" in *Prairie Dog.*

Peter Schmitt's "Thanksgiving: Visiting My Brother on the Ward" and "The Ropes" were first published in *Renewing the Vows* (David Robert Books, 2007) while "The Hands" originally appeared in *Tigertail Magazine* (2013).

Alexandrina Sergio's "Aspergillum" was previously published in *Caduceus* (Yale Medical Group, 2008) and "I Tell Her" in her book *My Daughter Is Drummer in the Rock 'n Roll Band* (Antrim House, 2009).

Christine Sikorski's "For the Brothers" was published in a somewhat different version in *Great River Review* (2001).

Cindy Stewart-Rinier published a slightly different version of "Stoichiometry" in *Crab Creek Review* (Winter, 2014).

Alison Stone's "Asperger's" previously appeared in the chapbook *Borrowed Logic* (Dancing Girl Press, 2014).

Loretta Diane Walker previously published "Breaking the Ice" and "Candidate for Statistics" in her collection *Word Ghetto.*

Michele Wolf's "Astigmatism" previously appeared in *Southern Poetry Review* as well as her chapbook *The Keeper of Light* (*Painted Bride Quarterly*) and her book *Conversations During Sleep* (Anhinga Press). "The Grieving Room" previously was published in her book *Immersion* (The Word Works).

Gary Young's "Family Matters" appeared in his book *No Other Life* (Heyday Books, 2005).

Photographs by Heather Tosteson, who thanks all those—including contributors, friends, and family—who so generously donated images to art with no idea what was coming next.

We are very grateful to our guest editors, Kathleen Housley, Kerry Langan, and Michele Markarian, indispensable members of the Wising Up Press Writers Collective, for so ably sharing their skills as writers, editors, and engaged and thoughtful readers. We couldn't do what we do without them.

CONTRIBUTORS

Laura Apol, associate professor at Michigan State University, is the author of three poetry collections: *Falling into Grace* (Dordt College Press, 1998); *Crossing the Ladder of Sun* (MSU Press, 2004, winner of the Oklahoma Book Award); and, most recently, *Requiem, Rwanda* (MSU Press, 2015) drawn from her work with survivors of the 1994 genocide against Tutsi.

Patricia Barone is the oldest of eight siblings. Her most recent book is *The Scent of Water*, a collection of poetry (Blue Light Press). *The Wind*, a novella, and *Handmade Paper*, poetry, were Minnesota Voices Award winners (New Rivers Press). Her short stories appeared in Wising Up Press, Peter Lang, and Plume/Penguin anthologies. She has received a Loft-McKnight Award of Distinction and a Lake Superior Contemporary Writers Award.

Carol Barrett holds doctorates in both clinical psychology and creative writing, and teaches for Union Institute & University. Her work appears widely, including *JAMA (Journal of the American Medical Association)*, *Poetry International*, *Poetry Northwest*, *American Journal of Art Therapy*, and *Journal of Consulting and Clinical Psychology*. Her books include the prize-winning *Calling in the Bones* (Ashland Poetry Press, 2005.)

Sarah W. Bartlett has published in *Aurorean, LiteraryMama, Minerva Rising* and *Ars Medica*. Her chapbook, *Into the Great Blue*, was published by *FinishingLinePress*. She contributed to *Women on Poetry* (2012) and *Contemporary American Women* (2009); and co-edited *Hear Me, See Me: Incarcerated Women Write* (2013), raw poetry and prose from Vermont's incarcerated women whose words she's midwifed weekly since 2010.

Rachel Squires Bloom has had poems in *Hawaii Review, Fugue, Poetry East, Main Street Rag, Panhandler, Mad Poet's Review, Bluster, 96 Inc., Bellowing Ark, Thin Air, Taproot Literary Review, True Romance, Lucid Stone, Green Hills Literary Lantern, Chest, A View from the Bed, Cities: An Anthology* and *Poet Lore*. She writes and teaches in Quincy, MA.

Deborah Burch-Lavis is Professor of the Practice of Writing and Communication at Rice University where she teaches creative nonfiction and academic writing and research. She has published numerous articles and essays, and her book, *Leadership Communication* (McGraw-Hill), is in its 4th edition. Her most recent published personal essay is "The Last Christmas" in the anthology *Shifts (Muse*Write Press*)*.

Brian Burns is a junior English major at Emmanuel College in Boston, MA. He was raised in New Jersey and New Hampshire. He is the recipient of a Gold Key from the Scholastic, Inc. Art and Writing Awards and an American Voices Award finalist. His future aspirations include a career in publishing and the evasion of mini-van ownership.

Katie Glauber Bush is the third of four children. She worked in public relations for nearly four decades. Her humor and memoir writing was honored by the San Francisco chapter of the National League of American Pen Women in 2012 and 2013. Her work appears in the anthology *Times They Were A-Changing* (She Writes Press).

Christa Champion coached collegiate basketball for two decades before beginning her second career as a writer. Like Thoreau, she has become rich by making her wants few, and supplying them herself. "The Sun Is the Center of the Universe" is her first piece of fiction to be published. A Massachusetts native, she currently lives in Oberlin, OH.

Lori DeSanti received her MFA Degree in Poetry from Southern Connecticut State University. Her works have appeared in journals including *Spry, Adanna, Winter Tangerine Review, Drunk Monkeys, Ekphrasis* and the 2014 Writer's Digest *Poem Your Heart Out* Anthology. She is a two-time Pushcart Prize Nominee, a Best of the Net Nominee, and the recipient of the 2014 William Kloefkorn Award.

Elizabeth Brule' Farrell has published poems in *Reflections On A Life With Diabetes, Poetry East, The Paterson Literary Review, Beyond Forgetting, Earth's Daughters, Proposing on the Brooklyn Bridge, The Healing Muse, Desert Call, Just Like A Girl, Calliope, The Onset Review, Poem, Revised,* and more.

Maureen Tolman Flannery is the author of eight books of poetry, including *Tunnel into Morning, Destiny Whispers to the Beloved,* and *Ancestors in the Landscape.* Over five hundred of her poems have been published in anthologies and literary reviews, among them: *North American Review, Xavier Review, BorderSenses, Wisconsin Review, Birmingham Poetry Review, Calyx, Pedestal, Poetry East* and *Atlanta Review.*

Diane D. Gillette writes, teaches, and tries to keep up with the voracious appetites of her cats. Her work has also appeared in other fine literary magazines and anthologies. She lives in Chicago with the love of her life and is probably working on a novel right now.

Rose Hamilton-Gottlieb has published her fiction in *The Chicago Tribune; Imitation Fruit; Ginosko; Make; Papier Mache Press* anthologies *Grow Old Along With Me, At Our Core,* and *Generation to Generation; Room of One's Own,* and *Faultline.* "Favorite Son" is from an unpublished novel set in her home state of Iowa, to which she recently returned after fifty years in California.

Grey Held is a recipient of a National Endowment for the Arts Fellowship in Creative Writing. His first book of poems, *Two-Star General,* was published in 2012 (Brick Road Poetry Press). His second book of poems, *Spilled Milk,* was published in 2013 (Word Press). He works closely with the Mayor's Office of Cultural Affairs in Newton, MA to direct projects that connect contemporary poets (and their poetry) with a wider audience.

Charlotte Jones promised herself she would do something more creative after a career in the oil industry and began writing. Her work has appeared in over eighty literary and commercial publications including *The Bellevue Literary Review, Nerve Cowboy* and *Barbaric Yawp.* When not writing, she enjoys golf, gardening, traveling, playing piano and singing.

Kavanaugh's poetry, prose and photographs have appeared in *Melancholy Hyperbole, When Women Waken,* and *Blotterature.* She travels the scenic route between St. Pete, FL and the Off Campus Writers Workshop (OCWW) in Winnetka, IL. When she's not writing, she's listening, picking up slices of life or shells on a beach.

J.S. Kierland is a graduate of the University of Connecticut and the Yale Drama School. He has published over sixty stories in literary journals like *Fiction International, Colere, International Short Stories, Trajectory,* and many others. His short story collection, *15 of the Best Short Stories,* was published by Underground Voices, and his novella *Hard To Learn* has just been released as an ebook by the same publisher.

Steve Koppman has contributed fiction to literary, regional and Jewish magazines including *ZYZZYVA, The Berkeley Monthly* and *Jewish Currents,* and anthologies. His short plays have been produced across the U.S. and anthologized. He was co-author of *Treasury of American-Jewish Folklore.* He has contributed to many other publications including *The Huffington Post, The Nation, The Village Voice* and *The San Francisco Chronicle.*

Susan Lanier, MFA, grew up in rural Ohio, taught elementary school and college level creative writing in Vermont and now lives in Santa Fe, NM. She has been published in *Harvard Magazine, MS., Passages North, The Poetry Miscellany,* and *THE Magazine of Santa Fe,* among others. She was the First Prize Winner of *Oberon Poetry Magazine's* 2012 International Poetry Contest.

Ruth Latta is the author of fourteen books including history, biography and fiction. Her most recent novel is *The Songcatcher and Me* (Ottawa, Baico, 2013).

Sharon Leder's fiction, about dynamics in Jewish families and the impacts of feminism, appears in *Connected: What Remains As We All Change* (Wising Up Press), *Jewish Fiction online, WIPs Online,* and *Femspec.* Her novel *She Needs To Know* was a semi-finalist in Merrimack Media's Outstanding Writer Award. Her novel-in-progress *Mirrors* features a teenage Holocaust refugee and a young Palestinian mother.

Roseann Lloyd has published four collections of poetry and four other books. Her most recent book, *The Boy Who Slept Under the Stars: a Memoir in Poetry,* which contains the prose poem in this anthology, was published in 2012 (Holy Cow! Press). *War Baby Express,* also from Holy Cow! Press, won the Minnesota Book Award for Poetry, 1997.

Katharyn Howd Machan is the author of thirty-two published collections, and her poems have appeared in numerous magazines, anthologies, and textbooks, including *The Bedford Introduction to Literature* and *Sound and Sense*. She is a full professor in the Department of Writing at Ithaca College in central New York State. In 2012 she edited *Adrienne Rich: A Tribute Anthology* (Split Oak Press).

Paula MacKay is currently finishing her MFA in Creative Writing at Pacific Lutheran University. For the past fifteen years, she has studied bears and other wildlife with her husband, Robert, with whom she co-edited *Noninvasive Survey Methods for Carnivores* (Island Press, 2008). Paula has written about conservation for numerous organizations and publications. She and Robert live in the Seattle area.

Susan Mahan has been writing poetry since her husband died in 1997. She is a frequent reader at poetry venues and has written four chapbooks and over three hundred poems. She has been published in a number of journals and anthologies.

Frances Ruhlen McConnel has published two full-length books of poems: *Gathering Light*, and *The Direction of Longing*, and the fine-arts chapbook, *White Birches, Black Water*. She is retired from teaching in the Creative Writing Department at the University of California in Riverside. She co-chairs the steering committee for the Claremont Library Poetry Reading Series. She hails from Seattle, Alaska, and Tennessee.

Beth McKim is an actress and writer who lives in Houston with her husband, Buddy, and their Labradoodle, Lucy. Her short stories, poetry, and essays have been widely featured in publications such as *Front Porch Review, Mayo Review, Birmingham Arts Journal, Long Story Short,* and others.

Greggory Moore lives in a historical landmark in Long Beach, CA. Once upon a time he was the Jerry Rice Jr. of the Top Gun Flag Football League, setting the all-time single-season record for receptions. His first novel, *The Use of Regret* (from which "How They Say It" is excerpted), was published in 2012. His follow-up is in-progress.

Tania Moore's short stories have appeared or are forthcoming in *Cleaver, The Madison Review, The Flexible Persona,* and many others. Having earned her MFA from Columbia University School of the Arts, she teaches creative writing at Riverdale Country School in the Bronx and lives along the mighty Hudson River.

Elaine P. Morgan is an award-winning poet, author and freelance writer. Her works have been published in numerous poetry journals, magazines, newspapers and anthologies, most recently Pixelita Press, *The Enigmatist, The Poet's Domain*, Whispering Angel Books, and *HaikuPix Journal.* She is a five-time Senior Poet Laureate for the State of Virginia. She published her first book, *Flying in Spirit,* and is working on another memoir, *From Fire to Ashes.*

Sharon Lask Munson was born and raised in Detroit, MI. She is the author of the chapbook, *Stillness Settles Down the Lane* (Uttered Chaos Press, 2010), a full-length book of poems, *That Certain Blue* (Blue Light Press, 2011), and *Braiding Lives,* (Poetica Publishing Company, 2014). She lives and writes in Eugene, OR.

Tim J. Myers is a writer, storyteller, songwriter, and senior lecturer at Santa Clara University. He's published three books of poetry, over 130 poems, and has made the *New York Times* bestseller list for children's books, been reviewed in the *Times,* and been read aloud on NPR.

Sarla S. Nichols earned her BA in French and Psychology at the University of Memphis in 1978 and since has worked in a variety of fields including dentistry, law, early childhood development, natural foods, and most recently, yoga. She took her first creative writing class in 2010 and since then has attended four writing conferences including the prestigious Sirenland Conference in Positano, Italy.

Ann Podracky has published her work most recently in *Newtown Literary, Hanging Loose, WSQ Journal, Poetry in Performance,* and *Revision's Journal.* She was an editor for the *Ozone Park Journal* and a Writer-In-Residence at the Louis Armstrong House. She lives in Queens, N.Y. and is working on a collection of short fiction.

Julie Preis has published her work in the *Innisfree Poetry Journal*, *Best Poem*, the Wising Up anthology *Love After 70*, and other journals and anthologies. She lives in Silver Spring, MD, and San Miguel de Allende, Mexico.

Andrea Rosenhaft is a licensed clinical social worker whose work has appeared in anthologies and literary journals, most recently the spring, 2015 issue of *The Intima*, from the Narrative Medicine Program at Columbia University. She writes primarily on the topic of mental health and recovery. If she isn't working or writing, she's home in Westchester, NY with her cat, Zoe.

Emily Rubin has published her writing in magazines, anthologies and newspapers, and has written a non-fiction book. Her fiction has been nominated for a Pushcart Prize, and has placed first in the White Pines Fiction Contest. Emily is on the faculty of the Psychiatry Department at UMass Medical School, where she conducts research on siblings of children with mental health needs.

Ira Schaeffer, an active member of Ocean State Poets, is the current recipient of the Editor's Choice Loft Chapbook Award. In addition, Ira's recent poetry has appeared in a variety of publications, including, *Penumbra*; *On the Dark Side: An Anthology of Fairy Tale Poetry*; *Tastes like Pennies*; *50 Haiku*; *Wising Up Press*; and *Silver Birch Press*. His poem *Primavera* was a 2014 nominee by *The Origami Poems Project* for the Pushcart Prize.

Peter Schmitt has published three full-length collections of poems: *Renewing the Vows* (David Robert Books), and *Country Airport* and *Hazard Duty* (Copper Beech). He is the recipient of The "Discovery"/*The Nation* Prize, The Lavan Award (Academy of American Poets), The Julia Peterkin Award, and multiple grants from The Florida Arts Council and Ingram Merrill Foundation.

Patti See has published work in *Salon Magazine*, *Women's Studies Quarterly*, *Wisconsin Academy Review*, *The Southwest Review*, *HipMama*, as well as other magazines and anthologies. She wrote the award-winning blog "Our Long Goodbye: One Family's Experiences with Alzheimer's Disease," read in over 90 countries.

Alexandrina Sergio has authored two poetry collections, *My Daughter is Drummer in the Rock 'n Roll Band* and *That's How The Light Gets In* (Antrim House). Her work has appeared in numerous journals and anthologies, received national and state awards, and been given multiple performances by a professional stage company. She frequently performs with her husband, pianist David Sergio.

Christine Sikorski's poems have appeared in *Waterstone*, *ArtWord Quarterly*, *Great River Review*, and elsewhere. She has received Academy of American Poets Prizes, a Gesell Award, a Minnesota State Arts Board Grant, and other awards. She teaches a creative writing class begun by Patricia Hampl forty years ago. Christine's brother Michael was killed by a motorist while cycling.

Jill Wilbur Smith received an MFA in creative writing from Hamline University in St. Paul, MN. Her work has appeared in *A Cup of Comfort for Parents of Children with Autism*, *Mothers Always Write*, and on her blog, "The Autism Fractal," which she co-authors with her oldest daughter. She has two grown daughters and lives in Minnesota with her husband.

Jane St. Clair has published fiction in over twenty literary journals and anthologies, and is the author of *Walk Me to Midnight*, a suspense novel from Oak Tara Press. She has also published eighteen children's books and fifty-four children's short stories. She likes Mortimer Brewster's words, "Insanity not only runs in our family, it practically gallops."

Cindy Stewart-Rinier holds an MFA in Creative Writing from PLU's Rainier Writing Workshop. Her work has appeared in *Calyx*, *The Smoking Poet*, *Crab Creek Review*, *Ascent*, *Naugatuck River Review*, *VoiceCatcher*, and *New American Voices*, with four of those poems having been nominated for Pushcarts. Cindy teaches pre-kindergarten and evening poetry writing workshops for the Mountain Writers Series in Portland, OR. She is one of six siblings.

Elizabeth Stoessl lives in Portland, OR. Her poetry has appeared in many journals and anthologies, most recently in *Naugatuck River Review*, *Measure*, *VoiceCatcher* and the *Main Street Rag* anthology *Creatures of Habitat*. Over the years, her relationships with two sons and four granddaughters have given her new perspectives on the joys and catastrophes of sibling dynamics.

Alison Stone wrote *Dangerous Enough, Borrowed Logic, From the Fool to the World,* and *They Sing at Midnight,* which won the 2003 Many Mountains Moving Award. She was awarded *Poetry*'s Frederick Bock Prize and *New York Quarterly*'s Madeline Sadin award. She created The Stone Tarot and is a licensed psychotherapist.

Heather MacDonald Storey traveled widely during her fifty-seven-year marriage to a Canadian career soldier. They happily retired to Fredericton, New Brunswick where she pursued her interest in creative writing. Heather's grandchildren and great-grandchildren inspired her first book, *Nana's Story Chest,* in 2013. Since then, a number of her stories were published in an anthology titled, *The Coffee Cup Companion.*

Donald R. Vogel holds a Masters in English from Stony Brook University and has published fiction and nonfiction in several print and online journals. He makes a living as a fundraiser in the non-profit sector and lives with his family in Long Island, NY.

Loretta Diane Walker has published her poetry in *Orbis International Journal, Haight-Ashbury Literary Journal, Concho River Review, 94 Creations, The Texas Observer, Her Texas,* the *2015 Texas Poetry Calendar, Red River Review, Illya's Honey, San Pedro River Review, Sugared Water, Perceptions Literary Magazine, Boundless,* and *Pushing Out the Boat.* Her manuscript *Word Ghetto* won the 2011 *Bluelight Press* Book Award.

Michele Wolf is the author of *Immersion, Conversations During Sleep* (Anhinga Prize for Poetry) and the chapbook *The Keeper of Light.* Her poems have appeared in *Poetry, The Hudson Review, North American Review* and many other journals and anthologies. She is a contributing editor for *Poet Lore* and teaches at The Writer's Center in Bethesda, MD.

Gary Young is the author of several collections of poetry including *Hands; Days; Braver Deeds; No Other Life,* winner of the William Carlos Williams Award; *Pleasure;* and *Even So: New and Selected Poems.* In 2009 he received the Shelley Memorial Award from the Poetry Society of America. He teaches creative writing and directs the Cowell Press at UC Santa Cruz.

GUEST EDITORS

Kathleen L. Housley is the author of nine books, including *Epiphanies* (2013) and *Keys to the Kingdom: Reflections on Music and the Mind* (2010) published by Wising Up Press. She has written extensively on the confluence of science, art and religion, with poetry and essays in many journals, including *Image* and *The Christian Century*.

Kerry Langan is the author of two collections of short fiction, *Only Beautiful & Other Stories* and *Live Your Life & Other Stories*. Her short stories have been published in dozens of literary magazines and anthologized often. Her non-fiction has appeared in *Working Mother* and *Shifting Balance Sheets: Women's Stories of Naturalized Citizenship and Cultural Attachment* (Wising Up Press). She is currently at work on her next collection of short stories. She resides with her family in Oberlin, OH.

Michele Markarian is a writer and actor based in Cambridge, MA. Her plays have been performed throughout the United States and the United Kingdom, and published by Dramatic Publishing, Heuer Publishing, Oxford University Press, and in anthologies by Smith and Kraus. She is editor of an anthology of plays, *The Unborn Children of America and Other Family Procedures* (Fomite 2015). Her short fiction can be found in various Wising Up anthologies.

Siblings: Our First Macrocosm Workshop
is available on our website as a free download.

See our booklist and calls for submissions for new anthologies.

www.universaltable.org
wisingup@universaltable.org

P.O. Box 2122
Decatur, GA 30031-2122

EDITORS/PUBLISHERS

HEATHER TOSTESON is the author of *Breathing in Portuguese, Living in English; Germs of Truth; The Sanctity of the Moment: Poems from Four Decades; Visible Signs;* and *God Speaks My Language, Can You?* She has worked as executive editor of two public health journals and in health communications with a focus on communication across disciplines, racism, social trust, and how belief systems develop and change. She holds an MFA in Creative Writing (UNC-Greensboro) and PhD in English and Creative Writing (Ohio University).

CHARLES BROCKETT has a PhD from UNC-Chapel Hill and is a recipient of several Fulbright and National Endowment for the Humanities awards. A retired political science professor, he has written two well-received books on Central America, *Land, Power, and Poverty* and *Political Movements and Violence*, and numerous social science journal articles and book chapters. With Heather Tosteson, he is co-founder of Universal Table and Wising Up Press and co-editor of the Wising Up Anthologies.

www.ingramcontent.com/pod-product-compliance
Lightning Source LLC
Chambersburg PA
CBHW020603270326
41927CB00005B/161